D1577334

THE IMPACT OF ITALY:

The Grand Tour And Beyond

Viaggio da Roma a Napoli, sono poste 19¼, Miglia 155; from Carlo Barbieri, *Direzione pe'
viaggiatori in Italia colla notizia di tutte le poste e loro prezzi* (Bologna, 1779), between pages 6
and 7. (*By kind permission of the British School at Rome. Photo: Mauro Coen*)

Published with the aid of a grant from the
Paul Mellon Centre for Studies in British Art

THE IMPACT OF ITALY:

The Grand Tour And Beyond

Edited by

CLARE HORNSBY

The British School at Rome, London

2000

ISBN 0 904152 32 4

Cover illustration: Untitled frontispiece to Carlo Barbieri, *Direzione pe' viaggiatori in*
Italia colla notizia di tutte le poste e loro prezzi (Bologna, 1779)
(By kind permission of the British School at Rome. Photo: Mauro Coen)
Cover design: Terry Wilkins

Typeset by Meeks & Middleton
Printed by Stephen Austin and Sons Ltd, Hertford, Great Britain

CONTENTS

'AFTER' THE 'GRAND TOUR'

LIST OF FIGURES

ACKNOWLEDGEMENTS

I wish to thank members of staff at the British School at Rome, particularly the Director, Professor Andrew Wallace-Hadrill, for supporting this publication project from its beginnings; the Librarian, Valerie Scott, who has allowed me very generous access to the collections; and the Publications Manager, Dr Gill Clark, for valuable guidance and for reading the manuscript. I acknowledge the kind assistance of Professor Edward Chaney at the early stages of the project and of Frank Salmon at a later stage. The Paul Mellon Center for Studies in British Art has helped the publication with a generous grant. Alexander Clark was always ready with invaluable advice on computer problems. In particular I would like to thank Professor Chris Wickham, who read and commented fully on my Introduction, providing me with important insights and much-needed constructive criticism.

I dedicate my part in the realization of this book to my children, Lily and Francis, who, by their enthusiastic attendance at school and willingness to go to bed early, have given me time to write.

Clare Hornsby
Rome

1

Introduction, Or Why Travel?

CLARE HORNSBY

Le conseil d'aller en Italie ne doit pas se donner à tout le monde ...[1]

CHOSEN FOR TRAVEL

Stendhal's fantasy itinerary with which he closes his *Promenades dans Rome* — 'manière de voir Rome en dix jours' — proposes an impossibly full sightseeing schedule, and not one that he himself attempted. The famous declaration which follows the admonition quoted above (in English in the original), 'TO THE HAPPY FĖW', adds to the élitism first suggested, the benediction of happiness as the result of being somehow 'chosen' to visit Italy. The visitors with whom we are concerned in this volume of essays did not all set out from their home country with such awareness; more prosaic interests predominated, as we shall see. It is as well, however, to bring to the fore this heightened expectation and response, which run through many of the accounts we will be examining. As Chloe Chard has noted, visitors who were 'incapable of hyperbole'[2] were considered inadequate, or considered themselves to be so.

This key response sets up a duality which can be used instructively as a framework for this examination of the Grand Tour — the hyperbolic and the bathetic, or high and low. This is manifested, for example, in the relationship established by the Reverenda Camera Apostolica with the English archaeologists for the granting of export licences for sculpture, contrasted with the construction of a lavatory for the use of the Duke of York while passing through the countryside near Vercelli, as presented in the essay by Ilaria Bignamini (Chapter 2). In this case, paradoxically, the 'high end' activity was undertaken by both parties for financial gain, whereas the lowly, even embarrassing, activity was

---

[1] Stendhal, *Promenades dans Rome* (ed. V. Del Litto) (Grenoble, 1993), 469 [original edition Paris, 1829].

[2] C. Chard, 'Introduction', in C. Chard and H. Langdon (eds), *Transports: Travel, Pleasure and Imaginative Geography, 1600–1830* (London, 1996), 2.

enhanced by a rare genre of artistic expression in the decoration of the toilet itself.

In the activities and responses of the writers, artists and architects who travelled to Italy there is, of necessity, a certain inbuilt enthusiasm and a tendency to note primarily what was of use to, or inspiration for, their particular creation. Already they are 'chosen' by virtue of their art; they are among 'the happy few'. Thus Thomas Jones, in the passage from his journal in which he writes of Italy as a 'Magick Land', notes that he 'I suppose, injoyed pleasures unfelt by my companions'.[3] Not so 'happy', and by no means 'few' in number, were the companions and their like; and by examining their motives it can be seen that their pleasures in the beauties of Italy were, Jones thought, so commonplace and slight that any higher degree of imaginative or spiritual engagement might seem hyperbolic by contrast. Again in the journal, this time at Tivoli, Jones maintains that: 'Seeing the Curiosities of Rome and its environs, is a task that they think must be got through — but the sooner the better'.[4] This is but one of the countless examples of what the 'cultivated' thought was the common artistic philistinism of the English visitor, of his or her ignorance and prejudice, which contrasts with the positive responses to the art of the past and the natural beauties of the country on the part of engaged and committed visitors — antiquarians, historians, writers, architects, archaeologists, painters and collectors.

The point at which the ignorance of the mere tourist is equalled by a more sophisticated, but identical, response in the artist is the moment at which a significant transformation takes place. The 'Idea of Italy' is altered from a site to be engaged with and psychically consumed, into a bit of 'abroad' that can be taken or left, as the visitor chooses. This comes alive in the work of Charles Dickens, as examined in the essay by John Bowen (Chapter 10). Dickens notes a group of Tourists: 'For a fortnight ... they were in every tomb and every church and every ruin and every Picture Gallery ... I don't think she [a member of the group] ever saw anything, or looked at anything'[5] — and then comes his own dismissal of the value of connoisseurship, when he prefers the opinion of a flock of geese 'to the discourses of Sir Joshua Reynolds'.[6] This prefigures the pride in ignorance that is the defence response of British philistines throughout the ages. Dickens's response is also debunking high art by comic effect. The image of the geese and the great Reynolds brings to mind one of William Hogarth's popular engravings satirizing the foreign (primarily French) influence on British art. I shall return to Dickens later.

---

[3] T. Jones, *Memoirs* (*Journal of the Walpole Society* 32 (1946-8)) (London, 1951), 55.
[4] Jones, *Memoirs* (above, n. 3), 66.
[5] C. Dickens, *Pictures from Italy* (with an introduction and notes by David Paroissien) (London, 1973), 177.
[6] See below, p. 209.

The mention of Reynolds introduces another aspect, the so-called 'Reynolds effect' on artists, inducing them to travel.[7] In his Fourth Discourse he urged: 'Gentlemen, the value and rank of every art is in proportion to the mental labour employed in it, or the mental pleasure produced by it. As this principle is observed or neglected, our profession becomes either a liberal art, or a mechanical trade'.[8] In his efforts to change the menial status of artists, Reynolds was up against the deeply-ingrained, self-satisfied ignorance of the visual arts so characteristic of the British, then as now. John Brewer writes: 'Both Johnson and Goldsmith blithely confessed their ignorance of painting and considered their lack of knowledge to be no stigma'.[9] This attitude is linked to the xenophobia of Hogarth, for example. None the less, Brewer has noted that through the *Discourses* the eighteenth-century 'Rule of Taste' becomes an implicit collaboration between artists and patrons, the Grand Tour being the most significant means of outwardly expressing the need to change, to learn and to 'be influenced'.[10] However, there were distinct practical advantages to be gained from making the Tour, and these, although not mentioned by Reynolds specifically, must have been in his mind during the writing of the *Discourses*. One advantage was, of course, the increase in 'market-share' (to use a twentieth-century expression) available to artists who were able to include Tour sites in their repertoire. I shall return to this subject when I discuss the essay by Michael Liversidge.

ART, TASTE AND VIRTUE

Together with the artists coming to Italy as to the fount of inspiration (or even at the next level, more self-consciously 'Let's go and see this so-called Fount of Inspiration'), there were those simply in search of a confirmation of their education: the élite, the would-be connoisseurs and gentlemen of taste.

One aspect of the effect of the Tour on the gentlemen amateurs and the merely curious who made up a large part of the travelling public in the eighteenth century, and who were also Reynolds's audience in Britain, is exemplified by James Boswell in a letter to Jean-Jacques Rousseau: 'I have almost finished my tour of Italy. I have viewed with enthusiasm classical sites, and the remains of the grandeur of the ancient Romans. I have made a thorough study of architecture, statues and paintings; and I believe I have *acquired taste to*

---

[7] J. Brewer, *The Pleasures of the Imagination — English Culture in the Eighteenth Century* (London, 1997), 313.

[8] J. Reynolds, *Discourses Delivered to the Students of the Royal Academy* (with notes and introduction by Roger Fry) (London, 1905), 71.

[9] Reynolds, *Discourses* (above, n. 8), 291.

[10] Brewer, *The Pleasures of the Imagination* (above, n. 7), 292.

a certain degree' (my emphasis).[11] We can trace the process by which this acquisition of Taste can have a transforming power if we look again at Reynolds. In the Ninth Discourse he states: 'The Art which we profess has beauty for its object' (thereby confirming his high aim announced, as we have seen, in the Fourth Discourse), 'conducting the thoughts through successive stages of excellence, till that contemplation of universal rectitude and harmony which began by Taste may, as it is exalted and refined, conclude in Virtue'.[12] That is to say — Art can transform Taste into Virtue. Taste also has the power to raise the connoisseur or even the amateur to the spiritual level of the artist: the Grand Tour was a recognized shortcut to this elevation.[13]

However, not all visitors to Italy, and certainly not the renowned lecher Boswell, displayed the beneficial and virtuous effects of their acquisition of Taste in their behaviour while travelling. Indeed, Boswell's frequent visits to prostitutes, not only in Venice (the traditional locus of licentious freedom), but in Rome also, seem to have been a deliberate experiment in comparative morality, by which his 'pretty doings'[14] could not be so harshly criticized, given the setting in which they were enacted. This is a theme that is often found in the literature on the experience of the Anglo-Saxon visitor to Italy: it involves simple issues, such as xenophobia, and also more subtle and complex ones, such as the comparison between the glories of the antique past of Italy and its degraded contemporary state. It is worth examining some examples of this attitude, since it runs throughout the responses of many significant visitors, and not only high status ones.

Boswell makes his opinion clear at the beginning of his visit, at Turin: 'my desire to know the world made me resolve to intrigue a little while in Italy, where the women are so debauched that they are hardly to be considered as moral agents, but as inferior beings'.[15] He expands his point, later on in the year, in a letter to his friend Deleyre, who had previously written to Boswell about the 'decadence of civilisation'.[16] 'Your ideas on the corruption of Italy have recurred to me many times. The worst is that in travelling there one becomes used to seeing people who think no more about the virtues of sensitive souls than an

[11] F. Brady and F.A. Pottle (eds), *Boswell on the Grand Tour: Italy, Corsica and France 1765–1766* [hereafter, Boswell, *Grand Tour*] (London, 1955), 85. From a letter to J.-J. Rousseau dated 11 May from Rome; the original is in French.

[12] Reynolds, *Discourses* (above, n. 8), 264.

[13] Brewer, *The Pleasures of the Imagination* (above, n. 7), especially pp. 464–5. This excellent book contains a full and fascinating discussion on the issues of Taste in the eighteenth century, amongst many other matters.

[14] Boswell, *Grand Tour* (above, n. 11), 109 — on the female attractions of Rome being equal to those of Venice. This is in a letter dated 19 July 1765 to his friend John Johnston. I would like to thank Professor Chris Wickham for making the point that Boswell had a similar attitude to that of the late twentieth-century sexual tourists in Thailand and the Dominican Republic, for example.

[15] Boswell, *Grand Tour* (above, n. 11), 29 — Thursday 10 January 1765.

[16] Boswell, *Grand Tour* (above, n. 11), n. 1, 110.

American savage thinks of the pleasures of civilised nations.'[17] This is the experience of travel as a corrupting factor on the stern morals of the Scottish gentleman. He continues, 'The Italians as well as the savages appear to pass their time very agreeably. Why then reproach the former [the Italians] for not possessing elegant and sublime virtues, when we do not blame the savages for having neither brilliant ballets nor serious operas. Virtue may be regarded as a luxury which all the world need not possess'. Even taking into account the level of irony in these comments, the Italy presented here is the playground of the morally hypocritical Anglo-Saxon; it is already so degraded that the activities of such as Boswell, in his cynical exploitation of the women, will not harm. What is admired is the past, always; the present in Italy is something that must be tolerated.

Even those, such as the poet Shelley, whom we have come to regard as having 'purer' souls than Boswell, express similar feelings — indeed, in even more hyperbolic terms:

> There are two Italies; one composed of green earth & transparent sea and the mighty ruins of antient times, and aerial mountains, & the warm and radiant atmosphere which is interfused through all things. The other consists of the Italians of the present day, their works & ways. The one is the most sublime & lovely contemplation that can be conceived by the imagination of man; the other the most degraded disgusting & odious.[18]

A postscript to this point comes in the form of an expression of the same type, but from an Italian. Crauford Tait Ramage, arriving at Maida in Calabria in the early summer of 1828 and talking with a group of 'respectable inhabitants of the village', quoted to them from Horace, and one of the group 'said that he was afraid that the Italians had changed places with the *Ultimi Britanni*, and that high civilisation had passed from Italy to Great Britain, which now occupied the noble position in the world which their ancestors had maintained in former times'.[19] This changing of places between Italy and Britain (clearly flattering, probably deliberately so, to this British traveller), wherein the teachers become the pupils in the study of the high concerns of civilized societies, is a thread running through the issues of Art, Taste and Virtue on the Grand Tour. The abasement of Italy has spread from the degradation of the personal morals of its women, as in

---

[17] Boswell, *Grand Tour* (above, n. 11), 111–12 — letter to Deleyre, 19 July 1765.

[18] T. Webb, '"City of the Soul" — English Romantic travellers in Rome', in M. Liversidge and C. Edwards (eds), *Imagining Rome — British Artists and Rome in the Nineteenth Century* (exhibition catalogue, Bristol City Museum and Art Gallery, 1996), 27. He quotes Shelley writing to Leigh Hunt: '[he] gave expression to a sense of division both in Italy and also perhaps in himself' (F.L. Jones (ed.), *The Letters of Percy Bysshe Shelley* (Oxford, 1964), II, 67).

[19] E. Clay (ed.), *Ramage in South Italy: the Nooks and By-Ways of Italy by Crauford Tait Ramage* (London, 1965), 64 [original edition 1868].

our example from Boswell, to the nationwide decay of its civic virtues, as pointed to by Ramage.

LEARNING TO TRAVEL

The expectations of the Anglo-Saxon visitor, arising from the education he or she had received, obviously have an important role in bringing to the fore the contrast between the ancient past and the present, particularly the identification of the political issues of contemporary Britain with those of ancient Rome.[20] Philip Ayres writes: 'for purposes of political self-justification the classical political heritage served too conveniently to be ignored ... Very few would have denied the continuing validity of the classical ideal of *libertas* or the social virtue obligatory in citizenship or *civitas*'. The successive generations of young men raised on the classics served to create an intellectual standard against which to measure the travel experience, while at the same time creating the élite that had the leisure to profit from this. Catharine Edwards has noted: 'The time and money spent on acquiring this difficult dead language [Latin] made it a most effective marker of social status'.[21]

What Francis Haskell has called 'the narrow obsession with the past that characterised the culture of the Grand Tourists'[22] clearly brought with it a predisposition to react in an intellectual way with what they saw, which was a marked divergence from the instinctive responses of the artists and writers, whether positive or negative. Gibbon, while in Florence, is very assiduous in his examination of the paintings and sculptures in the galleries, and in his descriptions of them in his Tour journal; however, he notes that: 'A L'avenir je dois faire une reforme que ne sera pas moins nécessaire pour les Voyages que pour les études. J'eviterai la tentation de donner des descriptions complettes ou je pourrais que copier Keysler ou Misson'[23] (a guidebook translated into English in 1695, frequently reissued). Despite his resolution not to keep too close to the material presented in the guidebook — thereby leaving space for a more personal response — he remains protected from the vitality of the direct experience of the art object because he was led to it by the book. The object — building, sculpture,

---

[20] On this subject see principally: P. Ayres, *Classical Culture and the Idea of Rome in Eighteenth Century England* (Cambridge, 1997), 2.

[21] C. Edwards, 'The roads to Rome', in Liversidge and Edwards (eds), *Imagining Rome* (above, n. 18), 8.

[22] F. Haskell, 'Preface', in A. Wilton and I. Bignamini (eds), *Grand Tour: the Lure of Italy in the Eighteenth Century* (exhibition catalogue, Tate Gallery, London, 1996), 12.

[23] G.A. Bonnard (ed.), *Gibbon's Journey from Geneva to Rome — His Journal from 20 April to 2 October 1764* (London, 1961), 224, in September on leaving Florence. This journal is in French until his arrival in Rome in December, when it stops after only a few entries in English on the paintings and antiquities. Boswell also is using a guidebook, in good scholarly fashion: Boswell, *Grand Tour* (above, n. 11), 59 — Sunday 17 March 1765, 'drove about and saw several churches (*vide* Cochin)'. He was using the *Voyage d'Italie* of 1758 as his guidebook.

ruin or painting —, when included in a guidebook, is raised to the higher, intellectual, plane by being presented in an educational framework; and yet this elevation of status at the same time dilutes the art object's power to provoke an engaged response. Once Gibbon gets to Rome, however, there is an indication of the soul of the man, rather than the mind of the classical scholar: 'Nous sommes arrives a ROME a cinq heures du soir. Depuis le Pons Milvius j'ai été dans un songe d'antiquité'.[24]

There were various directions in which the classical education of the British gentleman could lead. Only a mind such as Gibbon's could take the results of an education, add to it the stimulus of what he saw and thought in Rome, and over a long period of gestation be able to produce a piece of work on the scale of *The Decline and Fall of the Roman Empire*. Other intellects, however, were at least able to enrich their acquired knowledge of the classical past while in Italy, and thereby match even artists like Reynolds in their level of commitment to and absorption of the material available. The distinction of these two strands, intellectual response (historian, collector, antiquarian) and artistic response (painter, creative writer, architect), is, however, probably too modern a separation. Artists tended to be more hyperbolic, but they were dealing with nature and at the same time trying to live by their work, mixing the spirit of artistic creation with the daily anxieties of being, in Stendhal's famous phrase, 'en lutte·avec les vrais besoins de la vie'. The more educated classes had the leisure to travel freely and to collect antiquities, but did not always have the depth of understanding to raise their 'studies' above the level of 'been there, done that'. As I show below, when discussing museums, these visitors perhaps needed artificial stimulants for their experience to be truly thrilling.

The separation of intellectual versus artistic responses is useful, however, if it raises the question of which category of visitors to Italy was more significant in the development of Britain's close relationship with the antique past — a relationship that from the seventeenth century through to the beginning of the twentieth was to have such a widespread effect on British cultural life. Brewer writes of Horace Walpole's *Anecdotes of Painting in England* (published in 1762): 'His Anecdotes convey the impression that Britain's artistic heritage is best understood through the eyes of gentlemen amateurs who are also the best interpreters — as well as owners — of the paintings that make up the nation's artistic tradition'.[25] To this understanding, I would suggest, can be added the actual paintings and works of art collected by travellers on the Tour. Since their connoisseurship was a means of interpretation, by exercising choice in purchasing art, as well as commissioning it, they were modelling Taste. Brewer

---

[24] Bonnard (ed.), *Gibbon's Journey from Geneva to Rome* (above, n. 23), 235 — to Rome, 2 October. It has to be said, however, that collections and museums had, and retain into the present era, a particular power of their own which sapped that of the works therein. See section on the Museo Pio-Clementino (pp. 21–3).

[25] Brewer, *The Pleasures of the Imagination* (above, n. 7), 464.

speaks of 'the battle between artists and connoisseurs to arbitrate taste', in effect
between 'the amateur Walpole and the professional Reynolds'.[26] But Walpole, as
one of the educated élite, would clearly have claimed primacy in matters of Taste
and artistic judgement over the practitioner, despite Reynolds's efforts to raise
the social status of artists. Actually it was the Tour itself, and a period of time
spent outside the rigorous social framework of contemporary Britain, that could
enable some humble artists and architects to better their lot socially.

It is arguable which of these two groups, élite amateurs and artistic
professionals, had more 'right' to inherit the glorious mantle of the ancients. But
what is certain is that on the Grand Tour both groups needed each other; indeed,
neither could profitably exercise their particular calling without the other. Again
from Brewer, a comment by an amateur on the work of the artist George Romney
on his return from Italy is pertinent:[27] 'Such Pictures! And the pictures of such
People! I am lost in wonder and astonishment how all these things should be!
How so short a Travel could give such Excellence to his Pencil!'. Artists such as
Thomas Jenkins and James Byres became dealers and tour leaders to satisfy the
demands of the élite for pictures and sculptures and for sightseeing. The
expectations of both groups of travellers were to a certain extent fulfilled, the
level being determined largely by how far each individual was prepared to go in
the further voyage of discovery that began once they had arrived in Italy.

PURCHASING TASTE

The educated traveller was fully aware of the precedents for the sort of behaviour
in which he might indulge while abroad. Collecting is one activity which had a
particularly long and distinguished pedigree. The relationship between social and
political life in eighteenth-century Britain and the imagery of the antique past is
discussed by Ayres: 'The reduplication of antiquity by way of collecting
antiques, though it was underway for decades before the Revolution, naturally
came to be associated after 1688 with the cultural programme of the oligarchy'.[28]
Clearly the European monarchies and nobility for long had considered the
acquisition of objects from a glorious (because distant) past to be important in
the accretion of value and status to their family name. The British aristocrat,
newly wealthy at the beginning of the eighteenth century through the slave or
sugar trades, could follow their example. There was plenty of money to spend,
and dealers made sure of the supply — either by illegally selling valuable
antiquities, by concocting whole sculpted figures from fragments (Cavaceppi), or

---

[26] Brewer, *The Pleasures of the Imagination* (above, n. 7), 465.

[27] Brewer, *The Pleasures of the Imagination* (above, n. 7), 315. He quotes from a letter of
Thomas Greene ('benefactor' of George Romney, who had returned in 1775) to Romney's tour
companion, the painter Ozias Humphry, on entering Romney's studio.

[28] Ayres, *Classical Culture* (above, n. 20), 132. Here he mentions the Grand Tour without
capitalizing the words.

by providing simple copies or casts to satisfy demand: 'even copies of copies were proudly set up, as in the case of Le Sueur's duplicate of Charles I's much admired bronze copy of the Borghese Gladiator'.[29]

The collecting of paintings was more problematic. Since most of the so-called 'old masters' were already in established noble collections or in churches, and virtually no examples of antique painting survived, the educated visitor had to turn to contemporary works to fill the spaces on his walls. They principally bought landscape views, though the more wealthy might sit to Pompeo Batoni for a portrait *all'antica*. It is likely that by the end of the eighteenth century there were more painters, both Italian and British, than there were good (rich) patrons. However, paintings produced by contemporary artists in Italy were much in demand, and painters tended to make copies of their best views for the market.[30] At the next level, and for a different, larger, British home market, they had engravings made. Perhaps the painter Gavin Hamilton's generosity to his fellow Scot, Boswell, was merely canniness: 'Don't talk of price. I don't intend to make you pay much money for this picture. I shall make a great deal by the print'.[31] The general impression given by contemporary accounts of the business of producing and dealing in works of art in Rome and other major Italian cities is one of stiff competition, between artists for good patrons and between patrons for outstanding works or the work of outstanding practitioners, an active market that persisted beyond the Napoleonic invasion into the mid-nineteenth century.

Stendhal comments on an exchange between a penny-pinching English aristocratic visitor and a (nationality unknown, but presumably not English) painter, which, although laden with Stendhal's vivacious Anglophobia, sets the scene in the Roman art market-place beautifully:

> *Hier, un Anglais marchandait un tableau; il dit au peintre; «Monsieur, combien de jours ce tableau vous-a-t-il occupé? — Onze jours — eh bien! Je vous en donne onze sequins; vous devez être assez payé à un sequin par jour.» L'artiste indigné replaça sa toile contre le mur et tourna le dos à l'aristocrate. Ce genre de politesse livre les Anglais aux charlatans. J'ai vu des tableaux achetés 20 ou 30 louis et qui ne valent pas 100F; ce qui m'a fort réjoui. Mais, d'ici à un siècle, tous les tableaux d'Italie seront en Angleterre.*[32]

This comment of course sets out to mock the English in their relentless pursuit whilst on the Grand Tour of works of art to enhance their cultural aspirations. But Stendhal's prediction for the future destination of the pictures of Italy seems to be confirmed if one visits the interiors of many British country houses. It is

[29] Ayres, *Classical Culture* (above, n. 20), 141.
[30] Jones, *Memoirs* (above, n. 3), April 1779, 87.
[31] Boswell, *Grand Tour* (above, n. 11), 67. Thursday 4 April he discusses with the painter Gavin Hamilton a picture he has commissioned.
[32] Stendhal, *Promenades* (above, n. 1), 230, 5 June 1828.

interesting to note here the valuable insights on the British in Italy provided by French commentators. The French traveller in Italy was generally in a more privileged position than the British one, being already familiar with many of the religious and cultural practices that troubled visitors from the Protestant north of Europe. As France itself was a Grand Tour destination (for the painter William Marlow's travels in France and their importance for his later work see, for example, Michael Liversidge's essay (Chapter 5)) the French in Italy were well placed to observe — even if not as strictly unbiased observers — the habits, inclinations and foibles of the British abroad.[33]

CONNOISSEURSHIP

What turns a mere collector into a connoisseur: the same thing as transformed a mere tourist into a true traveller? (This second pair of terms is current in our own period — backpackers in southeast Asia are eager to describe themselves as the latter and would hate to be thought of as the former.) The distinction, if not the terminology, existed also in the eighteenth century. Engagement and motivation would seem to be the key. The intention of the translator of one early guidebook to Italy, addressed to 'our young Nobility and Gentry', was 'to inflame their minds and excite their industry'.[34] Social status, however, and wealth were, of course, other key markers that successfully set a man apart from the crowd. Stendhal was not alone in pinpointing the weaknesses of the English in Italy; the tendency for them to be seen as a group — and therefore as tourists — is noticeable also in the responses of their own countryman, Byron: 'at present it [Rome] is pestilent with English ... wishing to be at once cheap and magnificent'.[35] Byron would wish to be disassociated from this group, and was indeed able to rise above the common herd by virtue of his position in society and his creative aims, even though his reaction here is that of many 'intellectual' tourists — then and now.

The aims of the would-be connoisseur are more difficult to clarify. Ian Jenkins has written very perceptively of Sir William Hamilton,[36] who has become the archetype of the British connoisseur in Italy:

> To call Hamilton an archaeologist is to diminish his role as someone who would not have recognised the modern division of the arts and the sciences as discrete fields of inquiry. Hamilton loved art and

[33] I am indebted to Professor Wickham for raising this point.

[34] W. Lodge, *The Painter's Voyage of Italy ... Written Originally in Italian by Giacomo Barri, Venetian Painter. Englished by W.L. of Lincoln's Inne, Gent* (London, 1679), 'To the Ingenious Readers' (preface to the English edition).

[35] Webb, '"City of the Soul"' (above, n. 18), 22. He quotes Byron from 1817 on Rome.

[36] I. Jenkins, 'Contemporary minds: Sir William Hamilton's affair with antiquity', in I. Jenkins and K. Sloan (eds), *Vases and Volcanoes: Sir William Hamilton and his Collection* (exhibition catalogue, British Museum, London, 1996), 41, 'a new Pliny'.

nature as one, and shared the universal interests of the antiquaries of the past. Indeed, his very life on the Bay of Naples seems to imitate those ancient noble Romans who had their summer houses along the Neapolitan coastline.

I shall return to Hamilton's feelings for nature in discussing the essays (Chapters 7 and 8) which concern his mistress, later wife, Emma. It would seem, however, that this aspect of his character set him apart to some degree from others whose collecting had a perhaps more mechanical, methodical feel. An example of this is Richard Payne Knight, who, although as, or more, learned than Sir William, does not seem to have engaged as deeply with the objects of his collections; which had as their basis Payne Knight's great curiosity and a nascent scientific approach to what we would now call archaeology.[37] If, as Ian Jenkins has suggested, Hamilton is indeed like one of the 'ancient noble Romans', then it is perhaps in this that the similarity lies: the life of rural *otium* so beloved by the Romans cannot have been much different from the intense idleness of the role of British ambassador to Naples. Aside from his official writing of reports, what was a man like Hamilton to do profitably with his time except collecting, and once he had started and found he could not stop, except turn this pastime into an art? The passion that motivated his collecting and inspired his interest in the past was (literally) strong enough to breathe life into the forms of the dancers depicted on some of the many vases in his collection, and from them to create, with Emma, the artistic performances known as the 'attitudes'. His response to the past that he found in Italy (probably intensified by his long residence there) bridges the gap between the two categories I mentioned above, the intellectual and the creative; he raised to a spiritual level what was initially a scholarly pursuit.

'PERHAPS I SHOULD HAVE FALLEN OUT OF A GONDOLA'

We can distinguish, therefore, several layers of élite amongst the visitors who came to Italy on the Grand Tour, even though the very fact of travelling at all set them apart from those who stayed at home. In a last note before turning to examine the essays themselves (which will illumine the visits of some of the different individual visitors), a contrast to the passionate involvement of Sir William Hamilton might instructively be introduced, bearing in mind that both men concerned fall into the category of the English Gentleman in Italy. A diary entitled *A Journey to Italy in 1826*, by Robert Heywood, is the prosaic journal of a man of few words. He does not have many ideas either, and there is no

---

[37] There is no place here to examine this remarkable man's career in detail, but see the excellent catalogue M. Clarke and N. Penny (eds), *The Arrogant Connoisseur: Richard Payne Knight, 1751–1824* (exhibition catalogue, Whitworth Art Gallery, Manchester, 1982), especially chapter 5, N. Penny, 'Collecting, interpreting and imitating ancient art'.

evidence in his journal that his visit to Italy provided any mental or imaginative stimulus:

> We have visited ... the Capitol with its fine collection of paintings and statuary. I cannot but feel sorry for little children in many parts of Italy, they are wrapped up so tightly from the feet to the neck that it must be prejudicial to their growth and symmetry. Lotteries also abound here as at Naples. I have dined at a restaurant, for two pauls, having a dish of good potatoes and beef steak, two plates of bread and a bottle of wine.[38]

All are excellent observations. Later, however, his matter-of-factness attains an almost perceptive profundity. He is forced to exclude Venice from his itinerary due to a muddle with his passport: 'Thus I have lost two days and miss seeing the principal city. However, what cannot be cured must be endured, or rather all is for the best. Perhaps I should have fallen out of a gondola'.[39] He reveals in his journal his willingness to conform with a travel itinerary laid down by those whom he would probably readily accept were his betters in social and intellectual terms. The very idea of a modest provincial man of modest means undertaking such a journey is a tacit recognition of his desire to become associated with that higher status group. That he treats the whole enterprise as something to be endured rather than enjoyed indicates that here we are in the presence of a traveller *malgré lui*; yet there must be something of this attitude hidden in the thoughts of many visitors abroad. Here begins the argument 'why it is best not to travel', which I will not enter into.

* * *

THE BROAD PERSPECTIVE

Ilaria Bignamini's essay (Chapter 2) casts a wide net in order to catch some of the varied examples of 'active' participation by Italians during the time of the Grand Tour. The Italians to whom she refers are examined in a variety of social, artistic, cultural and service relationships with the visitors, from the builders of the ducal toilet to which I referred earlier, to the ladies of Venice ready to welcome the same English Duke, as described by local poets. Gibbon was in Italy at the same time as this visitor. When the young historian was in Florence he notes: 'On attendoit le Duc de York aujourdhui. Il nous a tous trompés au grand chagrin du ministre [Horace Mann] et a la joye extreme des autres

---

[38] R. Heywood [Robert Heywood, 1786–1868], *A Journey to Italy in 1826*, 48, Friday 9 June. This diary, privately printed in 1918, is in the Ashby collection of the British School at Rome Library.

[39] Heywood, *A Journey to Italy* (above, n. 38), 55, Thursday 15 June.

Anglois'.[40] He does not note the reaction of the Italians to the non-arrival of the royal guest; but we could assume that, unlike the English visitors, they were as eager to meet the Duke in Florence as they had been earlier in Venice. However, the two cities were profoundly different and, in terms of the Grand Tour, served different needs. As Bignamini notes: 'in the Golden Age of the Grand Tour, Venice identified itself with tourism ... No other Italian town shows such a degree of self-identification with festivals'.[41] This relates to the exploitation of the beauties, both physical and architectural, of the once-great Republic. As Boswell has noted, his principal souvenir of Venice, and perhaps that of many other male visitors there, was venereal disease.[42] Bignamini goes on to show that, in contrast, Rome was able to control the level of exploitation by political astuteness and skilful manipulation of the demand for 'souvenir' objects.

Boswell also provides an example of one of the ways the Italians reacted to the Grand Tour, here introducing the topos of comedy in the phenomenon of travel, which is looked at more closely in Chloe Chard's essay. Travelling with Lord Mountstuart to Loreto to see the Holy House, he wrote: 'My Lord was not much pleased but very tired. I made him laugh by showing him the signboard of a barber who had the impudence to put outside his shop a very crudely drawn, ugly figure standing beside a wig, with the inscription "*Al Milordo Inglese*"'.[43] Here the Italians are poking fun at those foreigners who visit their country, and this mockery in turn provides amusement and entertainment for the visitors — a welcome contrast to the depressing effect that too much sightseeing had (and still has) on the spirits. This is linked to the idea that great art made the viewers ill, as in Stendhal's syndrome. Museums and galleries, then and now, evoke this feeling of exhaustion and visual satiety; the modern urge to show a collection is undermined by a reaction to 'too much' art that began to be felt, as we have seen, at the beginning of travel literature.[44]

Towards the end of her essay Bignamini raises a significant point: 'Did some individuals or institutions make clever, planned use of the Grand Tour? And did their actions and reactions produce something solid, important and long-

---

[40] Bonnard (ed.), *Gibbon's Journey from Geneva to Rome* (above, n. 23), 124. He was at Florence on 28 June.

[41] On the subject of Venice, see B. Redford, *Venice and the Grand Tour* (London, 1996), especially chapter 3.

[42] Boswell, *Grand Tour* (above, n. 11), 109, 19 July 1765. From a letter to his friend John Johnston: 'At Rome I ran about among the prostitutes till I was interrupted by that distemper which scourges vice in this world. When I got to Venice I had still some small remains of disease, but strange, gay ideas I had formed of the Venetian courtesans turned my head, and away I went to an opera dancer and took Lord Mountstuart with me. We both had her; and we both found ourselves taken in for the punishment which I had met with at Rome'. This is excepting the pastel portraits by Rosalba Carriera. See Redford, *Venice* (above, n. 41), 93.

[43] Boswell, *Grand Tour* (above, n. 11), 95, Monday 17 June 1765.

[44] For more on this, see below the section on Collins's essay, and further, R. Wrigley, 'Infectious enthusiasms: influence, contagion and the experience of Rome', in Chard and Langdon (eds), *Transports* (above, n. 2), 75–116.

lasting for Italy and the rest of Europe?'. I hope this question can be answered after reading the rest of the essays in the volume.

David Watkin, in the first of his essays here (Chapter 3), considers architectural rather than social or cultural history, and discusses a sequence of visitors to Italy from Britain whose concerns were primarily architectural. From Henry Wotton — the 'spy turned aesthete' —, in Italy at the beginning of the 1600s, to Cockerell, the architect and founder of the Xeineion, a club of Greek-loving aesthetes in the nineteenth century, some of the lovers of classical architecture who went to Italy (and beyond) for inspiration and for discovery of the origins of the architectural vocabulary that they themselves employed are accounted for. Here, also, the primacy of the example of ancient Greece versus that of ancient Rome in the matter of architectural aesthetics is mentioned, a topic which Frank Salmon examines in more detail (Chapter 11).[45] While the visitors concentrated principally on the greatness of antique architectural practice, their reaction to contemporary or recent styles in architecture is noted. Inigo Jones responded to the architecture of the Baroque negatively, however: 'this style he largely ignored', Watkin writes.

The protagonists of this historical survey who came to Italy (and who in some cases stayed for the rest of their lives) when they did return, carried back not just the bare principles of classical architecture. They also must have been material in the transfer of ideas and talent in the opposite, northward, direction, resulting in a number of Italian architects coming to practise in Britain. I would like to set these creative and influential individuals beside the 'native' Italians that Bignamini examines, who also made constructive use of the Grand Tour, since, as Watkin notes, 'It is not unreasonable to regard Chambers, Mylne, Adam, Byres, Dance, Harrison, Soane, Gandy and Tatham as having become, in a sense, honorary Italians'.

THE ANTIQUARIAN

Dennistoun, in his memoirs of Andrew Lumisden, wrote: 'The history, antiquities and arts of Italy were a soil unexhausted by natives — unoccupied by foreigners'.[46] This was certainly not the case in the mid-eighteenth century, but the comment provides an interesting picture of Italy considered, 100 years later, as somehow having been comparable to the colonial concept of 'Darkest Africa' in the (cultural) booty it promised to the diligent explorer. It offers a convenient nineteenth-century apologia for the activities of people such as Lumisden, whom Michael McCarthy examines (Chapter 4) in his role as antiquarian and

---

[45] The literature on this subject is large. With specific relation to the Grand Tour see Penny, 'Collecting' (above, n. 37).

[46] See J. Dennistoun, *Memoirs of Sir R. Strange and A. Lumisden*, 2 vols (Edinburgh, 1855), I, 144–5.

acquaintance of Piranesi while in Rome as the secretary to the Stuart Pretender to
the English throne. Boswell visits Lumisden and describes him in his diary[47] as
'quite a Secretary of State', and later at Avignon gives a glimpse of how the
antiquarian was viewed by his contemporaries.[48] Walking around the town with a
friend of Lumisden's, a certain Dr Ray, he notes: 'At a corner of one of the
streets he showed me a singular thing. Not to encroach on the street, the corner
house, instead of having its corner fully built, retires at the bottom into the shape
of a *clam* shell, and supports the weight as an arch. Mr. Lumisden could write a
dissertation upon this'. Lumisden's interest in the curiosities of architecture and
antiquity, which are part of the British tradition of enlightened amateur inquiry
in the eighteenth century when much did remain to be discovered (as noted —
and, as we have seen, exaggerated — by his biographer), formed an essential
component of what gave the Grand Tour lasting meaning in the history of
European culture. A letter written by the great historian Count Leopoldo
Cicognara to his friend, the sculptor Canova, in 1817, discussed the stimuli that
had brought about the birth of neo-classicism. Concerning this, Christopher
Johns has written: 'According to Cicognara, one of the chief reasons for the
rebirth of art created in the true spirit of the ancients was the enthusiasm of
wealthy and cultivated British Grand Tourists for antiquities and for knowledge
of all things ancient'.[49]

Indeed, some Italians could be seen as having had an outright 'unscientific'
attitude to their own artistic and cultural heritage, which was shown up by the
greater commitment and response to the past by the foreigner, especially by the
Britons. Here, in a gem from Harold Acton's history of the Bourbon kingdom of
Naples, the sometimes casual attitude of the proprietor of the antiquities so

---

[47] Boswell, *Grand Tour* (above, n. 11), 67, Thursday 4 April.

[48] Boswell, *Grand Tour* (above, n. 11), 267, Sunday 29 December 1765.

[49] C.M.S. Johns, *Antonio Canova and the Politics of Patronage in Revolutionary and
Napoleonic Europe* (Berkeley, 1998), 145: 'describing the revolution in taste that had banished a
decadent, lingering baroque and engendered the classical 'gusto' of which Canova was the
ultimate and best exemplar' Johns's note 1, p. 255, gives the full listing and the source:

> According to the President of the Venetian Academy, other factors that led
> to the rise of what we now ... label neoclassicism were:-
> the massive archaeological excavations of the eighteenth century,
> the rediscovery of Herculaneum,
> the books with engraved illustrations of ancient monuments and Greek
> vases, the excavations and published drawings of the Imperial bath
> complexes,
> the publication of engravings after ancient sculpture in the Capitoline
> Museum, the works of Piranesi,
> the restoration of ancient monuments in Rome and elsewhere and
> the promotion of scholarship.
> This is the most comprehensive and insightful listing I have encountered.

See L. Rusconi (ed.), *Lettere inedite di Leopoldo Cicognara ad Antonio Canova* (Padova, 1839),
which I have been unable to trace in Italy, despite the kind assistance of Professor Johns.

sought-after by the foreigners is shown.[50] For the Villa Floridiana, residence of his mistress, the Duchess of Floridia, King Ferdinand had a menagerie built: 'Among the animals were eighteen kangaroos which the King had procured through Sir William A'Court in exchange for an equal number of papyri from Herculaneum'. The apparent equivalence of kangaroos with ancient texts is absurd. However, the exchange might be seen as fair if the animals are considered purely as an example of exoticism in Taste, and paralleled with the eighteenth-century view — not only a British view — of the classical past as a novelty, something new and strange, at the same time as being venerable in its immense age, an idea which is also present throughout Piranesi's work.

McCarthy notes Lumisden's 'marriage of literary evidence with archaeological evidence' when the antiquarian comes to conclusions about the antiquities of Rome; on his own admission, Lumisden had a 'passion for books'. We might add, based on the evidence that McCarthy presents, that he had a lesser interest in the creative aspects of the architecture of the Romans that he so admired. He finds fault with Piranesi on points of accuracy — he criticizes Piranesi's *Campus Martius* for 'misleading strangers' and judges the volume to be useful 'to artists', which implies the lesser status of artists as compared to antiquarians, since they can find a use for inaccurate data.

Of course we know that it was the 'misleading' aspects of Piranesi which exerted and still exert the greatest power over those who observe the antiquities of Rome. As William Beckford notes on seeing the Colosseum: 'for you must know I was very near being disappointed, and began to think Piranesi and Paolo Panini had been a great deal too colossal, in their view of this venerable structure'.[51] Since Panini is generally noted for his relative lack of exaggeration in his *vedute* manner when compared to Piranesi, it is significant that Beckford should link these two artists in this way. The importance of exaggeration and hyperbole as a response of some artist-visitors, as examined in the first part of this Introduction, is underlined by this comment; with Lumisden and the painter William Marlow — the subject of the next essay — the corresponding and opposite 'scientific' response can be noted.

'... IN REGIONS THAT LOOK LIKE PAINTINGS ...'

As Duncan Bull has written, 'The history of British depictions of the Italian landscape after about 1765 seems, at first glance, to reveal the triumph of topographical draughtsmanship over painting', and he mentions the work of

---

[50] H. Acton, *The Bourbons of Naples (1734–1825)* (London, 1998), 685 [first published 1957].

[51] From W. Beckford, *Dreams, Waking Thoughts and Incidents* (Rutherford N.J., 1971), 193 [original edition 1783]. Quoted by and commented on by E.S. Shaffer, '"To remind us of China" — William Beckford, mental traveller on the Grand Tour: the construction of significance in language', in Chard and Langdon (eds), *Transports* (above, n. 2), 232, n. 81.

Marlow, Francis Towne and John Robert Cozens. These can be opposed to Richard Wilson and then Turner, who had a romantic-nostalgic sensibility inherited from the 'sublime' Salvator Rosa and Claude Lorrain. Michael Liversidge (Chapter 5) notes that 'English painters responded to the market both by imitating what the collectors favoured and by extending their repertoires through travelling themselves', and in his essay he examines Marlow as an exemplar of what Brewer refers to as 'the Reynolds effect'. That a painter like Marlow was principally responding to the market, in what Liversidge calls 'the process of commodification' being undergone at the time, is not surprising. The extent of this process might come as a surprise to those happier with the concept of purely inspirational motivation in artistic creativity which pervades romantic literature. For example, in *Corinne*, by Germaine de Staël, when Lord Nelvil comes back into Italy towards the end of the novel, we read:[52] 'il semble, dans le pays de plaines, que la terre n'ait d'autre but que de porter l'homme et de le nourrir; mais, dans les contrées pittoresques on croit reconnaître l'empreinte du génie du Créateur et de sa toute puissance'. This remark of the fictional Lord Nelvil has strong echoes in the response of the painter Thomas Jones, written when he also was travelling south into Italy. On leaving Bologna in 1776 he wrote: 'The Scenery now was quite changed and I was almost in raptures at getting among rocks, precipices and Picturesque mountains after having travell'd so long over the flat, insipid tho' rich plains of Lombardy'.[53]

As we saw earlier, Jones was somewhat set apart from his travelling companions by this heightened sensibility; as a painter, however, he was as acutely aware of the exigencies of the market as any of his fellow artists.[54] Recognizing that he was running out of commissions and patrons in Rome, he moved to Naples in 1780: 'especially if I should be so fortunate as to obtain the patronage of Sr W'm Hamilton our Minister — at all Events I should there have fewer Rival competitors'. It is worth noting here that Jones's wonderfully intimate and informal pictures of the humble scenes and interiors of the city were seen by the artist himself as different from those done on commission or made up from sketches for sale on the market — they are written of as being done during 'many a happy hour in painting from nature'[55] and 'con amore'.[56]

Like many travellers, Marlow began his Tour in France and depicted French scenes in many of his works. His images of Roman sites in France (such as the bridge at Avignon) formed a particular, personal, niche in the highly competitive market for depictions of sites of the Grand Tour. Liversidge mentions the

---

[52] G. de Staël, *Corinne: ou, l'Italie* (Paris, 1849), 472. For a recent translation, see *Corinne or Italy* (with an introduction by A.H. Goldberger) (New Jersey, 1987).

[53] Jones, *Memoirs* (above, n. 3), 50, 18 November 1776.

[54] Jones, *Memoirs* (above, n. 3), 93, 1 April 1780. Frank Salmon has pointed out to me that one of Jones's companions was the architect Thomas Hardwick.

[55] Jones, *Memoirs* (above, n. 3), 112, June 1782.

[56] Jones, *Memoirs* (above, n. 3), 17 May 1781.

important role of the French *Salons* and of Vernet in the training of a Grand Tour painter. In a similar way, in architecture the influence of the work of the French architects of the 1740s in their *Prix de Rome* designs submitted to the Académie was important for the third of the individual visitors discussed in this section, the architect John Soane.

THE BRICKLAYER'S SON

Soane's Grand Tour, as David Watkin shows in the second of his contributions to this volume (Chapter 6), was highly significant for the later development of his own architecture. But it was also a very original one, in that the architecture he admired formed a collection of differing styles. He admired Bernini for his 'handling of light ... central to the preoccupation with nature in eighteenth-century architectural aesthetics' while at the same time worshipping the perfection (as he saw it) of the Corinthian order and sharing with the Emperor Hadrian 'a belief in the superiority of Greek over Roman architecture'. His passion for collecting not only focused on architectural styles, but, as can be experienced in a visit to his house in London, also on objects. Watkin notes: 'Soane liked to acquire objects already assembled by architects he admired'. While demonstrating again his fervent eclecticism, this activity shows his desire to enhance still further the meaning of the ancient object by adding another layer of reference, much as the great and noble collectors since the Renaissance had done. From his humble social background Soane could raise himself up by this activity to the level of his patrons and beyond.

Cardinal Albani and his collection at the Villa Albani in Rome is a clear exemplar for Soane's own house/museum, and the architect's admiration for this building and its decoration, including the ancillary garden buildings, can be contrasted with a contemporary opinion from another Grand Tourist. Gibbon visited the Villa in December 1764 and noted: 'I observed in the garden, which is but small, an artificial ruin, small and without taste in itself, it appears ridiculous in Rome. Perhaps all imitations of this kind are ill judged'.[57] This response is an example of the scientific approach to antiquity — of the British antiquarian taste, obsessed with the minutiae of the past — that we saw earlier with Lumisden. And this attitude is at odds with the spirit behind the creation of the ruins not long before, in 1760, and with the admiration of such as Soane.

WOMEN AND NAPLES

Although 'obsession with the past' is narrow and self-limiting, as are all obsessions and addictions, there can grow from this peculiar attitude various unexpectedly fruitful branches. The next two essays in this collection examine

---

[57] Bonnard (ed.), *Gibbon's Journey from Geneva to Rome* (above, n. 23), 159.

the role of two women — both performers — whose art was re-enacted to some degree in their lives. One is an historical figure — Emma — who emerged as a character from the obsession with the past on the part of her lover, and later husband, Sir William Hamilton; the other is fictional — Corinne — who exemplifies engagement and passion to such a degree that her life is literally given up at the altar of her commitment to her art. This is, of course, excusable for her, since she is a creation of de Staël's mind, but that Emma, in her increasingly sad life before and after her affair with Nelson, should echo the tragic experiences of the classical heroines she had depicted in her performances of the attitudes — her 'acting out' of poses suggested by events in ancient history or myth — is an extraordinary example of synthesis. Also interesting is that, while the performances had been admired, the physical reality was later found repellent, when she was caricatured as obese and promiscuous.

Lori-Ann Touchette's essay (Chapter 7) discusses the link between the attitudes and ancient pantomime, both in terms of what we know of it from literary sources and from the images of it depicted in art, as on the Greek vases in the famous collection of Sir William Hamilton. The antiquarian obsession for the recreation of the antique is discussed here, considering what influenced Sir William's 'conception of the Attitudes'; as an antiquarian would he not insist on correctness rather than free interpretation? Emma's poses were more Baroque when released from the 'box' that Sir William had placed her in at the early stages of the performances — like sculpture when released from its podium becomes less static and perhaps less 'classical'. This point raises the issue of the intersection of Nature and Art in Emma's attitudes, an intersection that also occurs in other contexts. In his memoirs, Thomas Jones speculates on the reason for the beauty and grace of the Roman women 'even among the lower Order'. He attributes this to the good weather and 'the variety of Antique Statues which are perpetually before their eyes'.[58] This was also true for Emma, a British woman transplanted to Italian soil.

Emma's famous personal beauty, although formed in distant places such as Wales and London, came to its full fruition when she was living in Naples, where all nature's beauties seemed enhanced and became art. This effect is described in a letter from Tischbein to Goethe, in July 1787, mentioning the swimmers employed for entertainment by Sir William: 'After dinner a dozen boys flung themselves into the sea; a very beautiful spectacle, with the many groups and various positions they assume in play among themselves'.[59] Here is evidence of a painter's eye for composition, but there are also parallels in the natural beauty and skill of Emma in her attitudes — summoning up the classical

[58] Jones, *Memoirs* (above, n. 3), 55, at Albano.
[59] From Goethe, *Italienische Reise* (Berlin, 1988), 359, quoted in C. Knight, 'William Hamilton and the "art of going through life"', in Jenkins and Sloan (eds), *Vases and Volcanoes* (above, n. 36), 15, n. 7.

past in its grace and formal beauty and associating it with the present day through the medium of the powerful, almost magical, nature to be found around Naples. Touchette asks the question at the beginning of her essay: 'what was the relationship between the attitudes and their setting within the landscape of a new-found knowledge of the ancient world as revealed in the excavations of the Campania region?'. So it is not simply the surface of the countryside around Naples which exerted its influence, but also what lay beneath the ground, and was at the time being gradually uncovered.

Emma was identified with Nature even before she arrived in Italy, as in the painting of her holding a puppy by Romney from 1782, commissioned by Charles Greville, Hamilton's nephew.[60] The verse below the engraving after this picture clarifies the point:

> Flushed by the spirit of the genial year
> Her lips blush deeper sweets they breathe of Youth
> The shining moisture swells into her eyes
> In brighter glow her wishing bosom heaves
> With palpitations wild.

Here Emma and dog are blended into one delicious and accessible fruit of nature. When she was performing the attitudes, this aspect of her image was enhanced (ennobled even) by association with the antique past. It is tempting to say that, while Emma was Nature, Sir William was Art in his management and arrangement of her for performance.

Chloe Chard's essay (Chapter 8) introduces itself: 'The two women [Emma and Corinne], compared to each other ... as rival sights of Naples, exemplify, respectively, the two traits of character that northern European travel writings regularly attribute to the Neapolitans themselves'. Also examined are the similarities they have in their 'gifted' abilities; Emma is 'invested with a power to reanimate', while Corinne has an 'extraordinarily animating effect on the musicians and the rest of her audience'. This power is, in both cases, primarily a force of Nature, and of Naples in particular:

> *Mais, en approchant de Naples, vous éprouvez un bien-être si parfait, une si grande amitié de la nature pour vous, que rien n'altère les sensations agréables qu'elle vous cause. Tous les rapports de l'homme, dans nos climats, sont avec la société, la nature, dans les pays chauds, met en relation avec les objets extérieurs et les sentiments s'y répandent doucement au déhors.*[61]

---

[60] From Jenkins and Sloan (eds), *Vases and Volcanoes* (above, n. 36), cat. no. 168, 269, a mezzotint by John Raphael Smith, published in 1784.

[61] De Staël, *Corinne: ou, l'Italie* (above, n. 52), 239.

This force is felt to be strong, subtle, potent and probably dangerous, and there is an implicit link between women and moral danger in *Corinne* which echoes the expressions of deprecation that we saw earlier in Boswell's journal. Lord Nelvil writes to Corinne: 'Les hommes, en Italie, valent beaucoup moins que les femmes, car ils ont les defauts des femmes, et leurs propres en sus'.[62]

Chard also looks at the theory of performance — Corinne's improvisations, which were long, unscripted, probably inspired, monologues on the art, literature and history of Italy; and Emma's attitudes, silent yet evocative renderings of the poses of antique women in art — and at the response this drew from the audience, particularly the travel writers who watched Emma's displays. This shades into the examination of the role of comedy; Chard quotes from De Boigne on Emma — 'il n'y a qu'un pas du sublime au ridicule'.

The novel gives us privileged insight to examine ideas on the contrast between two cultures — the Mediterranean and the Anglo-Saxon —, the meeting of which is central to the theory of the Grand Tour, but which are only hinted at in the diaries of those who witnessed Emma's performances. De Staël makes the point clearly in this episode when Corinne is invited by her beloved Scottish lord, Nelvil, to attend divine service aboard an English warship anchored in the bay of Naples:

> Corinne monta sur le vaisseau, dont l'intérieur était entretenu avec les soins et la propreté la plus recherchée. On n'entendait que la voix du capitaine, qui se prolongeait et se répétait d'un bord à l'autre par le commandement et l'obéissance. La subordination, le sérieux, la régularité, le silence qu'on remarquait dans ce vaisseau, était l'image d'un ordre social libre et sévère, en contraste avec cette ville de Naples, si vive, si passionnée, si tumultueuse.[63]

The restrained masculinity of the ship, in its intrusion in the luscious feminine image of the encircling bay, not only highlights the contrasts between the lovers in the context of the novel, but shows us that the idea of Italy as a repository of desirable objects to be plundered, yet not to become entangled with, that runs through many responses of travellers, is in many ways an accurate one.

'MUSE-EUM'

Jeffrey Collins's essay (Chapter 9) on the Museo Pio-Clementino and its architecture begins with a quotation from Goethe which is worth repeating here, since it also underlines the link between Nature and the antique past that was strongly evident in Naples: 'Standing amid antique statues, one feels as if all the

---

[62] De Staël, *Corinne: ou, l'Italie* (above, n. 52), 122.
[63] De Staël, *Corinne: ou, l'Italie* (above, n. 52), 246.

forces of Nature were in motion around one'.[64] Such feelings evoked by and in museums are new in the eighteenth century, as is the institution itself — as Collins points out: 'the Pio-Clementino's wholesale reconstruction of the ancient world inside the Vatican's walls advanced not just Italian neo-classicism but the development of the modern museum'. One turns, naturally, to Winckelmann, the great eighteenth-century writer on ancient art, for responses to the sculptures, but one could ask whether the architect Simonetti in fact already intended to create what Collins describes as a 'Winckelmannian mood' by the small *gabinetti* in which individual pieces were placed. A limited space enhances, yet contains, the power of the object displayed, and this could have affected Winckelmann's response to the work itself, for he certainly appreciated what he saw as the emotional control in the Laocoön: 'for Winckelmann, the aesthetic success of the Laocoön group depended as much upon the suppression as the expression of anguish'[65] (not an opinion that the modern visitor would share, I think). The less sensitized Boswell provides another, complementary view: '"Laocoon" supreme; equal to all ideas. Nerves contracted by it, so that beautiful "Apollo" could not be felt'.[66] This would suggest that the effect of the Laocoön was as that of a blow from a hammer, and the more subtle enchantments of the Belvedere Apollo are thence lost.

The particular, modern, activity of viewing the collection of a museum — in itself an extension of the process of travelling, and as such a microcosmic paradigm of the Grand Tour — is discussed by Collins: he mentions a nocturnal visit to the portico in 1783 which provokes a response that establishes 'an opposition between chaos and organization, ... past and present, viewer and viewed', which brings us back to Emma's attitudes and Corinne's improvisations. The nocturnal visits by torchlight are famous in the Romantic canon of the worship of art, a deliberate enhancement of the effect of examination of ancient buildings and sculpture to create a thrill beyond that which could normally be expected. The architectural historian Christian Elling has linked the Tourists' use of the artificial light of torches to view the works in the Museo with the *moccoli* held by the people at Carnival and the visiting of the catacombs, again by torchlight, — and both of these to the power of the past: 'An essential part of the secret of man's profound infatuation with the art of Antiquity was, in our opinion, that he did not always see the rooms of the museum in the ordinary light of day, the soberness of which is hostile to all

---

[64] J.W. Goethe, *Italian Journey* [1786–9] (translated by W. H. Auden and E. Mayer) (London, 1962; reprinted Harmondsworth, 1970), 489–90.

[65] See N. Spivey, 'The depiction of suffering in classical art: the audition of Laocoön's scream', *Apollo* (July 1998), 3; also J.J. Winckelmann, *Storia delle arti del disegno presso gli antichi*, 3 vols (translated and with notes by Carlo Fea) (Rome, 1783), II, 117.

[66] Boswell, *Grand Tour* (above, n. 11), 70, Tuesday 23 April.

illusions'.[67] The identification of the museum's architectural vocabulary with that previously reserved for the temple or church, which Collins explores in his essay, can be paralleled clearly with this intensification of the status of the viewing activity, now pulled out of the private domain of the *Wunderkammer*, or cabinet, and into the public sphere (albeit a restricted public in the eighteenth century). This leads to the now common modern practice of the secular religion of art, sanctified by romantic perceptions of creative figures such as Michelangelo and Van Gogh; a new Sunday activity in which all the family can participate, worshipping art intensified now by being placed in quiet, large, white spaces — objects that are validated simply by their inclusion in a collection.[68]

Space is too short here for a full discussion of the history of the museum.[69] I would just like to add a point about the discovery of Herculaneum and Pompeii which marries well with Collins's thoughts on the creation of the Museo Pio-Clementino. As Richard Hamblyn has written:

> It is untrue to say that the eruption of Vesuvius of AD 79 destroyed the two villages of Pompeii and Herculaneum, for it was the eruption of Vesuvius that created them and produced a renewed reason for northern Europeans to visit Naples rather than turn round at Rome. There would be no reason to recall the name of Pompeii, or any of the other two hundred or so similar settlements in the region, were it not for the circumstances of its burial, discovery and subsequent status during the mid-eighteenth century as an instant museum.[70]

That 'instant museum' provided the material for many subsequent collections and also was the impetus that turned the simple curiosity about objects from the ancient past into a legitimate learned activity.

'AFTER' THE 'GRAND TOUR'

To turn to the two essays whose subjects concerned visitors to Italy in the 1820s to 1840s, we can see that certain individual responses which were first voiced in the eighteenth century have developed by the nineteenth century into clear, identifiable, general attitudes on the part of the British visitors. Lumisden's

---

[67] C. Elling, *Rome. The Biography of its Architecture from Bernini to Thorvaldsen* (translated from the Danish by B. and I. Gosney) (Tübingen, 1975), 529.

[68] On Michelangelo in the nineteenth century see L. Østermark-Johansen, *Sweetness and Strength: the Reception of Michelangelo in Late Victorian England* (London, 1998).

[69] Valuable insight into this topic can be had from Johns, *Canova* (above, n. 49), esp. pp. 190 and 193, and from P. Liverani, *Dal Pio-Clementino al Braccio Nuovo in Vaticano* (as yet unpublished text of paper given at the conference on *Das Museum: Neue Tendenzen um 1800* at the Bibliotheca Hertziana, Rome, 1 and 2 March 1999).

[70] R. Hamblyn, 'Private cabinets and popular geology: the British audiences for volcanoes in the eighteenth century', in Chard and Langdon (eds), *Transports* (above, n. 2), 185.

antiquarian interest in architecture has become the rigorous scientific examination of Roman buildings by visiting architects, as we shall see in the essay by Frank Salmon (Chapter 11); and, as examined here in an essay by John Bowen (Chapter 10), the nascent progressivist philosophy linked with nostalgic yearning for the glories of a far-distant past, such as we saw in Boswell and in Shelley, has become an open, outright plea for reform in Dickens. At the end of *Pictures from Italy* he invokes progress: 'Italy with all its miseries and wrongs ... the wheel of time is rolling for an end and that the world is, in all great essentials, better, gentler, more forbearing and more hopeful as it rolls!'.

However, Dickens's responses to Italy are multifarious, mutually contradictory in many cases but always imbued with hyperbole — the key response of the visitor to Italy as signalled at the beginning of this essay. Bowen notes Dickens's constant recourse to the hyperbolic and points out that in the book 'good and bad are pushed to equal extremes'. His anti-clericalism and anti-Catholicism provide plenty of opportunities for hyperbole; these attitudes are given voice in his statements about the Roman church buildings themselves and his invective against the works of Bernini: 'the most detestable class of productions in the wide world'[71]and 'intolerable abortions'.[72] Yet his descriptions depend largely for their slant on the place he is in or the people by whom he is surrounded at any particular moment. His description of the Carnival procession and the ritual of *moccoli* is very positive: here he seems to like the people — they are no longer 'fierce and cruel', as at the Colosseum (p. 164 — his description of which contains the word 'ruin' five times in one paragraph alone) or 'coarse and heavy ... half miserable, half ridiculous' (p. 166), as they appear at Mass in Saint Peter's. Instead, he sees 'beautiful women ... delicate arms and bosoms ... graceful figures' (pp. 175–6). Bowen makes the point that in fact 'Dickens's writing is consistently interested in the grotesque ... extravagance, fancifulness, exaggeration: these are the charges that Dickens made against Bernini and Correggio, and that his detractors have always made against him'. And much as we saw with Emma, life began to imitate art for Dickens in Italy when he describes his encounter with Vesuvius, which, as Bowen notes, was 'astonishing and near-fatal'. This can be paralleled with the dangerous visit to the volcano by Corinne, and also, to extend the theme of the dangers of Italy for travellers, with the risks run by Winckelmann in the pursuit of his studies. Christian Elling notes that: 'The pioneers often ran great risks before they succeeded in creating harmony between the [ancient] texts and the monuments. Winckelmann just escaped with his life after nearly being crushed beneath a statue in the Villa Ludovisi when he was examining it at close quarters'.[73]

---

[71] Dickens, *Pictures from Italy* (above, n. 5), 196.

[72] Dickens, *Pictures from Italy* (above, n. 5), 197.

[73] Elling, *Rome* (above, n. 67), 497. His note 46 refers to K.W. Dassdorf (ed.), *Winckelmanns Briefe*, vol. I, 71. I would like to pay tribute to Christian Elling's book, first written in 1950 and with superb photographs of Roman buildings and sites by Lennart af Petersens, which gives the

These architectural pioneers included those whose visits to Rome and subsequent careers are examined in the essay by Frank Salmon (Chapter 11), which concludes this volume. His points on the chronological boundaries of the Grand Tour are important: 'there were in reality many different "grand tours"... if we take the year 1796 [Napoleon's invasion of Italy] as the endpoint of the Grand Tour we miss one of the most interesting episodes in the cultural linkage between Britain and the ancient Roman world'. Salmon mentions Taylor and Cresy's *The Architectural Antiquities of Rome* (1821–2) as an example of the insistence on scientific method. Perhaps reading Inigo Jones on Palladio, Lumisden on Piranesi and a thousand other commentaries pointed up the absolute necessity of 'getting it right' — the pure spirit of the ancients would no longer suffice; the chapter and verse quotation became necessary. The lure of Roman architecture was still strong for the British, despite the later eighteenth-century passion for all things Greek. The point made by Salmon that 'the symbolism of Roman buildings could become as much a part of a specifically British national identity as the supposedly indigenous Gothic' makes one think of Dickens, whose opinions on the architecture of Rome are in essence that there had been a corruption of the noble pagan style by the popish/Baroque. Roman architecture was adopted in Britain as Protestant architecture; and, as Salmon shows, as an official, municipal architecture.

To my own question in the title of this introduction — why travel? — there are, of course, too many answers. Perhaps at the time of the Grand Tour, as now, travel consisted in going, hoping to find one's preconceived opinions about a place, a people or a culture challenged, and instead often finding them confirmed — and being pleased about it. To conclude, as we began, with Stendhal in Rome, his mockery and exaggeration are valuable in highlighting the irreconcilable contrasts between peoples that made (and still make) travel such a satisfying, and at the same time frustrating, experience. On the British he wrote: 'le jury et l'esprit d'association, la machine à vapeur, les dangers de la navigation, les ressources dans le péril, lui seront choses familières; mais comme homme, il sera fort inférieur au Romain'. [74]

---

fullest and most detailed account of the fabric of Roman architecture in the late Baroque and neo-classical periods, with much insight into the work of earlier periods. Architecture is the framework for a wonderfully written extended essay in praise of the city and an opinionated examination of its traditions and institutions. The last chapter is a marvel in Grand Tour studies *avant la lettre*, focusing as it does on the magnetism of the ancient ruins that drew so many travellers to Rome.

[74] Stendhal, *Promenades* (above, n. 1), 232.

THE PROTAGONISTS

2

The Italians As Spectators And Actors: . The Grand Tour Reflected

ILARIA BIGNAMINI

Studies of the various aspects of the eighteenth-century Grand Tour are usually focused on foreign travellers, on the impact of Italy upon them as individuals and, more generally, on their home countries. The other side of the Grand Tour has hardly been explored so far. The question is what the Italians thought of the Grand Tourists; what were their actions and reactions? Were the Italians simply spectators, or were they active participants and, if so, what were the different levels of their participation? More generally, did the Grand Tour cause substantial changes to Italy and to the Italians? This essay does not aim to discuss all these issues in full, but is intended to serve as an introduction to a new and largely unexplored area of research, which, I believe, deserves to be investigated in all its aspects, from the most banal to the most culturally significant. As a consequence, the examples selected here range from naive paintings produced by little-known artists to vulgar poems and comedies of no literary quality; from roads and bridges built for royal travellers to toilets provided for them and meals cooked for them, both modest and grand. More 'serious' examples show how far the British (and also the German, Scandinavian and Russian) conquest of the marbles of ancient Rome was counterbalanced — thanks to a clever policy in granting excavation and export licences — by the creation of new museums in Rome and, more generally, by the Roman conquest of Europe. These examples of the activity of the Italians in the context of the Grand Tour will answer, at least in part, the questions raised above and, I hope, stimulate further thought on the dichotomous nature of the Grand Tour — those who travelled and those who responded to this activity.

FIG. 1. Canaletto, *Regatta on the Grand Canal, c.* 1730–1. Oil on canvas, 147 × 218 cm. Woburn Abbey. *(By kind permission of the Marquess of Tavistock and the Trustees of the Bedford Estate)*

FIG. 2. Gabriel Bella, *Women's Regatta on the Grand Canal*, after 1764. Oil on canvas, 94.5 × 146 cm. *(Reproduced courtesy of the Fondazione Scientifica Querini Stampalia, Venice)*

A VENETIAN VISIT

Clashing images can be shocking, but they are liable to capture the attention of curious viewers and make important points in purely visual terms, without the need for lengthy, written commentary. This was the case in the room devoted to *Festivals and Folklore* in the *Grand Tour* exhibition, held at the Tate Gallery in 1996, where the superb *Regatta on the Grand Canal*, painted by Canaletto in *c.* 1730–1 (Fig. 1), was juxtaposed with the *Women's Regatta on the Grand Canal* (Fig. 2), depicted by a little-known, minor, Venetian painter called Gabriel Bella, sometime after 1764.[1] In the accompanying text in the catalogue, Marini and I commented that 'Spectacular Canalettos were produced for the export market, for wealthy tourists and foreign collectors, while modest, naïve, Bellas were kept in town to preserve the memory of the age of the Grand Tour in Venice and for the Venetians'.[2] The works of Bella remind us that the Italians were themselves part of the Grand Tour, and that their views, tastes and budgets might be different from those of the tourists.

The Canaletto *Regatta* (Fig. 1) and its magnificent companion piece, the *Bucintoro leaving from the Molo on Ascension Day*,[3] were part of a series of 24 paintings by Canaletto that Joseph Smith, the British Consul in Venice, purchased on behalf of John Russell, fourth Duke of Bedford, a Grand Tourist and art collector. By contrast, the naive *Regatta* (Fig. 2) was part of a larger and, in many respects, more important series of 95 canvases that Bella painted for two Venetian noblemen, Girolamo Ascanio Giustinian and his friend Andrea Querini.[4] Altogether, these canvases form a unique visual history of Venice, which parallels the historical account written by Pietro Gradenigo, a Venetian nobleman.[5]

---

[1] This provocative comparison is less noticeable in the exhibition catalogue, where the two paintings were separated visually from each other.

[2] I. Bignamini and G. Marini, 'Venice', in A. Wilton and I. Bignamini (eds), *Grand Tour: the Lure of Italy in the Eighteenth Century* (exhibition catalogue, Tate Gallery, London, 1996), 187; and also, *Grand Tour: il fascino dell'Italia nel XVIII secolo* (exhibition catalogue, Palazzo delle Esposizioni, Rome, 1997), 193. For paintings by Canaletto and Bella, see Wilton and Bignamini (eds), *Grand Tour: the Lure*, 194–5, no. 145, and 189–90, no. 140; and Wilton and Bignamini, *Grand Tour: il fascino*, 201–2, no. 145, and 197–8, no. 140.

[3] See Wilton and Bignamini (eds), *Grand Tour: the Lure* (above, n. 2), 194–5, no. 144; and Wilton and Bignamini (eds), *Grand Tour: il fascino* (above, n. 2), 201–2, no. 144.

[4] See G. Busetto (ed.), *Cronaca veneziana. Feste e vita quotidiana nella Venezia del Settecento. Vedute di Gabriel Bella e incisioni di Gaetano Zompini dalle raccolte della Fondazione Querini Stampalia di Venezia* (exhibition catalogue, Strauhof, Zurich, 1991); G. Busetto (ed.), *Cento scene di vita veneziana. Pietro Longhi e Gabriel Bella alla Querini Stampalia* (Venice, 1995).

[5] He spent most of his life writing several manuscript volumes, which are now preserved in the Biblioteca Correr and the Marciana. Biblioteca Correr, Venice, *Cod. Gradenigo* 191/I–II and 52; Biblioteca Marciana, Venice, *Cod. It.* VII 164 and 707. For Gradenigo, see G.A. Moschini, *Vite di tre ... Gradenigo* (Venice, 1809).

These remarkable histories of eighteenth-century Venice — Gradenigo's written history and Bella's visual history — tell us something that no Canaletto will ever disclose. As we have seen, Canaletto worked for the export market, while *nobile* Gradenigo was writing for the Republic of Venice and 'modest' Bella was painting for the Venetians; we can be sure that no foreigner bought a Bella. Gradenigo and Bella remind us that, in the Golden Age of the Grand Tour, Venice identified itself with tourism and with the spectacular festivals organized by the Venetian Government in honour of royal and other important travellers. In an age of booming tourism, these festivals attracted huge crowds of tourists, who converged on Venice from all over Italy and Europe.

These festivals became very important for the economy of Venice. Countless prints were produced by local engravers, such as Antonio Baratti, Giuseppe Baroni, Giambattista Brustolon, Domenico Fossati, Giacomo Leonardis and Giambattista Moretti.[6] Popular among the Venetians, and also the tourists, were prints of boats richly decorated for festivals organized in honour of royal travellers (Figs 3–5).[7] Their success is demonstrated, amongst other things, by the fact that they were reproduced in best-selling illustrated volumes, such as Domenico Lovisa's *Il gran teatro di Venezia* of 1720 (Fig. 3), and in standard guidebooks, such as Giambattista Albrizzi's *Forestiero illuminato*, first published in 1740 and reprinted until 1822.[8] No other Italian town shows such a degree of self-identification with festivals and, more generally, tourism as Venice. The *Serenissima* had always held spectacular festivals — during previous centuries they had been organized to celebrate visits which had important political, diplomatic and commercial consequences for the Republic. In the eighteenth century, however, they were sadly reduced to the role of celebrating important tourists.

In fact, during the eighteenth century, the Government of Venice was primarily concerned with administration relating to tourism, and its State Inquisitors spent most of their time reading countless lists of the misspelt and unpronounceable names of British, French, German, Austrian, Dutch, Scandinavian, Polish and Russian tourists that were sent to the Inquisitors by all the innkeepers of Venice and the towns of the *Terraferma*.[9] The Venetians, of

---

[6] See Wilton and Bignamini (eds), *Grand Tour: the Lure* (above, n. 2), 176–81, nos. 129–34; and Wilton and Bignamini (eds), *Grand Tour: il fascino* (above, n. 2), 183–7, nos. 129–34. Also D. Succi (ed.), *Da Carlevarijs ai Tiepolo. Incisori veneti e friulani del Settecento* (exhibition catalogue, Museo Correr, Venice, 1983).

[7] See *Bissone, poete e galleggianti* (exhibition catalogue, Museo Correr, Venice, 1980).

[8] See Wilton and Bignamini (eds), *Grand Tour: the Lure* (above, n. 2), 129, no. 88; and Wilton and Bignamini (eds), *Grand Tour: il fascino* (above, n. 2), 133, no. 88.

[9] The names of British travellers and the dates of their stays in the various inns have been recorded for the Brinsley Ford Archive at The Paul Mellon Centre, London. For a selection, see J. Ingamells (ed.), *A Dictionary of British and Irish Travellers in Italy 1701–1800* (New Haven and London, 1997) (hereafter *DBITI*).

course, benefited significantly from the presence of so many tourists. The innkeepers were certainly pleased, as were the traders in all sorts of commodities and souvenirs. Printers were very busy; they printed beautiful books and engravings, music and operas, comedies, newspapers, and also poems and ballads (possibly the most vulgar to be found in any archive or library) — Venice is a real joy for the eclectic scholar. In fact, the Grand Tour contributed greatly to the increase of poetasters. Their very particular expression is clearly evinced, in 1764, when the most memorable of all the royal travellers, Edward Augustus, Duke of York, arrived in Venice.[10]

The arrival in Venice — capital city of prostitution and libertinism — of the English Duke, himself allegedly a libertine, is celebrated by a certain Pipina Sinviesti in the following words:

> *De Yorck el Duca,*
> *Prencipe Inglese,*
> *che Annoverese,*
> *oriundo el xè.*
> *Re d'Inghilterra,*
> *xè sò Fradello,*
> *Glorioso quello,*
> *sè nò il savè.*[11]

She, 'la bella VENEZIA' (in Venetian *canzonette* the city is always described as a beautiful woman), embraced him tenderly. He immediately forgot about everything else, even Justice and Prudence, and followed her to the *Canalazzo in Gringola*, to the sumptuous regatta:

> *Un numero infinito*
> *De barche, e de barchette,*
> *Batteli, e gondolette. (Mi gho mai più visto*
> *Spettacolo più belo.) Ricchi abitoni*
> *Visetti da basar. (Mi son restà de sasso.)*[12]

---

[10] For the Duke of York, see Wilton and Bignamini (eds), *Grand Tour: the Lure* (above, n. 2), 77–8, no. 35, and 189–90, no. 140; and Wilton and Bignamini (eds), *Grand Tour: il fascino* (above, n. 2), 81–2, no. 35, and 197–8, no. 140. Also Bignamini's entry in Ingamells (ed.), *DBITI* (above, n. 9), 1,033–5.

[11] P. Sinviesti, *Descrizione della famosissima Regata seguita li 4. Giugno 1764*, in *Raccolta di tutto quello che fu stampato in questa città nell'occasione della venuta di Sua Altezza Reale Odoardo Augusto Duca di York, contro-Ammiraglio, e conte d'Ulster nell'Irlanda* (hereafter *Raccolta*) (Venice, 1764). Translation: 'Of York the Duke, / English Prince, / of Hanoverian origins he is. / King of England, / his brother is, / glorious that one, / if you did not know it.'

[12] Translation: 'An immense number / of boats, and little boats, / larger boat, and gondolas. (I have never seen / such a beautiful scene.) Sumptuous dress / faces to be kissed. (I was quite astounded.)

FIG. 3. Anonymous, *Veduta del Canal Grande dirimpetto la Pescaria di Rialto*. One of the prints issued to celebrate the regatta organized in honour of Frederick Augustus of Saxony, later King of Poland, in 1716. From Domenico Lovisa, *Il gran teatro di Venezia*, 1720. Etching and engraving. *(Reproduced courtesy of the Museo Correr, Venice)*

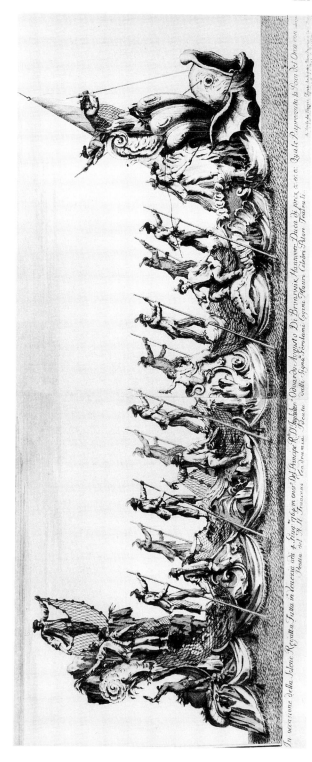

FIG. 4. Giorgio Fossati, *La pesca dell'orca*. From a series of five boat prints issued to celebrate the regatta of 4 June 1764 in honour of Edward Augustus, Duke of York. Engraving. *(Reproduced courtesy of the Museo Correr, Venice)*

Bissona fatta construire dalla Seren.ma Sign.ria di Venezia per la Regatta a sua Maestà Gustavo III Re di Svezia

LI CAMPI ELISI

FIG. 5. Anonymous, *Li Campi Elisi*. From a series of six prints issued to celebrate the regatta of 8 May 1784 in honour of Gustav III, King of Sweden. Engraving. *(Reproduced courtesy of the Museo Correr, Venice)*

He sat there, among 'tutte le persone che ghiera stravacae su le Bissone' (all the people who were there, sprawled out on boats). He listened to poems and songs written for him by Silvestro Ferrara Dilettante, Pietro Ségala Barcariol Niovo Poeta, Arobald Coma fra i Poeti Infimo, all writing for him (a royal prince and a foreigner) in Venetian and also *rustego* dialect (lower class Venetian) because 'la curiosità de tutto el Mondo ve mette in giubilio giocondo' (the curiosity of all the world puts one in a state of joyful jubilation). He, 'El Prencipe ODOARDO, De York el Duca, gran Inglese, Eroe BRITANNO, Ammiraglio della Flotta Turchina' (Prince Edward, Duke of York, great Englishman, British hero, Admiral of the blue fleet), listened to them. And they, 'famosissimi poeti dei spiantati' (the most famous poets of the penniless), recited poems for him in praise of women, songs full of joy, of sweetness and some malice. The arias were 'Spettacolo più vago, Fra tutti ispassi, Più bella della Luce, Per quell'affetto che l'incatena, Non si ama più da vera' (More charming spectacle, Among all the fun, More beautiful than the light, For that affection that held him in chains, No real love any more). One of the best of these is 'Me xè saltà in testa un bel pensier' (I have suddenly had a wonderful idea).[13]

The fragments quoted above come from poems and songs published for the regatta held on 4 June 1764 (see Fig. 3). This event included a regatta of rowing women held, on the Grand Canal, especially for this important male visitor; although, as shown in his portraits, he seems to have been physically unattractive, he was apparently successful with women.[14] The Venetian deputies in charge of assisting him during his stay described the Duke as being young, lively, rather intelligent, informal, easy and very accessible.[15] Although the deputies produced this sympathetic portrayal of him for the Doge, countless malicious reports were written by agents and spies of other Italian courts. A Venetian agent reported to the Court of Turin that the Duke of York was superficial, indifferent, and inconstant, like *Don Giovanni*. He added: 'Va in giro da queste nostre Dame, e vorrebbe visitarle in Casa senza riserve, ma non può avere tutta la libertà, che spiegasi desiderare, perché sempre assistite al fianco dai loro Cavalieri serventi'.[16]

Moreover, the Duke misbehaved with the wife of the Commander of Trieste. He visited her every night at the inn where she was lodging with her husband, and claimed that, because of his love for her, he wished to see Trieste;

---

[13] All these quotations come from *Raccolta* (above, n. 11).

[14] For example, the portrait by Pompeo Batoni, shown in Wilton and Bignamini (eds), *Grand Tour: the Lure* (above, n. 2), 77–8, no. 35; and Wilton and Bignamini (eds), *Grand Tour: il fascino* (above, n. 2), 81–2, no. 35.

[15] Archivio di Stato di Venezia, *Senato, Corti*, fol. 319: *Relazione dei Deputati sul Duca di York*.

[16] Archivio di Stato di Torino (sez. I), *Cerimoniale, Inghilterra*, mazzo 1 d'add., ins. 13: *Venezia 2. Giugno 1764*. Translation: 'He goes around and visits our ladies, would like to visit them at home without any restrictions, but cannot have all the freedom he himself would like to have because they are always escorted by their swains'.

but, the agent reported that it seemed that the Commander did not approve of such declarations. Such a visitor was indeed the ideal honorary spectator of the memorable *Regatta delle Donne*.

A poem describes him as he is shown in Bella's painting, seated in the prow of the beautiful boat on the left (Fig. 2):

> *Ghe xè nella più bela*
> *El Prencipe ODOARDO*
> *Che zira intorno el sguardo*
> *Mostrando gran stupor.*[17]

One might speculate on the relationship between the poetasters writing in dialect and Bella. From a cultural and social point of view, he was similar to them, the major difference being that while the poets were writing for the man in the street, Bella was painting for Venetian noblemen, Giustinian and Querini. However, by examining the poetic production of some Venetian noblemen, it can be seen that their work did not differ greatly from that of the lower class of poets. Two samples of risqué aristocratic writing, which relate to the Ducal visit, are to be found at the Biblioteca Correr. The first is a poem describing the Duke's arrival in Venice and of his welcome by the populace, who were so busy, friendly and charming. Also mentioned is the risk posed to the chastity of Venetian women by the Duke's presence, and the preventive measures to be taken by their partners:

> *Odoardo Fratell dell Rè d'Inghilterra*
> *vien a Venezia con un gran corteggio*
> *doppo haver visto Roma, Parma, e Reggio*
> *Turin, e tanti altri gran Paesi.*
> *I Veneziani Splendidi, e Cortesi*
> *i ghe prepara un Trattamento Reggio*
> *e de vera amicizia i se fà preggio*
> *darghe i Segni pui vivi, e pui palesi.*
> *Per far feste, Regatte, e Recreazion*
> *è in motto, e in allegria ogni Persona*
> *Solo i morosi xe in agitazion*
> *Savendo che ghe piase assae la Donna*
> *i pensa alle morose con rason*
> *de metterghe un Luchetto sulla mona.*[18]

---

[17] 'In the most beautiful of the boats there is / Prince Edward, / who is looking round / in astonishment'. *El Canalazzo in Gringola*, in *Raccolta* (above, n. 11).

[18] Biblioteca Correr, Venice, *Cod. Cicogna* 1486, fol. 59: *Nella venuta del Duca di York a Venetia 1764. Sonetto.* (Translation: 'Edward, brother of the King of England / arrives in Venice with a great following / after having visited Rome, Parma, and Reggio / Turin, and many other grand places. / The Venetians, splendid, and courteous, / have prepared a princely reception for him, / and of real friendship they are keen to give him the most vivid and sincere signs. / Organising receptions, regattas, and recreations / everybody is joyfully active. / Only lovers are in a state of agitation; / and since they know how much he likes the female sex / they are considering, wisely enough, locking the vaginas of their beloved'.)

The descriptions of the characters of a comedy set at a regatta on the Grand Canal are even more scurrilous than this poem, but offer an ideal comment on the scene depicted by Bella. A group of witty Venetian nobles — both men and women — on a balcony overlooking the Grand Canal, comment and gossip about the participants in the regatta:

Li deputati del Duca
Il Nobile Zuanne Grimani.........Propone tutto
Il Nobile Marco Priuli..........S'oppone a tutto
Il Nobile Francesco Pesaro........Guasta tutto
Il Nobile Vettor Pisani............Accorda tutto.
Il Duca ... Hà in cesto tutto.

Sopra le Bissone, Malgarotte, e Ballottine fatte nella
Regatta 4. Giugno 1764.
Fratelli Mocenighi: Castore e Polluce trasformati in Polastrelli.
Giacomo Foscarini: L'Eunuco a diporto.
Cattarin Corner: Non est de Sacco tanta farina suo.
Pietro Marcello: Il Convitato di Pietra, ò sia Don Giovanni.
Fratelli Pesari: Col tempo faranno qualche cosa.
Francesco Savorgnan: Il Porco in Trionfo.
Giovanelli, e Soranzo: Và paroli, e sette a levar.
Fratelli Venieri: Li Figli di V[u]lcano.
Domenico Michiel: Quando faremo giudizio? Mai.
Mario Savorgnan: Dò; Re; Mi, Fà, Là, Là, Là, Sol fà mi rè, dò.
Girolamo Giustinian: E chi ha d'aver aspetta.
Li Fratelli Manini: Omnia & pecuniam facta sunt.
Antonio Bollani: Homo sine pecunia; Imago Mortis.
Li Fratelli Redetti: Una voglia di compania.
Trifon Valmarana: Compatilo; l'à robba di Casa.
Fratelli Zani: L'Ecconomia beffata da Cupido.
Bortolo Vittari: Mercurio balordo.

Cariche dispensate da S.A.R. Duca di Yorch alle Dame di Venetia
N.D. Procuratoressa Rezzonico....Dama di Corte.
N.D. Lodovica Zaguri....La Favorita.
N.D. Marietta Corner....Dama di Trattenimento.
N.D. Katterina Cappello....Maestra di bone creanze.
N.D. Cecilia Minotto....Governatrice dei Paesi bassi.
N.D. Lucrezia Pisani...Commissaria d'Affari.
N.D. Cecilia Corner...Bibliotecaria.
N.D. Morosina Gradenigo....Novizza alle Dismesse.[19]

---

[19] Biblioteca Correr, Venice, *Cod. Cicogna* 3345, fol. 70. (Translation: The deputies of the Duke / The noble Giovanni Grimani...Proposes everything / The noble Marco Priuli...Opposes everything / The noble Francesco Pesaro...Spoils everything / The noble Vettor Pisani...Reconciles everything / The Duke...Has everything in his basket // On board all sort of boats (bissone, malgarotte and ballottine) taking part in / the regatta of 4 June 1764. / The Mocenigo brothers: Castor and Pollux turned into chickens. / Giacomo Foscarini: The eunuch on board. / Cattarin Corner: Does not have much of his own flour in the sack. / Pietro Marcello: The

The English Duke is described as a lucky man who has everything 'in his basket' (implying that he has given proof of his libertinism), while Girolamo Ascanio Giustinian, Bella's patron, is unlucky since he is kept waiting. By contrast, Venetian sexual success is represented by Pietro Marcello, who is described as a Don Giovanni. However, Pietro Marcello was not alone; the list of the alleged conquests made by the English Duke on his Grand Tour is almost as long as that of Don Giovanni himself.[20]

IN THE PROVINCES

The scene now moves to Vercelli, not a renowned tourist site, nor an exciting town, surrounded by rivers between Piedmont and Lombardy. It was a cloudy day at the beginning of March 1764, and the Governor of Vercelli, Marchese Morozzo della Rocca, and the soldiers of the garrison had been waiting for the Duke since 9 a.m — he eventually arrived at 2 p.m. According to documents, the Duke was travelling in a great hurry from Turin to Milan, which he had to reach before darkness. At Vercelli everything was ready to welcome such a distinguished traveller. Due to so many hours delay, the light meal, a sort of breakfast, that those hapless soldiers had prepared for him had to be transformed into a lunch worthy of a prince. They had worked very hard on it, and thought about the most minute details, not only of food but also about all sort of 'modern' facilities. In case he needed one, they had built a toilet especially for him; they made a hole at the harbour on the river Sesia and erected a very fine structure. The Governor proudly reported to the Court of Turin that he had ordered: 'un gabinetto tappezzato e coperto, provvisto di un cadregone e sedia a Braccia per maggior comodo'.[21] Here

---

'Convitato di Pietra', or Don Giovanni. / The Pesaro brothers: Sometimes they will do something. / Francesco Savorgnan: The pig in triumph. / Giovannelli, and Soranzo: [?] / The Venier brothers: The sons of Vulcan. / Domenico Michiel: When will he become sensible? Never. / Mario Savorgnan: Dò; Re; Mi, Fà, Là, Là, Là, Sol fà mi rè, dò. / Girolamo [Ascanio] Giustinian: He who gets, waits. / The Manin brothers: Omnia & pecuniam facta sunt (the personification of everything, including money) / Antonio Bollani: Homo sine pecunia; Imago Mortis (A man with no money, image of death). / The Redetti brothers: A desire for company. / Trifon Valmarana: Pity him; he's got family things. / The Zani brothers: Economy mocked by Cupid. / Bortolo Vittari: Foolish Mercury. // Honours bestowed by His Highness the Duke of York to the [noble] ladies of Venice / Dame procurator Rezzonico...Lady-in-waiting. / Dame Lodovica Zaguri...The Favourite. / Dame Marietta Corner...Entertainment lady. / Dame Caterina Cappello...Mistress of good manners. / Dame Cecila Minotto...Governess of the Low Countries. / Dame Lucrezia Pisani...Chargée d'affairs. / Dame Cecilia Corner...Librarian. / Dame Morosina Gradenigo...Novice at the dismissed.)

[20] To realize how literally the young Duke was a 'Don Giovanni' (like one of the several pre-Mozart *Don Giovannis* performed in the Italian theatres), see G. Macchia, *Vita, avventure e morte di Don Giovanni* (Milan, 1991).

[21] Archivio di Stato di Torino (sez. I), *Cerimoniale, Inghilterra*, mazzo 1 d'add., ins. 12: *Ricevimento, e Trattamento*. The toilet, according to the description of the Governor of Vercelli, was a proper room, covered by a roof and papered with wallpaper; it was furnished with two lavatory pans, a conventional big chair and a more refined armchair so that the Duke 'could feel more comfortable'.

we have a mock-serious example of the way in which the very soil of Italy was radically transformed by eighteenth-century tourism.

The Piedmontese were very meticulous and much preoccupied with details during the Duke's visit. For his part, the Governor of Vercelli reported to his Court that guards had been placed outside the toilet on the river Sesia while the Duke was there so that there should be no accidents ('acciò non succedesse nessun incidente').[22] While preparing the meal, the Governor and his soldiers also realized that their garrison dishes, glasses and cutlery were not worthy of a royal duke. As a consequence, they went to the richest nobleman in town, Conte Arigliani, and to the Bishop, and returned to their headquarters with the most splendid silver. The soup was ready but the visitor was not there. Eventually he arrived and pointed out that he could not stay. Their disappointment was so evident that he relented. The Governor proudly reported to the Court of Turin that at table the Duke ate very heartily. Besides having 'una buona porzione di riso; ha gustato varie pietanze, e massimamente una magnifica trutta [sic] in Carboglione spiegandosi che molto le piaceva tal pesce, come di fatti se ne servì più volte' (he had a big portion of rice and enjoyed various courses, notably a magnificent grilled trout; he said that he liked that fish very much and, in fact, he helped himself more than once). The Duke also drank some glasses of burgundy and champagne. Enquiries were made about his stay in Turin: the Duke was good-natured, he told them of the Court, the balls and the ladies. With a glass of champagne he proposed a toast to the health of the women of Turin and left. The Duke of York's toast to the women of Turin on the 'stage' of Vercelli anticipated one of the typical scenes of Mozart's opera *Don Giovanni*. Like the eponymous hero, the Duke was joyful but eventually tragic. His death three years later, while again on the Grand Tour, was a long and painful agony, the same destiny as Don Giovanni himself.[23]

The toilet on the river Sesia was only one of several minor engineering works carried out for the Duke's visit. He crossed a bridge over the river Bormida which had been specially constructed; and on his way to Milan he travelled on a road newly built for him in less than three days, since the old road of Ponte Boffalora, by the river Ticino, was so damaged by heavy rain ('così fonduta e piena di acqua e fango') that his coach certainly would have been turned over. Countless trees were cut down overnight by workers employed by the local mayor and consul who, in their turn, had received strict orders from Karl Joseph von Firmian, the Minister Plenipotentiary of the Austrian empire in Milan, 'prontamente [da] eseguire per non incorrere nelle disgrazie di Sua

---

[22] See above, n. 20 for all quotations regarding the Duke's stay in Vercelli.

[23] Macchia, *Vita* (above, n. 19), 152. The scene of toasting the women of the various towns where the opera was performed was typical of the repertoire of the *Convitato di Pietra, o Don Giovanni*. But it appears that the scene was first officially introduced in 1787 (the same year as Mozart's *Don Giovanni*), when Giuseppe Gazzaniga's *Convitato di Pietra* with Giovanni Bertati's libretto was performed at the Giustinian theatre in Venice.

Maestà' (the works to be carried out immediately so as not to incur the displeasure of the Empress of Austria). The road was built, and the mayor and consul were able to sign their report, the mayor signing for the consul who was illiterate ('per non sapere esso scrivere'). They noted the impressive number of beautiful trees they had had to cut down and the complaints of the landowner. The new road (mentioned above) that had miraculously been built for the English Duke was also mentioned in the report.[24]

Italian collections, archives and libraries are filled with evidence of minor painters, vulgar poets, poor soldiers and illiterate officials, who, as has been shown, were intricately involved with the Grand Tour. Documents, including account books, tell long-forgotten stories of the Grand Tour observed and lived through by countless lesser people, such as the shopkeepers and pedlars of Milan, who carried tons of food to the Palazzo Simonetta so that the 'Duca de Orcho'[25] could eat as much as he wished of *Polastri*, *Polastrini*, *Galine*, *Galinaze*, *Poline*, *Anadre* and *Ostreghe* (chickens, hens, pullets, ducks and oysters). They tell stories of servants, who were able to observe all the travellers very closely; of Catterina Branbilla [sic], a maid who could not spell her name well but had beautiful handwriting and who also signed for her colleague, Maria Ripamonti, who could not write but was a very good maid.[26] We learn of musicians and singers who entertained royal and non-royal travellers, of famous chapel-masters such as Giovanni Battista Sammartini,[27] and also of countless musicians who earned their living with great difficulty, playing for a few coins for the splendid tourists. All these Italians, great and lesser people, played active roles in the Grand Tour. It is difficult to visualize most of them, but their voices still survive and are waiting for somebody to tell their naive and unimportant stories. Much work remains to be done on this aspect of the Grand Tour.

ROME AND ARCHAEOLOGICAL EXCAVATIONS

The Grand Tour brought much wealth to Italy — it transformed the Italian soil and created new jobs and also artists. Pompeo Batoni, for instance, originally intended to become a history painter, but he soon realized that in Rome, the principal destination of the Grand Tour, there was a great demand for tourist portraits and an insufficient supply. It was the Grand Tour that created Batoni,

---

[24] Archivio di Stato di Milano, *Potenze estere* 52: *Inghilterra 1764*.

[25] The derivation is York, Orch, Orcho, an ogre.

[26] The name should read 'Caterina Brambilla'. Archivio di Stato di Milano, *Potenze estere* 52: *Inghilterra 1764*.

[27] Sammartini's concerts in honour of the Duke of York, which were held in Milan on 12 March and 9 July 1764, are not recorded in S. Sadie (ed.), *The New Grove's Dictionary of Music and Musicians* (London, 1980), but are documented in manuscripts preserved in Milan (see above, n. 21).

FIG. 6. *Statue of Discobolous*. Marble, height 1.65 m. British Museum, Townley Collection, no. 250.
(© The British Museum; reproduced courtesy of The British Museum)

the great specialist in souvenir portraits,[28] and it was the Grand Tour that stimulated the production of all sorts of souvenir objects. There were bronze statuettes from the Roman foundry of Giacomo and Giovanni Zoffoli, porcelain figures from the Roman factory of Giovanni Volpato, cork models of ancient monuments made by Neapolitan and Roman craftsmen such as Giovanni Altieri and Antonio Chichi, casts of engraved seal-stones, souvenir plates and glasses, fans and countless other objects which filled the houses of the Grand Tourists in England and elsewhere in Europe.[29] These objects could be either purchased on the spot or ordered by post. Like Josiah Wedgwood and Matthew Boulton,

---

[28] See A.M. Clark, *Pompeo Batoni. A Complete Catalogue of his Work* (Oxford, 1985). Also Wilton and Bignamini (eds), *Grand Tour: the Lure* (above, n. 2), 59 no. 16, 61-2 nos. 18-19, 77-8 no. 35, 82 no. 39, and Wilton and Bignamini (eds), *Grand tour: il fascino* (above, n. 2), 60 no. 16, 63 no. 18, 64 no. 19, 81-2 no. 35, 86 no. 39.

[29] The Grand Tour exhibition included a small selection of souvenir objects. See Wilton and Bignamini (eds), *Grand Tour: the Lure* (above, n. 2), 280–9, 298–303; and Wilton and Bignamini, *Grand Tour: il fascino* (above, n. 2), 290–9, 309–13, 319.

FIG. 7. *Statue of Discobolous*. Marble, height 1.33 m without plinth. Vatican Museums,
Sala della Biga, inv. 2346. *(Reproduced courtesy of the Vatican Museums)*

Italian artists, craftsmen and manufacturers issued catalogues which were sent to collectors and occasional buyers all over Europe. The Grand Tour also saved some Italian craftsmen from unemployment. For example, by the late 1750s the mosaic decorations for Saint Peter's had been completed. It was the risk of losing their jobs that led the Vatican mosaicists to undertake the independent production of souvenir micro-mosaics for the newly expanding tourist market.

In this paper, discussion so far has concentrated on certain aspects of the Italian participation in the Grand Tour. On the whole, this picture does not indicate a particularly pro-active participation, but is this really the case? Did some individuals or institutions make clever, planned use of the Grand Tour? And did their actions and reactions produce something solid, important and long-lasting for Italy and the rest of Europe? To answer these question is not easy, but one example, at least, can be cited — that of Rome and the papal states.

The popes' advisers and members of successive papal governments succeeded in making the best possible use of the new European order resulting from the Treaty of Paris, which concluded the Seven Years War in 1763. They responded to growing tourism and the expansion of the general demand for works of art, particularly ancient sculpture, by opening the Museo Capitolino to the public in 1734 and the Museo Pio-Clementino in 1771. The potential of one of the most valuable 'resources' on the territory of the papal states, that is to say of archaeological sites in and near Rome, as well as elsewhere in Latium, was realized, a source which fed Rome and Europe with countless ancient marbles. The cardinals succeeded in designing a rigorous and, at the same time, liberal policy for the granting of excavation and export licences, regulated by law, which produced long-lasting results. The Museo Pio-Clementino and, later, the Museo Chiaramonti, as well as virtually all the European collections of classical sculpture (including the Townley collection, now part of the British Museum), were primarily the result of Italian and British excavations in these areas at this time — excavations which were paid for in part by the papal government but also in part by British and other European patrons and Grand Tourists. The complimentary nature of the collections of the Vatican and the British Museum is significant here.[30] Two famous statues of *Discobolous*, both unearthed at Hadrian's Villa at Tivoli in 1791, demonstrate this, and, above all, show how scrupulous, careful and choosy the cardinals and commissioners were. The so-called *Townley Discobolous* (Fig. 6) was discovered first; it was acquired by the art dealer and excavator Thomas Jenkins, who applied for the export licence but was, at first, denied it. Although the statue was in bad condition, the commissioner, Filippo Aurelio Visconti, thought the Museo Pio-Clementino should have it and Jenkins was ordered to keep it in Rome. When, a few months later, a better-preserved *Discobolous* (Fig. 7) was found and purchased for the Vatican, Jenkins was granted the export licence for his *Discobolous*, which was purchased by Townley.

The evidence of great liberality in the release of excavation and export licences during a period of over 30 years is represented by sculptures such as these. When the demand was booming and growing as fast as it did in the years 1764–98, a liberal policy was almost certainly the best option, since prohibition would have resulted in a spectacular increase in illegal excavations and exports. However, those who are liberal can make deals, and those who are both liberal and clever can make very good deals. The Reverenda Camera Apostolica, its cardinals, commissioners and antiquaries, retained the legal right of deciding what could and could not be exported. No rigid rules, much common sense and a

---

[30] This comparison was visualized by the curators of the room devoted to the antique in the Grand Tour exhibition by selecting the two caryatids from the *Triopion* of Herodes Atticus on the Via Appia, the two pairs of dogs from Monte Cagnolo, and views of the rooms of the Museo Pio-Clementino and of the collection originally displayed by Charles Townley at his house in London. See I. Bignamini and I. Jenkins, 'The antique', in Wilton and Bignamini (eds), *Grand Tour: the Lure* (above, n. 2), 203–70; Wilton and Bignamini (eds), *Grand Tour: il fascino* (above, n. 2), 211–79.

great ability in selecting the pieces were the strategies employed to great effect, an effect which can still be admired in the rooms of the Vatican Museums and elsewhere in Britain and Europe. This example, and the others given earlier, do indeed prove that there were some Italians, and some well-run Italian institutions, who made the best possible use of the Grand Tour.

3

The Architectural Context Of The Grand Tour: The British As Honorary Italians

DAVID WATKIN

One of the most intense evocations of the impact of Italy on the English visitor occurs in the course of George Eliot's account in *Middlemarch* of the disastrous honeymoon in Rome of Dorothea Casaubon. Eliot describes Rome evocatively as 'the city of visible history, where the past of a whole hemisphere seems moving in funereal procession with strange ancestral images and trophies gathered from afar'. Explaining that Dorothea was 'brought up in English and Swiss Puritanism, fed on meagre Protestant histories and on art chiefly of the hand-screen sort', Eliot describes how the girl was overwhelmed by:

> Ruins and basilicas, palaces and colossi, set in the midst of a sordid present, where all that was living and warm-blooded seemed sunk in the deep degeneracy of a superstition divorced from reverence; the chiller but yet eager Titanic life gazing and struggling on walls and ceilings; the long vistas of white forms whose marble eyes seemed to hold the monotonous light of an alien world.

Eliot went on to recall that:

> Our moods are apt to bring with them images which succeed each other like the magic lantern pictures of a doze; and in certain states of dull forlornness Dorothea all her life continued to see the vastness of St Peter's, the huge bronze canopy, the excited intention in the attitudes and garments of the prophets and evangelists in the mosaics above, and the red drapery which was being hung for Christmas spreading itself everywhere like a disease of the retina.

To escape from the drugged intensity of these visions, Dorothea often chose 'to drive out to the Campagna where she could feel alone with the earth and the sky, away from the oppressive masquerade of ages'.[1]

---

[1] G. Eliot, *Middlemarch* (1871–2) (Oxford, 1986), 187–8.

It is a passage to set beside the famous reactions to Rome of Edward Gibbon and of Horace Walpole, the former conceiving his ambition of chronicling its decline and fall as he 'sat musing amidst the ruins of the Capitol, while the barefooted friars were singing vespers in the Temple of Jupiter',[2] the latter responding to Piranesi's vision of Rome by expressing the hope that:

> our artists would study the sublime dreams of Piranesi, who seems
> to have conceived visions of Rome beyond what it boasted even in
> the meridian of its splendour ... He piles palaces on bridges, and
> temples on palaces, and scales heaven with mountains of edifices.
> Yet what taste in his boldness! What grandeur in his wildness![3]

Piranesi succeeded in attracting many British patrons, descendants of those who, from the time of Elizabeth I, had escaped from the cultural isolation and the grey northern climate of England to the warmth and romance of classical Italy. The importance of the Grand Tour from Britain depended partly on the isolation of the nation from Italy, for the theological break with Rome at the Reformation had cultural, as well as religious, implications. In this essay a chronological selection of these British travellers is presented, concentrating on those for whom the grandeur of the classical past had its principal expression in architecture.

SOME RENAISSANCE TRAVELLERS

Sir Thomas Hoby (1530–66) studied at Cambridge and Strasbourg, making an Italian tour in 1549–50 to complete his education and equip himself for his career abroad as a diplomat during Edward VI's reign. His brother was in touch with Titian and with the leading scholars and men of letters in Venice. Thomas described his travels in a lengthy journal,[4] and in 1561 translated as *The Courtier* that classic Renaissance text on manners and education, Baldassare Castiglione's *Il libro del cortegiano* (1528). The men of Edward VI's court, bent on governmental and social reform, sympathized with recent Italian writings on architecture which emphasized the role of buildings as promoting the public good. Somerset House, built in the Strand for the Lord Protector Somerset in 1547–52, was remarkable for its Italianate sophistication. As Howard has explained of these years, 'it was some time before the educated Protestant

---

[2] E. Gibbon, *Memoirs of My Life and Writings* (1796) (ed. A. Cockshut and S. Constantine) (Keele, 1994), 170.

[3] H. Walpole, 'Advertisement', *Anecdotes of Painting in England* (fourth edition, 1786), IV, 398.

[4] T. Hoby, *The Travaile and Lief of me Thomas Hoby (1547–1564)* (*Camden Society* VII) (London, 1902).

Englishman withdrew into the peculiarly insular and priggish attitudes to Continental art that characterised the late sixteenth and seventeenth centuries'.[5]

Travel in Catholic countries was made increasingly difficult for the Elizabethans, thanks to the war with Spain, the excommunication of Queen Elizabeth in 1570, and the Inquisition. The Privy Council refused to issue travel licences to Rome until well into the seventeenth century, while Milan and Naples were virtually inaccessible. However, some cities in northern Italy, in particular Venice, Vicenza and Padua, were open to English visitors, of whom one of the most remarkable was John Shute (d. 1563). He was sent to Italy in 1550 by John Dudley, Viscount Lisle, the future Duke of Northumberland, with the specific aim of meeting modern architects and studying antique monuments. That this was part of a programme of enabling English architecture to catch up with Italian architecture is clear from the book which Shute published on his return, *First and Chief Groundes of Architecture* (1563), with a dedication to Queen Elizabeth. Drawing on Vitruvius, Serlio and Philander, as well as on his studies of Roman buildings, this was not only the first book on architecture in English, but also one of the earliest English textbooks.[6] Before publishing this, Shute showed the fruits of his labours to Edward VI, who died in 1553, the same year in which Shute's patron, the Duke of Northumberland, was executed for treason. However, Shute's book was popular, and went into four editions by 1587. Elizabeth I encouraged future diplomats to travel on the continent in order to learn languages and act as unofficial spies on foreign princes. Sir Henry Wotton (1568–1639), scholar-diplomat and poet, travelled abroad from 1588 to 1595, acting latterly as an intelligence agent for Robert Devereux, 2nd Earl of Essex. However, a great change from the increasingly insular and parsimonious character of the Elizabethan regime came with the arrival on the English throne in 1603 of the Scottish king, James I, and in particular with the cultural ideals of his son, Henry, Prince of Wales (1594–1612). December 1611 saw the publication of an English edition of Serlio dedicated to Henry, Prince of Wales. Published by Robert Peake (*c.* 1551–1619), Serjeant-Painter, or court picture-maker, this book has been connected to the Italianate gardens, fountains and grottoes then being planned for the Prince of Wales at Richmond Palace by

---

[5] M. Howard, *The Early Tudor Country House: Architecture and Politics 1490–1550* (London, 1987), 187. The aims of those who commissioned post-Reformation tombs featuring classical motifs were 'those of status, power and allegiance, not of aesthetics', according to N. Llewellyn, 'Accident or design? John Gildon's funeral monuments and Italianate taste in Elizabethan England', in E. Chaney and P. Mack (eds), *England and the Continental Renaissance: Essays in Honour of J.B. Trapp* (Woodbridge, 1990), 143–52. Certainly, the word 'classicism' was not used until the nineteenth century. For a development of this argument, see L. Gent (ed.), *Albion's Classicism: the Visual Arts in England 1550–1660* (New Haven and London, 1995).

[6] In considering the influence of this book, it is worth bearing in mind that only ten copies are now known, eight of the first edition, two of the fourth edition of 1587, and none of those of 1579 and 1584.

Costantino de'Servi (*c.* 1554–1622).[7] A Florentine architect, painter and garden designer, de'Servi had been brought from the Medici court of Cosimo II to that of the Prince of Wales in June 1611, and remained in England until 1615.

James I and his 'favourites', the young men whom he gathered round him, took a sensuous pleasure in Italian art, forming a world in which Sir Henry Wotton was to play an important part. After the Treaty of Vervins of 1598, when Venice had once more opened diplomatic relations with England, James I appointed Wotton as Venetian Ambassador in 1603 on the recommendation of Sir Robert Cecil, the future Earl of Salisbury. Cecil was thus able to use Wotton to acquire Italian paintings for his galleries at Salisbury House in the Strand and Cranborne Manor, Dorset.[8] Acquiring a passion for Palladio in Venice, Wotton became the first Englishman to collect drawings by him.

An anti-papalist, Wotton nourished a vain hope that the Italian states of Venice and Savoy might form an alliance against the pope, Spain and the Empire, thus allowing Protestants to gain a foothold in Italy. He turned his palace in Venice, where he hung a portrait of Henry, Prince of Wales, into the equivalent of a miniature Oxford or Cambridge college: it played a key role in introducing Italian culture to England, from the architecture of Palladio to paintings of the Venetian school.

Living in Italy for seventeen years, studying classical and Renaissance texts as well as antique and modern buildings, Wotton formed friendships with patrons and scholars such as Marc Antonio Barbaro (for whom Palladio built the Villa Maser) and provided the illustrations for his edition of Vitruvius. Armed with this knowledge, Wotton wrote *The Elements of Architecture* (1624), which, improbably, he published as part of his bid to secure the Provostship of Eton College. A neo-Platonist Vitruvian essay, this book has recently been interpreted as a plea for a modern minimalist architecture.[9] It doubtless played a part in the architectural education of Sir Christopher Wren, who did not visit Italy himself, but whose architecturally-minded father annotated the copy which his friend, Wotton, gave him.[10]

Wotton found valuable patronage in James I's favourite, the flamboyant George Villiers, Marquess of Buckingham (1592–1628), a fabled collector of Italian paintings who was created Duke of Buckingham by the king in 1623. Jones designed Lodgings for him in 1619–21 at Whitehall Palace, and worked

---

[7] H.M. Colvin (ed.), *The King's Works*, vol. III, *1485–1660*, part 1 (London, 1975), 125–6, and T. Wilks, *The Court Culture of Prince Henry and his Circle 1603–1613* (Oxford D. Phil. thesis, 1987).

[8] Wotton to Salisbury, dated Venice 1608, referring to the acquisition of paintings for 'your Lordship's galleries'; see L. Pearsall Smith (ed.), *The Life and Letters of Sir Henry Wotton,* 2 vols (Oxford, 1907), I, 420.

[9] T. Mowl and B. Earnshaw, *Architecture without Kings: the Rise of Puritan Classicism under Cromwell* (Manchester, 1995), 67–9.

[10] The volume is in a private collection and I am grateful to Dr John Adamson for supplying me with a copy of the unpublished annotations.

for him at New Hall, Essex, in 1622–3, while Wotton obtained for him a plan and elevation of Vignola's celebrated Villa Farnese at Caprarola.[11] Influenced by the sculpture collected by the Earl of Arundel for the gallery which Jones had created for him in *c.* 1618 at Arundel House, Wotton wrote in 1624 to Sir Thomas Roe, Ambassador to Constantinople, requesting his help in the acquisition of antiquities.[12] It was, in turn, Wotton's agent, the French-born Daniel Nys, long settled in Venice as a merchant, dealer and diplomat, whom the Countess of Arundel asked to provide a model of the Ducal Palace at Mantua, either on her return from Italy in 1614 or on her return there in 1622. Together with full descriptions of the interiors, this was intended for Charles, Prince of Wales, the future Charles I. It was, indeed, Nys who acquired the Gonzaga collection at Mantua for Charles I in 1627–8, one of the greatest collections in Europe after those of the Vatican, Philip IV and Ferdinand II. Wotton is the vital transitional figure who turned from spy to aesthete, thus anticipating the shift in the history of travel from that current in the sixteenth and first half of the seventeenth centuries, to the Grand Tour proper.

Inigo Jones brought not only pure Italian Renaissance architecture to England, but also the stage effects of the royal masques of the Medici court in Florence, with their threads of Platonic and Pythagorean allegory woven into a political portrait. As part of the associated world of royal Stuart propaganda, Jones designed the funeral catafalque for James I at Westminster Abbey in 1625, with pennons and shields of arms surrounded by statues of the virtues.[13] This was the first time that allegorical overlay of this Renaissance type had been applied to an English royal funeral. Remarkably, Jones used as a model the catafalque that had been designed for the funeral of Pope Sixtus V by the papal architect Fontana. In 1606, Jones's Catholic friend, the Cambridge antiquarian Edmund Bolton, had given him a book of Latin poems published in 1588 celebrating Sixtus V for having combined ecclesiastical reforms with the architectural transformation of the city of Rome and the restoration of ancient monuments.[14] Bolton inscribed this book with praise of Jones as someone 'through whom there is hope that ... all that is praiseworthy in the elegant arts of the ancients, may one day find their way across the Alps into our England'.

We tend to find what we want to find when we go abroad or when we investigate the past, bringing expectations to what we find or think we find. Inigo Jones, for example, went to Italy when Mannerism was about to turn into

---

[11] Pearsall Smith, *Henry Wotton* (above, n. 7), II, 286–7. An elaborately arcaded and terraced set of external stairs, inspired by Caprarola, had already been created at Wimbledon House, Surrey, for Sir Thomas Cecil, the future Earl of Exeter, as early as 1588. See M. Girouard, *Robert Smythson and the Architecture of the Elizabethan Era* (London, 1966), pl. 10.

[12] D. Howarth, *Lord Arundel and his Circle* (New Haven and London, 1985),197.

[13] J. Peacock, 'Inigo Jones's catafalque for James I', *Architectural History* 25 (1982), 1–5.

[14] G.F. Bordini, *De rebus praeclare gestis a Sixto V Pon. Max.* (Rome, 1588). Jones's copy is in Worcester College Library, Oxford.

Baroque and he lived until 1652, when Baroque was at its height. This style he largely ignored, and instead looked in Italy to the buildings by Palladio and Scamozzi of about 60 years before. His second Italian tour of 1613–14, with the Earl of Arundel, seemed to imply that it was essential for an architect to travel and study in Italy. In creating a sculpture gallery on his return, Arundel also set an example that was to be widely followed, just as his commissioning of Wenceslaus Hollar to make drawings while they were in Germany together in 1636 was followed by numerous noblemen taking artists with them on their Grand Tours.

TRAVEL IN ITALY AND THE CIVIL WAR

The Civil War encouraged travel in Italy by those anxious to escape the turmoil, including the Earl of Arundel, who travelled again after 1642, dying in Padua in 1646, and Sir Roger Pratt (1620–85), who travelled in France, Italy, Flanders and Holland from 1643 to 1649. Becoming a friend of John Evelyn in Rome in 1644, Pratt matriculated in law at the University of Padua in January 1645. He assembled a handsome library of architectural books and compiled 'Rules for the Guidance of Architects' and 'Notes on the Building of Country Houses', in which he recommended the owners of houses to obtain plans from those who had travelled abroad and studied Palladio, Scamozzi and Serlio.[15] However, Pratt's own designs for houses, notably Coleshill, Berkshire (1649–62), and Kingston Lacy, Dorset (1663–5), were dependent on Italy as filtered through the work of Inigo Jones and of contemporary Dutch architects. One important guidebook to Rome, published in London in 1654, the first year of Cromwell's Protectorate, and little noted in modern studies of the Grand Tour, is by Henry Cogan: *A Direction for Such as Shall Travell unto Rome*. It is arranged as a series of five day-long visits, complete with itineraries.

John Evelyn (1620–1706) avoided the Civil War by travelling abroad from 1643 to 1647. After passing through France, he visited the principal cities of Italy, studying languages, gardening, architecture and antiquities. Hugh May persuaded him to persevere with his translation of Fréart de Chambray's *Parallèle de l'architecture antique et de la moderne* (1650). Published as *A Parallel of the Antient Architecture with the Modern* in 1664, this was one of the most influential architectural books of the seventeenth and eighteenth centuries. Evelyn dedicated it to Charles II, whom he revered as a second Augustus, seeing himself as a second Vitruvius. Since Vitruvius had dedicated his *Ten Books of Architecture* to Augustus, Evelyn thought it appropriate that he should be seen as 'presenting you [the King] with those antiquities on which the ancient master formed his studies'.

---

[15] Pratt Collection, Ryston Hall, MS L. See N. Silcox-Crowe, 'Sir Roger Pratt 1620–1685, the ingenious gentleman architect', in R. Brown (ed.), *The Architectural Outsiders* (London, 1985), 3.

Despite the lengthy and fulsome dedication in which Evelyn described Charles II's building projects in London, the book bore a second dedication, to Sir John Denham, Surveyor of the King's Works, whose paving of London much resembled 'the Reformation of Rome'. Evelyn saw the 'promotion of ... building [as] a certain indication of a prudent government, of a flourishing and happy people'.[16] He argued elsewhere that, as a result, 'this Glorious and Ancient City ... from wood might be rendered brick; and (like another Rome) from Brick made Stone and Marble'.[17] Evelyn was also important for persuading Henry Howard, 6th Duke of Norfolk (1620–84), to give to Oxford University the first and one of the greatest of all Grand Tour collections of antiquities, begun by the Duke's grandfather, the 14th Earl of Arundel.

ENLIGHTENMENT IDEALS

The term 'Grand Tour' seems first to have been used in print by the Catholic priest and travelling tutor, Richard Lassels, who argued in his *Voyage of Italy or a Compleat Journey through Italy* (1670) that no one could understand Livy and Caesar if they had not performed exactly the 'Grand Tour of France and the Giro of Italy'.[18] The first comprehensive guidebook to Italy in English, this was also translated into French and German.[19] Joseph Addison's *Remarks upon Several Parts of Italy* (1705) and Jonathan Richardson's *An Account of Some of the Statues, Bas-reliefs, Drawings and Pictures in Italy, France etc.* (1722) promoted the Grand Tour as part of a process of moral improvement, as well as being educational and entertaining.

Before the second half of the seventeenth century, travel in Italy was undertaken for a variety of reasons, dominated by political and diplomatic considerations. The Grand Tour proper coincided with the eighteenth-century Enlightenment, which promoted new ideals of international brotherhood and sociability, of intellectual and moral improvement in a secular context. Some modern studies of the Grand Tour tend to have an anecdotal and picaresque flavour, concentrating on carriage accidents and the purchase of silk waistcoats, while ignoring the role of the Tour as an intellectual as well as a social *rite de*

---

[16] J. Evelyn, *A Parallel of the Antient Architecture with the Modern* (London , 1664), preface.

[17] Evelyn, *Fumifugium: or, The inconvenience of the aer, and smoake of London dissipated* (1661), preface. Evelyn's friend Hugh May (1621–84), who may not have visited Italy, produced at Windsor Castle in 1675–84 the most complete examples of the Italianate Baroque ever created in England. In Saint George's Hall and the King's Chapel, he brought together for the first time Antonio Verrio and Grinling Gibbons.

[18] R. Lassels, *The Voyage of Italy* (1670), and see E. Chaney, *The Grand Tour and the Great Rebellion: Richard Lassels and 'The Voyage of Italy' in the Seventeenth Century* (Geneva, 1985).

[19] See E. Chaney, 'The Grand Tour and the evolution of the guide book', in A. Wilton and I. Bignamini (eds), *The Grand Tour. The Lure of Italy in the Eighteenth Century* (exhibition catalogue, Tate Gallery, London, 1996), 95–6.

passage.[20] A full study of the Grand Tour would require knowledge of architecture, art and archaeology, as well as the history of religion, literature, music and educational systems, and an understanding of the social, political and diplomatic structures of *ancien régime* Europe.[21]

The Grand Tour traditionally has been seen as an essentially British phenomenon, although travel as the completion of education was common in Renaissance Europe, where it was known in Italy as the *peregrinatio academica* and in Germany as the *Kavaliersreise.* Moreover, the international nature of the Enlightenment meant that the Grand Tour became by definition something fundamentally pan-European, involving, for example, the French,[22] the Dutch,[23] and the Germans, who established a famous colony in Rome. It also involved travel throughout Europe. One example is the tour of Prince Franz of Anhalt-Dessau (1740–1817) and his friend, the architect Friedrich Wilhelm von Erdmannsdorff (1736–1800), which constitutes a spectacularly fruitful example of the Grand Tour at its most international. In 1761 the Prince sent Erdmannsdorff on a study tour of Italy, while in 1763 they travelled together in England, and in 1756–7 in Italy, where they moved in the circle of Clérisseau, Piranesi, Winckelmann, Cardinal Albani and Sir William Hamilton. This extended study tour culminated in Schloss Wörlitz and its vast landscaped setting, which Erdmannsdorff created for the Prince from 1766 to 1799.[24] The range of styles and of building types adopted for the numerous garden buildings at Wörlitz were the consequence of the Prince's intention, in accordance with Enlightenment idealism, to educate his subjects, to bring the Grand Tour to them.

The educational role of the Grand Tour is also clear from the youthful age at which many Englishmen undertook it. A good example is provided by the Blathwayt brothers, who were aged fourteen and sixteen in 1705 when they began a four-year tour.[25] Their father, William Blathwayt, Secretary at War to William III, having made his own continental tour in 1672, employed the French Huguenot architect Samuel Hauderoy in 1692 and William Talman in 1698–1704 to rebuild Dyrham Park, Gloucestershire, in a style dependent on Rubens's

---

[20] For the biographical information necessary for such a study, see J. Ingamells, *A Dictionary of British and Irish Travellers in Italy 1701–1800* (New Haven and London, 1996).

[21] Edward Chaney's recent study has achieved something of this synthesis: *The Evolution of the Grand Tour: Anglo-Italian Cultural Relations since the Renaissance* (London, 1998). Other recent examples of a broader approach include B.M. Stafford, *Voyage into Substance: Art, Science, Nature, and the Illustrated Travel Account, 1760–1840* (Cambridge, Mass., 1984), and C. Chard and H. Langdon (eds), *Transports: Travel, Pleasure and Imaginative Geography, 1600–1830* (London, 1996).

[22] M. Roland Michel, *Artistes en voyage au XVIIIe siècle* (Paris, 1986).

[23] R. de Leeuw (ed.), *Herinneringen aan Italie: Kunst en Toerisme in de 18de Eeuw* (Zwolle, 1984), and A. Frank-van Westrienen, *De Groote Tour: Tekening van de Educatieris der Nederlanders in de Zeventiende Eeuw* (Amsterdam, 1983).

[24] R. Alex, *Schlosser und Gärten von Worlitz* (Leipzig, 1988).

[25] N. Hardwick (ed.), *The Grand Tour: William and John Blathwayt of Dyrham Park 1705–08* (Bristol, 1985).

Palazzi di Genova as well as on contemporary French and Dutch architecture. Blathwayt employed a French Protestant, Monsieur de Blainville, as tutor to his sons, of whom John, the younger, a harpsichordist and musical prodigy, was expected to form a collection of music while abroad. In Geneva, additional tutors were hired to instruct the boys in mathematics, languages and horsemanship, while in Rome they were taught Italian and mathematics. John also studied and performed music, whereas William was taught architecture, apparently by James Gibbs.[26]

Such a course of education is emphatically European and non-insular in its character. William Blathwayt, though a prominent Whig, had no qualms about his sons being received in Rome in the cultivated household of Cardinal Ottoboni, and even in that of Cardinal Alessandro Caprara, who had dealt with the affairs of James II in Rome in the 1690s.[27] That the English had a particular trust in the quality and value of continental education is clear from those who sent a son abroad in his early teens, with the result that by the time he returned he would have changed from a boy into a man without their having seen him.

George Berkeley (1685–1753), the future Bishop of Cloyne, was tutor to the sixteen-year-old St George Ashe, the frail son of the Vice-Chancellor of Dublin University, during an exceptionally intensive four-year Italian tour from 1716. Berkeley's journals and letters reveal a mind of great independence and subtlety, capable of appreciating both Roman Baroque and Greek Doric architecture.[28] It was also at the age of sixteen that William Beckford (1760–1844) was sent with his tutor to Geneva University, where he stayed for eighteen months, studying languages, natural history, philosophy and experimental science.

Thomas Coke (1697–1759), future 1st Earl of Leicester, went on his Grand Tour at the age of fifteen in 1712 with a Cambridge tutor, returning six years later aged 21.[29] He studied at the Turin Academy, exchanged gifts with the Grand Duke of Tuscany, had Italian lessons, and was taught architecture by 'Signor Giacomo'. In the studio in Rome of the painter Benedetto Luti, he met William Kent (1685–1748), who spent his formative years from the age of 24 to 34 in Rome, studying ancient and modern architecture and painting. With Kent, Coke undertook an extensive architectural tour of the main Italian cities, palaces and villas. At Aix-les-Bains he studied architecture, geography and mathematics, bought antique marbles in Rome and numerous books throughout Europe, including Geneva, Frankfurt and Florence. It was not only patrons who collected, but also architects: Inigo Jones, Lord Burlington, William Talman, Robert Adam,

---

[26] B. Ford, 'The Blathwayt Brothers of Dyrham in Italy on the Grand Tour', *National Trust Year Book* (1975–6),19–31.

[27] A point made by R. Oresko in 'The British Abroad', *Durham University Journal* (1986), 349–63.

[28] Chaney, *The Evolution of the Grand Tour* (above, n. 20), ch. 13.

[29] A. Moore, *Norfolk and the Grand Tour* (Norwich, 1985).

Henry Holland and John Soane all formed collections of enormous importance which they used in their work as designers.

Architects as well as patrons undertook these foreign studies at an early age. George Dance (1741–1825) was dispatched to Rome at the age of seventeen for architectural training and education, remaining there for six years. James Gibbs was sent to train for the priesthood at the Scots College in Rome, at the age of 21, in 1703. Quickly switching to architecture, he became a pupil of the leading architect of papal Rome, Carlo Fontana, a pupil of Bernini and chief architect to Pope Clement XI. Gibbs remained for six years in Italy, a country he said he never wanted to leave. Architects of more humble birth found the Grand Tour socially, as well as educationally, advantageous, for the British social hierarchy seems to have been temporarily forgotten abroad: thus Inigo Jones, the son of a clothworker, could travel with the Earl of Arundel; William Kent, humbly born in Bridlington and early apprenticed to a coach-painter in Hull, was transformed through his association with the Earl of Burlington in Rome; James 'Athenian' Stuart, left penniless by the early death of his father, a Scottish mariner, in 1742 set off on foot to Rome, where he was taken up by the Society of Dilettanti of which he even became a member; Robert Adam wanted to be taken for a gentleman grand-tourist, not a professional architect while he was in Rome; Soane, the son of a bricklayer, also met numerous members of the peerage and the social élite who subsequently became his patrons.

THE ACADEMIES

In common with many other Renaissance ideas and institutions, the academy arrived late in England. In 1753, fifteen years before his involvement with the foundation of the Royal Academy in London, William Chambers (1723–96) was elected to the Academy in Florence. In 1757, Robert Adam (1728–92) was elected to the Accademia di San Luca in Rome, as well as to membership of the academies of Florence and Bologna. In the following year, Robert Mylne (1733–1811) became the first British architect to win the Silver Medal for architecture in the Concorso Clementino of the Accademia di San Luca, and, like Adam, was also elected to those at Bologna and Florence.[30] George Dance was a member of the Accademia di San Luca as well as of the Accademia degli Arcadi, a Roman society devoted to the study of literature, poetry and philosophy. The architect James Byres (1734–1817), son of a Scottish laird of Jacobite and Catholic sympathies, won the third prize in the Concorso Balestra at the Accademia di San Luca in 1762 and lived for over 30 years in Rome, where he became one of the most famous of the *ciceroni*, in which capacity he took Edward Gibbon on an eight-month tour in 1764. Thomas Harrison (1844–1829), in Rome from 1769 to

---

[30] See F. Salmon, 'British architects and the Florentine Academy', *Mitteilungen des Kunsthistorischen Instituts im Florenz* 34 (1990), 199–214.

1776, was admitted as academician of merit into the Accademia di San Luca. John Soane (1753–1837), his future amanuensis, Joseph Gandy (1771–1843) and Charles Heathcote Tatham (1772–1842) followed these architects in their association with Italian academies. It is not unreasonable to regard Chambers, Mylne, Adam, Byres, Dance, Harrison, Soane, Gandy and Tatham as having become, in a sense, honorary Italians.

PIRANESI THE CATALYST

From the mid-eighteenth century Giovanni Battista Piranesi (1720–78) was one of the most influential figures in Rome, having an impact on William Chambers on his Grand Tour from 1750–55, and an even more powerful one on Robert Adam, in Italy from 1754 to 1758. Chambers told his pupils to meet Piranesi when they were in Rome, sending them a letter of extraordinarily broad sympathies, originally written in 1774, in which he urged them to: 'Converse much with artists of all countrys, particularly foreigners, that you may get rid of national prejudices. Seek for those who have most reputation young or old, amongst which forget not Piranesi, who you may see in my name'.[31]

Piranesi dedicated to Adam his great plan of ancient Rome, *Ichnographia*, published in his book, *Il Campo Marzio dell'antica Roma* (1762). The wreathed heads of Adam and Piranesi appear in a medallion on the title-page, as a duumvirate of Roman emperors, in one of the most extraordinary tributes ever paid by an Italian to a British subject during the whole course of the Grand Tour, though it should be noted that Adam knew from the outset that he would be obliged to purchase up to 100 copies at considerable expense. Piranesi, not successful as a practising architect himself, recognized in Adam a brilliant designer, sympathetic to his Roman cause, who was capable of expressing in built form his own vision and ideas. In his boldly anti-Vitruvian design philosophy, Piranesi declared that:

> an artist ... must not content himself with copying faithfully the ancients, but studying their works he ought to open himself a road to the finding out of new ornaments and new manners ... New pieces are daily dug out of the ruins and new things present themselves to us capable of fertilising and improving the ideas of an artist who thinks and reflects. Rome is certainly the most fruitful magazine of this kind.[32]

It was at Syon House, in the Hall, Ante Room and Dining Room of 1762–9, that Adam first achieved the rich ornamental synthesis, this 'novelty and variety', as

---

[31] A.T. Bolton (ed.), *The Portrait of Sir John Soane, R.A.* (London, n.d.), 11–12. For a fuller quotation from this letter see essay on Soane (Chapter 6).

[32] G.B. Piranesi, *Diverse maniere d'adornare i cammini* (Rome, 1769), 33.

he called it, which he and Piranesi must have discussed together in Rome. Piranesi now made four large engravings of the hall at Syon from Adam's designs, which Adam published in his *Works of Architecture*, vol. II (1778). Of the 110 plates in Piranesi's *Vasi, candelabri, cippi, sarcofagi, tripodi, lucerne ed ornamenti antichi* (1778), 63 bear the names of English patrons and collectors to whom he cleverly dedicated them in somewhat obsequious terms, hoping that they might buy the objects depicted. Many were for sale in his show-rooms or *Museo*, as he called them, in the Palazzo Tomati in Rome.[33]

ITALIANS BROUGHT TO ENGLAND

While Piranesi influenced English patrons and designers without having visited their country, several Italian architects and decorators came to England to seek commissions. These included Alessandro Galilei, a Florentine architect who arrived in 1714 at the invitation of the Hon. John Molesworth, British envoy to the court of Tuscany. With two friends, Molesworth formed 'the new Junta for Architecture', with the intention, even before Burlington, of pushing English architecture in a classical or Palladian direction. The Venetian architect Giacomo Leoni, in England by 1714, published the first English translation of Palladio in 1715–20 and was a prolific country-house architect. Other visiting architects and decorators included Giuseppe Maria Borgnis and his son, Giovanni Battista Borra, and Vicenzo Valdré (Valdrati), as well as Joseph Bonomi, who was brought to England in 1767 by the Adam brothers.

In the 4th Earl of Aylesford (1751–1812), Bonomi found the dream patron for any Grand Tour architect: a gifted painter, an architect *manqué*, a traveller and connoisseur, whose friends included the Picturesque theorist, Sir Uvedale Price, and the collector, Sir George Beaumont. Bonomi and Lord Aylesford designed the Pompeian Gallery of 1787 at Packington Hall, Warwickshire, with painted panels on the walls and a ceiling based on engravings in Nicolas Ponce's *Description des bains de Titus ou collection des peintures trouvées dans les ruines des thermes de cet empereur* (Paris, 1786).[34]

Fresh light on the cosmopolitan flavour encouraged by the Grand Tour may be gained by comparing the similar approaches to the creation of a monumental interior by two superficially very different patrons, the 8th Baron Arundell of Wardour (1740–1808), excluded by his Catholic faith from holding public office, and the 1st Marquess of Lansdowne (1737–1805), President of the Board of Trade and George III's prime minister in 1782–3. Succeeding his father in 1756 at the age of sixteen, while studying at the English College of St Omer, Arundell went on a Grand Tour in 1758 with a Jesuit priest, the Rev. John Thorpe.

---

[33] On the sale of antiquities, see H. Gross, *Rome in the Age of Enlightenment: the Post-Tridentine Syndrome and the Ancien Regime* (Cambridge, 1990).

[34] What Ponce knew as the Baths of Titus were the remains of Nero's Domus Aurea.

Arundell and Thorpe, who remained in Rome, exchanged two or three letters a month for 24 years,[35] many of which concerned the design and fittings of the ambitious Catholic chapel filling one wing of Wardour Castle, Wiltshire, the vast Palladian mansion which Arundell built from designs by James Paine in 1771–6.

At the same time that Lord Arundell was creating his great Anglo-Italian chapel, with the help of designs by Giacomo Quarenghi sent from Rôme, Lord Lansdowne was commissioning designs for a library or gallery in a closely similar style at Lansdowne House, London, again with the help of an English agent in Rome. The gallery at Lansdowne (then Shelburne) house, designed by Robert Adam, had been in an unfinished state when Lansdowne bought it in 1765.[36] In 1771, following his wife's death, he went to Italy, where he met Gavin Hamilton (1723–98), dealer, archaeologist and painter, resident in the city from 1756. He began to buy sculpture from Hamilton, at whose suggestion he commissioned Francesco Panini, son of the painter of Roman *vedute*, to prepare designs for the Lansdowne House gallery. He also obtained designs from Clérisseau, François-Joseph Belanger and Bonomi, though the commission was eventually given to George Dance.

* * *

The advice of Chambers to 'get rid of national prejudices' produced a late flowering in the Xeineion which C.R. Cockerell (1788–1863) formed in Greece, in November 1811, with Haller von Hallerstein, the Liverpool architect John Foster, Jakob Linckh from Württemberg, the Hon. Frederick North (later Lord Guilford), Baron Otto von Stackelberg and the Danish archaeologist, Peter Brondsted. They gave each other bronze rings inscribed 'Xeineion' (token of friendship), depicting the owl of Minerva.[37] The foundation document, written in French, described how:

> every worthy man of every country, every religion and every age can aspire to become a Xenios, the only essential quality being enthusiasm for Greece, ancient literature and the fine arts. The Xenioi themselves constitute a nation or people, and the moment the ring is on the finger it never leaves it. The arbitrary differences between the nations are abolished and one becomes wholly and uniquely a Xenios.[38]

---

[35] Only Thorpe's half of the correspondence has survived. See P. Caraman SJ, *Wardour: a Short History* (Bristol, 1984).

[36] D. Stillman, 'The gallery for Lansdowne House: international neo-classical architecture and decoration in microcosm', *Art Bulletin* 52 (March 1970), 75–80.

[37] See H. Bankel (ed.), *Carl Haller von Hallerstein in Griechenland: 1810–1817* (Berlin, 1986), 188–9.

[38] See D. Watkin, 'C.R. Cockerell and the role of archaeology in modern classical architecture', *The Classicist* 2 (1995–6), 16–24.

In 1819, two years after his return from his seven-year-long Grand Tour, during which he had helped excavate the Temple of Apollo Epicurius at Bassae, Cockerell became a founder-member of the Travellers' Club. The aim of this Club was to provide a setting where members could return hospitality to foreigners who had assisted them while much of the continent was difficult of access during the Napoleonic Wars. It thus enshrined the ideals of the eighteenth-century Grand Tour, as expressed in the Enlightenment vision of an international community, rooted in scholarship, archaeology, connoisseurship and fraternal sociability. The scholars and statesmen on the first committee included, in addition to Cockerell, the Earl of Aberdeen, prime minister from 1852 to 1855 and author of *An Inquiry into the Principles of Beauty in Grecian Architecture* (1822),[39] William Hamilton, secretary to Lord Elgin, Viscount Palmerston, the Earl of Auckland and the Marquess of Lansdowne. In 1830 the committee commissioned a new club-house in Pall Mall from the architect Charles Barry, who had made his own Grand Tour in 1817–20. The interiors behind the serenely Italianate façades of Barry's Travellers' Club (1830–2) contain casts of Greek figured friezes from the Temple at Bassae, which Cockerell had excavated, and from the Parthenon.[40] The building thus encapsulates the Grand Tour vision of Italy as the channel for transmission to the modern world of the cultural ideals of antiquity, at the last moment before such ideals were subsumed by the growing nationalism of the nineteenth century.[41]

---

[39] First published in 1812 as the preface to William Wilkins's edition of Vitruvius, a book which Wilkins dedicated to Lord Aberdeen. The copy in the Club library is inscribed 'from W. Wilkins'.

[40] The Bassae frieze survives in the Library, but the Parthenon frieze, installed in the Billiard Room by 1839, has disappeared. See D. Watkin, 'The Travellers' Club and the Grand Tour: Raphael corrected', *The British Art Journal* 1 (autumn 1999), 56–62.

[41] I wish to thank Professor Edward Chaney and Dr John Adamson for advice on an early draft of this paper.

THREE INDIVIDUAL VIEWS

4

Andrew Lumisden And
Giovanni Battista Piranesi

MICHAEL McCARTHY

The protagonists of this essay, Andrew Lumisden and Giovanni Battista Piranesi, were likely to have become acquainted with each other in the society of eighteenth-century Rome, since Lumisden (Fig. 1) was a Scot and Piranesi had many professional and personal contacts with Lumisden's fellow-countrymen.[1] Piranesi's *Bird's Eye View of the Campus Martius,* of 1762, shows in the lower left a frieze inscribed 'Roberto Adam Architecto', testifying to the intimacy of connection between the works of Piranesi and those of Scottish architects and collectors on the Grand Tour.[2] That this extended to Piranesi's theoretical concerns and polemical writings may be demonstrated by the long letter he addressed to Robert Mylne on 11 November 1760, referring to the publication of *Della magnificenza ed architettura dei Romani,* a work prompted in part, the letter informs us, by a pamphlet on Taste, written by another Scottish artist who spent much time in Rome, Allan Ramsay.[3] Mylne's greatest commission, won directly upon his return from Rome, was celebrated by Piranesi in the plate *Blackfriar's Bridge under Construction.*[4] There we see Piranesi's interest in structural engineering respond to the comparable interest of his Scottish friend, who had earlier supplied Piranesi with the drawings and analysis he had made of *The Temple of Concord at Agrigentum*, which in its raking chiaroscuro foretells the response Piranesi will make to the solemn grandeur of the Paestum temples twenty years later.[5] Piranesi also paid Robert Adam the compliment of engraving six plates of his designs for Syon House; a compliment returned by Adam in the design of the final room of the suite he designed for Osterley House, the

---

[1] B. Skinner, *Scots in Italy in the Eighteenth Century* (Edinburgh, 1966).

[2] C.D. Denison, M.-N. Rosenfeld and S. Wiles, *Exploring Rome: Piranesi and his Contemporaries* (Montreal, 1993), no. 61, 109–12.

[3] J.A. Gotch, 'The missing years of Robert Mylne', *Architectural Review* 130 (657) (Sept. 1951), 179–82.

[4] J. Wilton-Ely, *Giovanni Battista Piranesi: the Complete Etchings*, 2 vols (San Francisco, 1994), II, no. 1014.

[5] Wilton-Ely, *Piranesi: the Complete Etchings* (above, n. 4), II, no. 782.

Etruscan Room, which depends upon the plates of his Roman friend and mentor.[6] The Hope family of Amsterdam was also Scottish, and they responded to the furniture designs of Piranesi, published in *Diverse maniere d'adornare i cammini* (1769), by commissioning the table to Piranesi's design now in the Rijksmuseum.[7]

ANDREW LUMISDEN ESQ.ᴿ

FIG. 1. *Andrew Lumisden*; engraving by W. Dickinson, after a medallion by James Tassie.
(By kind permission of the British School at Rome)

We should therefore have an established context within which to place Andrew Lumisden, who was born in Edinburgh in 1720 and was to die there in 1802. In fact, he has almost disappeared from the constellation of scholars, artists and architects around Piranesi, and of recent authors only Jonathan Scott mentions him, and then by way of a footnote.[8] He is worthy of notice in his own right, however, and also because his career illuminates an aspect of the Rome of

---

[6] Wilton-Ely, *Piranesi: the Complete Etchings* (above, n. 4), II, nos. 1,010–13.
[7] Denison, Rosenfeld and Wiles, *Exploring Rome* (above, n. 2), no. 64, 115–18.
[8] J. Scott, *Piranesi* (New York , 1975), 315–16.

Piranesi to which attention has not been sufficiently drawn, but which had obvious relevance to the Scottish community in Rome — that is, the presence of the exiled Stuart family, the so-called King James and his son (who was to be romanticized as 'Bonnie Prince Charlie'), who held court, in continually diminishing splendour, at the Palazzo Muti in the Piazza Santi Apostoli. Andrew Lumisden became their secretary and was to spend the years from 1750 to 1769 in Rome.

Lumisden was to publish in London in 1797 *Remarks on the Antiquities of Rome and its Environs*, a book which was reissued in 1812. He is a great name-dropper, and it must be remembered that, writing his book late in life and in the far north, he was dependent upon the books of prints he had brought back with him from the city of his exile. But he drops the name of Piranesi no fewer than 54 times in his text, and in the footnotes to the text he refers to Piranesi's prints more than 150 times. His is therefore a very rare instance in which we can chart a contemporary's reaction to the work of Piranesi, and for that reason alone a re-examination of the connections between Lumisden and Piranesi is in order.

Nor is it only through his book on the antiquities of Rome that Lumisden finds common cause with Piranesi. His sister Isabella married Robert Strange (subsequently Sir Robert Strange), one of England's leading engravers of the eighteenth century, and Lumisden acted as coordinator between Strange and Piranesi in an unhappy business deal connected with plates of Dorigny, a subject to which we shall return.[9] It should be noted also that Robert Mylne, an effective agent for the sale of Piranesi's prints in England just as Piranesi was effective in spreading Mylne's fame for the design of Blackfriars Bridge throughout Europe, was an intimate friend of Isabella Strange, and thereby of her brother, Andrew Lumisden.

Why then has Lumisden disappeared from Piranesian studies? The answer may be that neither of the great Scottish artists in Rome at this period — Allan Ramsay and Robert Adam — were sympathetic to him, and their letters, diaries and drawings are the fullest record of Rome at the mid-century.[10] Both had their minds set on a career at the Hanoverian court in London, and it would have done them no good to be associated with a staunch supporter of the Stuart cause such as Lumisden, personal secretary to the Old and the Young Pretenders. Lumisden, so far as we know, never sought acquaintance with Robert Adam, and it is unlikely that he would have made that acquaintance, since Adam's hostility to Robert Mylne (and thus, we might infer, to one of his intimates) is only too apparent in his letters of the period. But he did seek a friendship with Allan Ramsay, whose father had been a warm friend of his own father. He was

---

[9] For their correspondence see J. Dennistoun, *Memoirs of Sir R. Strange and A. Lumisden*, 2 vols (Edinburgh, 1855).

[10] For Ramsay see A. Smart, *Allan Ramsay: Painter, Essayist and Man of the Enlightenment* (London, 1992); and for Adam see J. Fleming, *Robert Adam and his Circle in Edinburgh and Rome* (London, 1962).

met by a frosty reception and ceased to pursue the matter. Ramsay, on his first visit to Rome, had raised suspicions of Jacobite sympathies by having been admitted to the Masonic Lodge of the *Strada Paolina*, which was reputed to have the young Prince Charles for its Grand Master. Returning to Rome in 1754 as a happily married man and established court painter, he had no wish for association with known Jacobites. Lumisden evidently knew well Ramsay's sister, Catherine, who had accompanied Ramsay and his wife to Rome. His rueful comment is that he cared little for Ramsay and his bad figure drawings, but longed to have heard again a song from the 'lips of Katty!'.[11] He was to be disappointed.

A second reason for the relative disappearance of Andrew Lumisden from studies of the Rome of Piranesi is that his biographer and the publisher of his papers in two volumes in 1855, James Dennistoun, adopted a rather patronizing tone in his account of Lumisden's book on the antiquities of the city and its environs. 'On the whole', he wrote, 'although now in some measure superseded by works produced under the influence of modern taste, and with the aids of German research and criticism, Mr. Lumisden's volume is highly creditable to his industry, and may still be read with pleasure and profit'.[12] He could hardly have said less! But in fact in an earlier passage Dennistoun had denied to his subject even the boring virtue of industry:

> A man of genius, enthusiasm, or taste would, however, have made far more of his position. The history, antiquities and arts of Italy were a soil unexhausted by natives — unoccupied by foreigners. Through his master's influence, libraries, archives, and galleries, the muniments as well as the monuments of Rome, would have been patent to his researches. But, devoid of ambition and originality, he was usually content to gather and peruse the works of others, chiefly his contemporaries, in an age when most authors were satisfied to follow beaten tracks in monotonous routine.[13]

With a biographer like Dennistoun, who needs enemies?

Lumisden is modest in the conventional manner of self-deprecation when introducing his book. There is the usual talk about his having written it solely for his own amusement and then having his arm twisted to make it public 'by tasteful and learned friends'.[14] We can identify these friends by his references in the text — they are mainly Scottish friends from Roman days, sharing his retirement in Scotland, such as Gavin Hamilton, James Byres and Colin Morison, all well-known experts in the Roman antiquities and experienced

---

[11] Dennistoun, *Memoirs* (above, n. 9), I, 279–80.
[12] Dennistoun, *Memoirs* (above, n. 9), II, 171.
[13] Dennistoun, *Memoirs* (above, n. 9), I, 144–5.
[14] A. Lumisden, *Remarks on the Antiquities of Rome and its Environs* (London, 1812), The Advertisement.

ciceroni and dealers. But when he closes his account, there is a ring of authenticity to his remarks: 'This enquiry, full of variety and ancient anecdote, has afforded much pleasure to my own mind; and after a long lapse of time, I still, in imagination, frequently tread over this classical ground, and never without the recollected satisfaction I enjoyed in the agreeable pursuit'.[15]

It is time to offer a brief synopsis of the career of Andrew Lumisden, whose profile was engraved in a medallion by Tassie (Fig. 1). Born in Edinburgh in 1720, he was trained, like his father, for the law. But his father had been involved in the Jacobite rebellion of 1715: as a result, he was denied practice at the Scottish bar and acted as law agent rather than lawyer. The sins of the father were not visited upon the son, who practised law in Edinburgh until the Stuarts revisited their curse on the country, 30 years later. Andrew Lumisden was secretary to Bonnie Prince Charlie and held the seals of the Pretender during the rebellion of 1745, which ended in the Massacre of Culloden early the following year. Meanwhile, his sister, Isabella, had attached herself emotionally to Robert Strange, an apprentice engraver whose skills were used by the Bonnie Prince for the printing of paper money for the payment of the troops — most of whom never lived to cash it in; which was just as well, since it was worthless. After Culloden, Andrew Lumisden had a price on his head and a warrant was taken out for his arrest on the charge of treason; though, strangely, his future brother-in-law was not named in the Bill of Attainder and was subsequently to be knighted by King George III. They spent several months in hiding in the mountains and islands of Scotland, and with considerable daring Lumisden eventually went in disguise to London, thence to Dover and so to Rouen. He was so reckless that he actually visited some of his Jacobite friends imprisoned in London, and his father was heard to remark that he deserved hanging for that act of stupidity rather than for his political allegiance! It is clear that old man Lumisden had learned by his youthful folly and had no sympathy whatsoever for the Jacobite tendencies of his offspring, Andrew and Isabella (who had by this time eloped to marry Robert Strange). As a result, he was very slow to send money to his son in exile and Andrew's letters from Rouen show him in constant penury. But the stay in Rouen is important in the history of art, because it led him to induce his brother-in-law to come to Rouen and perfect his engraving technique, first at the studio of Descamps in Rouen, and subsequently at that of Le Bas in Paris. Just such a progress of training in engraving was followed by two of the best bookmen of the eighteenth century in London — Richard Bentley, who illustrated Gray's *Odes,* and Thomas Major, who was to issue *The Ruins of Paestum* in 1768 and who executed the most ambitious plates of Robert Wood's books on Palmyra and Baalbek published in the previous

---

[15] Lumisden, *Remarks* (above, n. 14), 390.

decade.[16] It is a chapter of the history of the graphic arts in England that would merit detailed research.

Lumisden had hoped to get a start in the import and export business while at Rouen, but this never materialized, and eventually he accepted the offer of a fellow-Jacobite, Mr Daniel, to accompany him to Rome, where he hoped to find employment with the Stuart King or to become a *cicerone* or travelling tutor. 'As I have not given over thoughts of travelling with some person of fortune, it would be no small recommendation my having made a Roman journey', he wrote to his father from Rouen on 27 June 1749.[17] We learn from a letter of his sister that he was in Rome for the opening of the Jubilee Year of 1750, and within a year he had received the appointment of Assistant Secretary to Mr Edgar, Principal Secretary to the King, which involved residence at Palazzo Muti, at the north end of Piazza Santi Apostoli. He assumed the post of Principal Secretary on the death of Mr Edgar in 1762 and was confirmed in it at the death of the Old Pretender in 1766. But two years later, in a fit of drunken pique, Bonnie Prince Charlie dismissed all his Scottish attendants. Andrew Lumisden moved to Paris early in 1769. Allowed to return to England in 1773, he was finally pardoned in 1778 and lived in Edinburgh till his death in 1802.

From this summary of his life, it is clear that his interest in the antiquities of Rome pre-dated his actual arrival in the city. Such an interest explains the circle of his friends, noted students of Rome and its antiquities such as Gavin Hamilton, James Byres, Colin Morison, James Stuart (of whom he speaks very highly) and, of course, Piranesi. There can be little doubt that his studies were propelled by intellectual and historical curiosity; but they probably had a practical end also. His employment at the court of the Pretenders was always tenuous, its permanence dependent upon the shaky health of the Old Pretender, the shifting policies of the papal court and the waywardness of the Young Pretender. It was sensible of him to equip himself with detailed knowledge of the Roman antiquities to prepare himself for an alternative career, as *cicerone* and dealer, in the event of a collapse of the exiled Stuart household at Palazzo Muti.

Lumisden's text, by and large, is exactly what one would expect of an armchair traveller dependent on the books in his collection, which he was to describe as the mainstay of his life. 'A passion for books', he wrote from his retreat in Paris, 'has made my collection larger than is convenient for one who is not in a fixed state of life. However, they are such companions as I cannot think of parting with. They will become the more necessary as I reckon to spend the remainder of my days in retirement'.[18] He assured Strange at the same time: 'I

---

[16] For Bentley see L. Jestin, *The Answer to the Lyre* (Philadelphia, 1990), and for Major see M. McCarthy, 'Una nuova interpretazione del "Paestum" di Thomas Major', in J. Raspi Serra (ed.), *La Fortuna di Paestum*, 2 vols (Florence, 1986), I, 39–57.

[17] Dennistoun, *Memoirs* (above, n. 9), I, 131.

[18] Dennistoun, *Memoirs* (above, n. 9), II, 124.

am now likely to converse more with the dead than with the living. I still intend to correct and put together the remarks I have collected on the Antiquities of Rome and its environs'.[19]

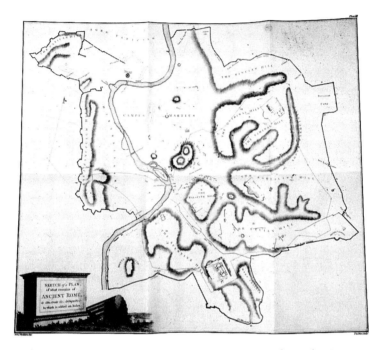

FIG. 2. *Ancient Rome and the Seven Hills*, from Lumisden, *Remarks on the Antiquities of Rome and its Environs*, p. 135. *(By kind permission of the British School at Rome)*

Therefore it is to the Paris years, 1769–73, that the bulk of the writing may be assigned, and clearly the author was dependent on graphic sources. He mentions some drawings in his collection, specifying a view of the Roman forum by Zocchi, and these guaranteed the accuracy of the few plates he had printed in London. They are fourteen in all, the most interesting of which are the two maps, both large nine-sheet fold-outs, one of the 'Gates and Environs' and the other of 'Ancient Rome and the Seven Hills' (Fig. 2). These are still extremely helpful and are, for their date, remarkable for clarity and accuracy. Modern scholarship would concur with him in the location of the Villa of Pliny, for instance, always a very vexed subject. In some instances they serve to supplement the text. He writes: 'Whether Titus's Baths were erected in the gardens of Maecenas, as Piranesi supposes, or whether these gardens, and his celebrated tower, lay further east on the hill, I shall not venture to determine'.[20]

---

[19] Dennistoun, *Memoirs* (above, n. 9), II, 125.
[20] Lumisden, *Remarks* (above, n. 14), 193.

Such diffidence is not possible in the map, which shows the Baths of Titus set squarely on the Esquiline.

Lumisden is never slow to contradict Piranesi, and his book serves as the best contemporary running commentary on the works of the master, especially the volumes of *Antichità romane*, to the plates of which he refers the reader, as I mentioned earlier, over 200 times. Certainly Piranesi was to the fore of his mind when he wrote the tribute in his Introduction to 'the industry of many ingenious artists, who have measured and delineated these ruins, models of perfection in architecture, and by means of the graver, thus transmitted them to posterity'.[21] His range of reference is wider than the works of Piranesi, encompassing Desgodets and Pietro Santi Bartoli, as well as older authors, Serlio, Palladio and, on one occasion, Pirro Ligorio, of whose plan of the Villa Adriana he did not think highly, remarking that Ligorio was 'a better architect than accurate antiquary'.[22] Lumisden's frankness is one of the most attractive features of his book. 'It is indeed very uncertain', he generalizes, 'if the antiquaries of Tivoli are right in the places they assign to the different villas. Men will swallow down any story rather than appear ignorant'.[23] His most cutting remark, however, is reserved for the prejudiced anti-Catholic and anti-Italian traveller Gilbert Burnet, later bishop of Salisbury, 'who seems unhappily', he wrote, 'to have had a reluctancy to tell the truth, even when he had no interest to do otherwise'.[24] I should remark here that, even though he was a loyal Jacobite, Lumisden was born Protestant and remained so throughout his life.

Only one aspect of Piranesi, his antiquarian activities, was of interest to Lumisden. Aspects of the master's work that are of consuming interest to us, the *Grotteschi*, the *Carceri* and the imaginary works of the *Prima parte,* receive no comment from Lumisden. This may be accounted for by their pre-dating his arrival in Rome and his introduction to Piranesi in 1750, but I do not think that is the full explanation for the blind spots. He was fully conversant with Piranesi's work as architect at the Church of Santa Maria del Priorato and the Piazza dei Cavalieri di Malta from 1764 to 1768. Yet when on page 168 he mentions that church, he says not a word about its having been restructured by Piranesi. Nor does he have anything to say about Piranesi as designer of interiors and furniture, though the *Diverse maniere* would have been known to him, as would the decoration of the English Coffee House with Egyptian murals in 1766. Such indifference to what many aficionados of Piranesi would regard as essential is typical of a man of Lumisden's age and background. For instance, when Sir Roger Newdigate in 1775 ordered two sets, each of twelve bound volumes, of the works of Piranesi — one for himself and one for the Bodleian Library — he pointedly omitted the same works, though he was a principal

---

[21] Lumisden, *Remarks* (above, n. 14), 5.
[22] Lumisden, *Remarks* (above, n. 14), 411.
[23] Lumisden, *Remarks* (above, n. 14), 420–1.
[24] Lumisden, *Remarks* (above, n. 14), 149.

patron of the artist. And Newdigate is just as silent about Piranesi's architecture when he revisited the Aventine to see Santa Maria del Priorato, on which he had made two pages of notes on his first visit there in 1740. Indeed the only contemporary comment (apart from Bianconi's diatribe in the *Eulogium*) that I have come across is that of Prince Poniatowski, who, visiting the Priorato on 1 January 1786, remarks that it is 'defiguré par la mauvaise église de Piranesi'.[25] Such eloquent silences and downright denunciation must have relevance to a Piranesian problem I have never seen addressed — why the great engraver of ancient and modern Rome never published or caused to be published prints of his own architecture, though he was ready to publish the works of Robert Adam and Robert Mylne, and those of his Italian contemporaries, Galilei, Fuga, Salvi and de Sanctis. As the drawings in the Pierpont Morgan and Avery Libraries in New York demonstrate, materials for a printing of the Aventine designs were prepared, as were those for the rebuilding of San Giovanni in Laterano.[26]

It has relevance also to a Piranesian topic perhaps too much discussed, his quarrel with Lord Charlemont over the dedicatory plates of the *Antichità romane* and his consequent issuing of the *Lettere di giustificazione*.[27] Piranesi was never less than a sensible businessman, and there can be little doubt that he sensed the lack of appeal that idealized architecture had for his English clientele and the need to cater to their passion, which was for antiquity. Staking his claim therefore to their patronage upon his work as an antiquary, by undertaking the enormous labour of charting the antiquities of Rome and its environs, the shoddy treatment that one way or another attended that crucial venture in his career was of the greatest importance; and his committing himself to public denunciation of the behaviour of Lord Charlemont (or the apparent behaviour of the young Milord) was necessary to his ability to fulfil the task he had undertaken. In the exhibition of his works at Smith College in 1961 there was a copy of the *Lettere* which bears a manuscript list of names interpreted as being the names of the recipients (Fig. 3).[28] One can read *Lomysdael*, and I feel sure that Andrew Lumisden is the persona lurking behind this unintelligible cipher, because the following name is that of Mr Edgar. It may well be, therefore, that Lumisden, the practised diplomat, played a role in solving that international incident with the election of Piranesi to the Society of Antiquaries of London in 1757. That the incident was solved with the greatest success is evident from the fact that precisely 40 years later Lumisden could issue in London his book on the antiquities of Rome and its environs using the *Antichità romane* for illustrations. He could safely assume that his readers would have a copy of Piranesi to hand.

---

[25] Manuscript account in the Gabinet Rycin of Warsaw, kindly communicated to me by Dr Elżbieta Büdzinska.

[26] Denison, Rosenfeld and Wiles, *Exploring Rome* (above, n. 2), nos. 30–6, 48–55.

[27] Denison, Rosenfeld and Wiles, *Exploring Rome* (above, n. 2), nos. 57–8, 99–104.

[28] P. Hofer, K. Lehmann and R .Wittkower, *Piranesi* (Northampton, Mass., 1961), 66, pl. 15.

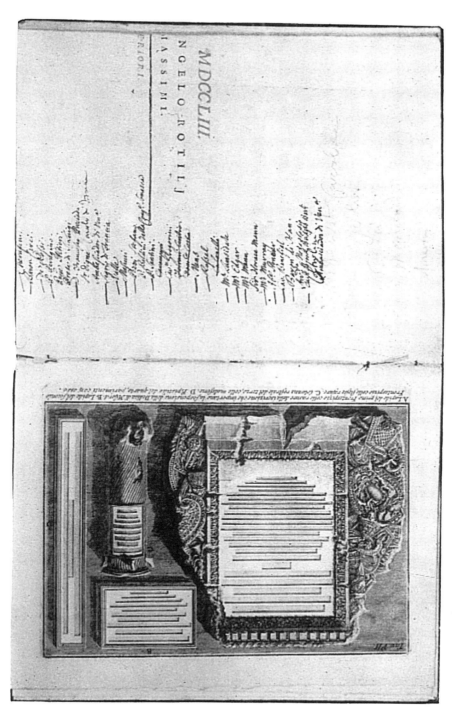

FIG. 3. Giovanni Battista Piranesi, *Lapide del primo frontispizio*, from *Le antichità romane* (1757), letter to Charlemont.
(By kind permission of the British School at Rome)

Lumisden certainly acted the diplomat in the troubled relations of Piranesi with his brother-in-law, Robert Strange, in 1763. This had to do with two plates of Dorigny that Strange gave Piranesi to print, and with which Piranesi was disappointed. I will not bore you with the details: there is nothing more unsatisfactory than attempting with hindsight to solve clashes of personality. What one can say in this case is that if Piranesi was an awkward fellow to deal with on occasion, Robert Strange was positively paranoid because of a persecution complex that he nurtured, as his tortuous letters to Allan Ramsay and Lord Bute demonstrate beyond shadow of doubt.[29] Piranesi in this case was content to leave bad enough alone and was even so good as to chair the meeting of the Accademia di San Luca at which Strange was admitted to a fellowship: a kindness Strange returned by failing to deposit with the Academy the sample of his work that he had promised. Besides Lumisden, the Abbé Grant and the papal nephews, Cardinal Giambattista and Don Abbondio Rezzonico, were dragged into this potentially international incident, which ended so tranquilly that its trace survives only in the letters of Lumisden to Strange. It is in that context that we must read Lumisden's sentence about Piranesi: 'I am against your having hereafter any considerable dealings with so wrong-headed and dangerous a man'.[30] That this is not an adequate account of Lumisden's attitude to Piranesi may be pointed to by the letter to Strange of 3 July 1765, that is, eighteen months later. 'I shall communicate to Piranesi what you say of him: he and all your friends here, long much to see *Justice* and *Meekness*', two personifications from Raphael that Strange was then in process of printing in Paris.[31] How ironic the titles are in the light of Strange's litigious spirit!

What then was Lumisden's true assessment of his friend Piranesi? He clearly thought him a muddled thinker about the antiquities of Rome. One instance will suffice:

> But Piranesi places the Pons Milvius above a mile higher up the river, opposite to the Tor di Quinto, and makes the Via Flaminia to have passed through the Porta Pinciana, and from thence, by many turnings, to have reached the Pons Milvius. The reasons offered by Piranesi to support his singular opinion do not seem satisfactory. The Romans never made their consular roads in winding lines, but in cases of absolute necessity, which cannot be pleaded here. But this question, I think, is decided by Suetonius, who tells us that Augustus built his mausoleum 'inter Flaviam viam ripamque Tiberis'. Now, had the Flaminian Road led to the Porta Pinciana, it must have passed by the south end of the Collegio di Propaganda Fidei, and consequently the mausoleum could with no propriety be said to stand between it and the river; whereas, if this road led to the Porta del Popolo, the historian's description answers exactly; for the

[29] Dennistoun, *Memoirs* (above, n. 9), I, 272–82; II, 176–9, 293–306.
[30] Scott, *Piranesi* (above, n. 8), 319.
[31] Scott, *Piranesi* (above, n. 8), 33.

remains of the monument are yet to be seen, near the church of St. Roch.[32]

I could hardly have found a passage better calculated to demonstrate the marriage of literary evidence with archaeological evidence that forms the basis of Lumisden's judgement of the antiquities of Rome. If we look at Piranesi's view of the Ponte Milvio (Fig. 4), we find that he shows the stub of an arch in the foreground, next to the Tor di Quinto; and the current Ponte Milvio is in the background. Piranesi has decided that the ruined stub of the arch is the real Ponte Milvio because it is in *opus incertum*, and Vitruvius had said that the Ponte Milvio was in *opus incertum*, as Piranesi's letterpress to the plate indicates.

Let me tie in that discussion with one other, Lumisden's passage on to the Temple of Rome and Venus:

> Some writers call it a temple of the Sun and Moon, or Serapis and Isis, others that of Venus and Rome; but Piranesi supposes it was a double triclinium of Nero's Golden House; the one fronting the east having served for a summer, and the other to the west for a winter eating-room, agreeable to a rule laid down by Vitruvius for the construction of such buildings.[33]

What Lumisden and other antiquaries seem to have forgotten is Piranesi's statement of intent in the Preface to *Antichità romane*: 'to illustrate by means of the ruins here portrayed the precepts of Vitruvius on the division, durability, grandeur and beauty of buildings'. To return to a point I made by other means in my essay 'The theoretical imagination in Piranesi's shaping of architectural reality': Piranesi's intent in publication of the *Antichità romane* was polemical and made no pretence to the objectivity or archaeological exactitude that Lumisden practised and expected others to practise.[34]

I do not wish to exaggerate the dissonance between these contemporary accounts of the antiquities of Rome. In the majority of instances where he cites the works of Piranesi, Lumisden does so without any critical comment and often with undisguised admiration. 'See Piranesi's beautiful large view of the inside of this church', he writes in connection with San Paolo fuori le mura.[35] Sometimes he gives Piranesi half the argument and begs to differ with the second half, as in the case of the Arch of Drusus: 'Piranesi however makes it one of the arches of Aqua Antoniana. It might indeed have been an arch, either of the Aqua Marcia or the Aqua Appia. But at any rate it has more the appearance of an arch of an aqueduct than of a triumphal arch'.[36]

<hr/>

[32] Lumisden, *Remarks* (above, n. 14), 34 (misprinted 43).
[33] Lumisden, *Remarks* (above, n. 14), 345–6.
[34] Published in *Impulse* (Toronto, Winter 1986), 6–12.
[35] Lumisden, *Remarks* (above, n. 14), 121.
[36] Lumisden, *Remarks* (above, n. 14), 85–6.

FIG. 4. Giovanni Battista Piranesi, *Remains of the Milvian Bridge*, from *Il Campo Marzio dell'antica Roma* (1762).
(By kind permission of the British School at Rome)

FIG. 5. Giovanni Battista Piranesi, *The Substructure of the Appian Way*, from *Antichità d'Albano e di Castelgandolfo*.
(By kind permission of the British School at Rome)

One notable feature of Lumisden's book is that, whilst his references to other authorities are quite widespread in the early part — I counted nineteen different authorities cited —, he insensibly gets more selective as the work proceeds, and by the end of the main text he routinely offers three only, namely Palladio, Desgodets and Piranesi. That is, I think, the measure of his true estimate of Piranesi's greatness. Even when he is critical of Piranesi, Lumisden sees the wider relevance of his works beyond the interests of antiquaries:

> Piranesi, in his elegant plan of the Campus Martius, has completely traced all the buildings, which the Roman writers have mentioned to have stood there, as if he had seen and measured them all; though of the greatest part of them, no vestige remains. But this magnificent work, which is a proof of the fertile invention of its ingenious author, will be apt to mislead strangers and future antiquaries, whilst it must afford many noble ideas and useful hints to architects.[37]

Again, in connection with the Pons Aelius, now the Ponte Sant'Angelo, he asserts:

> Piranesi, as an architect, seems with attention to have examined this bridge and the mausoleum: he has given plates to explain their construction, to which I beg leave to refer the reader. He has traced their foundations so minutely, that one would think he had assisted at the building of them. I am indeed afraid that much of this is ideal; but his ingenious remarks may be useful to artists.[38]

The importance of Piranesi's graphic work to artists and architects, therefore, is clearly recognized by Lumisden: I need hardly stress what the entire book shows, that Piranesi was of great use to antiquaries, and to none more than Andrew Lumisden. Was the debt ever repaid? Was the antiquary of use to Piranesi in ways other than diplomatic? Fortunately the fifth and final appendix of the book provides us with an important instance of antiquarian study informing art and giving occasion to one of Piranesi's most sublime plates, *The Substructure of the Appian Way* (Fig. 5), from the collection *Antichità d'Albano e di Castelgandolfo*, which was published in 1764, but not with this plate, which is not earlier than 1769, as the text of Lumisden demonstrates:

> Between the Stella and La Ricia there is a remarkable part of the Via Appia, which deserves the attention of the curious. It is a long and vast mole or levé, carried across the vale of La Ricia, to facilitate the passage. Arches are constructed at various distances, to carry off the water that may collect there. This mole remains a monument of Roman grandeur, and gives an high idea of the expense they

---

[37] Lumisden, *Remarks* (above, n. 14), 252.
[38] Lumisden, *Remarks* (above, n. 14), 371.

bestowed on their consular roads. To see it to advantage, it is
necessary to go down to the vale, for its sides are now so covered
with trees and shrubs, that one may travel along it without
perceiving its greatness. Such has happened even to the ingenious
Piranesi, to whom, on publishing his elegant work on Albano, I
observed that he had taken no notice of this part of the Via Appia:
he promised to supply this neglect, but which, as far as I know, has
not been done.[39]

This is indeed an unnumbered plate, added to the collection in later years. Let us
hope that before his death in 1802 Andrew Lumisden had been made a gift of it,
since it may stand as Piranesi's testament to their long friendship.

Lumisden's removal to Paris in April 1769 did not entirely break his
relationship with Piranesi, since he acted as adviser to another generation of
Grand Tourists passing through Paris on their way to Rome and the recovery of
antiquity. One such was Charles Burney, who travelled in 1770 to prepare a
history of music in antiquity. He has left us a vivid pen-portrait of our author
during the years Lumisden was writing his book:

> My first visit [after arrival in Paris] was to Mr. Lumisden, whom I
> found to be all I expected, and more, as to intelligence, good
> breeding, good nature etc. With him I had a long conference on the
> object of my Italian journey, and he kindly undertook to make out a
> route for me — and gave me much information as to customs,
> manners, books etc. I found him to be a man of taste and learning,
> and though no musician, he was able to give me satisfaction on
> several subjects relative to my chief errand, such as libraries, Pope's
> Chapel, conservatories etc. He has a very pretty and well-chosen
> collection of books made at Rome during 19 years residence there
> where he had been secretary to the Chevalier St. George. He showed
> me several tracts on music necessary for me to consult and to get
> when in Italy and lent me others.[40]

On his arrival in Rome, Charles Burney immediately contacted James Byres
— 'who received me very kindly. He had already been apprised of my journey
and errand by Mr. Lumisden'.[41] Their conversation was, however, about Byres's
designs for Sir William Wynn's house. His visit on Monday 24 September was
to the Cavaliere Piranesi, and there he struck gold, finding several ancient
monuments in Piranesi's collection, not actual instruments of course, but relief
sculptures depicting ancient instruments. He left for Naples in mid-October but
not before having had dinner with James Byres and Piranesi (on 13 October).
When he returned a month later he noted with excitement:

---

[39] Lumisden, *Remarks* (above, n. 14), 457.

[40] H.E. Poole (ed.), *Charles Burney's Grand Tour in 1770* (London, 1969), 10.

[41] Poole, *Charles Burney* (above, n. 40), 130.

Il Cavaliere Piranesi, while I was at Naples, had sent his draughtsman all over Rome in search of ancient instruments — and he had made drawings from several of the most antique and curious — however, as I came here to see with my own eyes I determined to examine the originals and compare the copies myself — for which purpose I set off this morning as soon as it was light in company with Piranesi's young man — and walked about till I was ready to lye down in the street. However I was glad I took this method of having the drawings correct, for several things had been mistaken, and others were very obscure till I had seen the whole figure who held or played the instrument, and sometimes even seeing the whole group in a *basso relievo* was necessary to my forming any conjecture about the occasion and manner of playing it.[42]

The visit of this music historian was brief, since he departed Rome on 21 November, but it is apposite to record here that his final visits were to two of Andrew Lumisden's great friends: 'At six went out in the most violent rain, thunder and lightening that can be imagined — to make partenza visits and to examine Piranesi's things, from which I had had some ancient instruments drawn. Thence to Mr. Hamilton the painter whose pictures I saw and whose prints I bought'.[43]

That is the Rome of Piranesi and his contemporaries I would like to leave with you — a Rome in which older scholars, artists and architects went out of their way to assist the younger generation and to stimulate their study of antiquity; and, amongst other reasons, they did so from respect and affection for their friend and fellow-antiquary, Andrew Lumisden.

---

[42] Poole, *Charles Burney* (above, n. 40), 204.
[43] Poole, *Charles Burney* (above, n. 40), 211.

5

'... A Few Foreign Graces And Airs ...': William Marlow's Grand Tour Landscapes

MICHAEL LIVERSIDGE

Among the various factors that contributed to the rise and development of landscape painting in England in the eighteenth century, by far the most important in terms of educating taste and sustaining an informed appreciation of the fine arts was the Grand Tour. From the Treaty of Utrecht in 1713 until the outbreak of the wars with France at the end of the century, English gentlemen who had already received a classical education flocked across the Continent to Italy, where they inspected the sites made famous by historical events in antiquity and enjoyed the scenery described by the poets and writers of ancient Rome.[1] Crossing the Alps, the English traveller might recall Hannibal and Longinus on *The Sublime;* further on, in the tranquil atmosphere of the Roman Campagna, on ground hallowed by history, the golden visions of Virgil's pastorals might come to mind; and in the south, near Naples, there could be discovered scenes reminiscent of the enchanted Arcadia described by Theocritus. By observing the correspondences between the landscapes they were travelling through and the evocative accounts of the countryside they had read in classical literature, they learned to respond to nature with poetic sensibility, and they also learned to recognize the resemblance of real scenery to the idealized vision they encountered in the pictures of seventeenth-century painters like Claude Lorrain, the Poussins or Salvator Rosa.[2] The Grand Tour also contributed a renewed stimulus to connoisseurship and collecting, and it was from that stimulus that landscape began to play an increasingly prominent role in English art and literature — so much so that by the end of the eighteenth century it had become

---

[1] See D. Bull, *Classic Ground. British Artists and the Landscape of Italy 1740–1830* (New Haven, 1981), for a general account of British landscape and the Grand Tour.

[2] E. Manwaring, *Italian Landscape in Eighteenth Century England. A Study Chiefly of the Influence of Claude Lorrain and Salvator Rosa on English Taste 1700–1800* (London, 1925), provides the fullest account of English responses to Italianate landscapes in art and literature.

one of the principal vehicles through which the British creative genius expressed itself, in poetry, in painting, in garden design and in philosophical enquiry.[3]

As the demand grew for pictures that expressed the cultural and associational values with which landscape was invested by the Grand Tour, English painters responded to the market both by imitating what the collectors favoured and by extending their repertoires through travelling themselves in order to supply the kinds of subject, especially views, that patrons wanted. The English demand for souvenirs of the Grand Tour largely sustained the practices of several of Italy's leading view painters, among them Canaletto and Panini, and there were other painters like Claude-Joseph Vernet whose clientele included a high proportion of British buyers. Some Italian painters, because of their success with British travellers, moved to England, the most notable being Canaletto and Zuccarelli, both of whom spent prolonged periods in London.[4] The Grand Tour equally offered English artists the opportunity of lucrative employment: sometimes as draughtsmen travelling with patrons to record their journeys, as in the cases of William Pars and John Robert Cozens; or as painters residing abroad for a time and finding employment from British visitors; or there were those who toured the Continent in order to gather material from which to produce Grand Tour subjects back in England. There were a great many artists who followed the advice anonymously published in 1764 in *Lines to an English Painter:*

> Go abroad — take your palette and pencils to Rome,
> And when you return from your tour
> If a few foreign graces and airs you assume
> You will charm a complete connoisseur.[5]

One who did, and whose career illustrates particularly well the impact of the Grand Tour on English landscape art in the eighteenth century, was William Marlow. Both in his origins as a view painter before he travelled abroad, and subsequently in the pictures from which he mainly earned his livelihood, Marlow exemplifies the different ways in which English painters were affected by, responded to, and commercially exploited the Grand Tour.

Marlow learned his trade as a view painter in the studio of Samuel Scott, to whom he was apprenticed for five years between 1754 and 1759, staying on afterwards for one or two years as Scott's assistant. Scott was the first of the English painters working in the 1740s and 1750s — when Canaletto was in London — fully to comprehend his example and adapt it to the native tradition

---

[3] For the Grand Tour, collecting and landscape see J. Hayes, 'English patrons and landscape painting: eighteenth century collecting', *Apollo* (1966), 188–97; 'The response to nature in the eighteenth century', *Apollo* (1966), 444–51; 'Eighteenth century patronage', *Apollo* (1967), 254–9.

[4] For Canaletto, in England 1746–56, see M. Liversidge and J. Farrington (eds), *Canaletto and England* (Birmingham, 1993). Zuccarelli stayed in England 1752–62 and 1765–71.

[5] Quoted by W.T. Whitley, *Artists and their Friends in England 1700–1799*, X vols (London, 1929), I, 199.

of topographical painting, and it was through Scott that Marlow emerges as a view painter working in a manner that directly derives from a source that had been introduced into English painting as a result of the Grand Tour. All three artists worked at different times for the same patrons, the most important of them Sir Hugh Smithson (created Earl of Northumberland in 1750, and then Duke in 1766), for whom Canaletto painted six pictures when he was in England. Marlow's London views carry on the Canaletto-Scott tradition, and there are also other early pictures which show that he must have known paintings like Canaletto's views of Warwick Castle and Alnwick Castle.[6]

By the middle of the 1760s the professional context in which a painter working in London operated was changing rapidly and radically. The annual public exhibitions of the Society of Artists, which began in 1761, made it imperative for a landscape or view painter who aspired to attract the most discerning patrons to expand his repertoire beyond the kind of picturesque English prospects, views of country houses and other architectural subjects, or urban scenes which made up the great majority of such exhibits. With artists like Richard Wilson showing landscapes that related to the Italianate tradition and others who attracted attention with views of the kinds of scenery that appealed to tastes refined by the Grand Tour, a young painter such as William Marlow had to respond to the growing market for such subjects. So in 1765 he set out for Italy. His journey through France and Italy furnished him with a completely new range of material which he drew on continuously for the rest of his career, until he more or less retired from painting towards the end of the 1790s. How his practice changed as a result of his tour, and the particular influences that he absorbed, offer some interesting insights into how the Grand Tour fashioned different aspects of English landscape painting at the time.

There are only two documents that provide firm dates for Marlow's tour. One is an inscription dated 8 July 1765, on a drawing of an English river scene, which states that 'William Marlow the Author of this Drawing ... is now studying in Italy'.[7] Probably all it implies is that Marlow had left for Italy by then, rather than that he was already there. He cannot have set out much earlier, as he was still in London in April and May, when the Society of Artists exhibition was on view. The only dated record of his presence in Italy occurs in John Hayward's list of artists in Rome in February 1766. The next we know of his whereabouts is that he was back in London in the following year, when he showed his first Italian subjects, four oil paintings, at the Society of Artists exhibition which opened on 22 April 1767. Since there is no evidence that he painted any pictures when he was abroad, he probably prepared his exhibits over the winter months after returning to London, so a tour lasting around a year, from the summer of

    [6] The connections between Canaletto, Scott, Marlow and their patrons are discussed in Liversidge and Farrington (eds), *Canaletto and England* (above, n. 4).
    [7] Sold at Sotheby's, London, English Drawings and Watercolours, 1 April 1976 (lot 166).

1765 until the autumn or so of 1766, is the likely duration of the time he was abroad. All we know about it otherwise, apart from the drawings he made while travelling and what we can infer from the paintings that subsequently resulted from the tour, is that according to an obituary notice dated 14 January 1813 he 'went on his travels to France and Italy in 1765 by the advice of the late Duchess of Northumberland' — that is, the wife of Sir Hugh Smithson who became Duke of Northumberland and who had been Canaletto's patron. As there are still in the Northumberland collection at Alnwick Castle a group of eight early Italian paintings by Marlow (of Tivoli, Ariccia and scenes in the Bay of Naples) the source can be trusted.

When Marlow left London in 1765 he was an accomplished performer in view painting, following in the Canaletto-Scott tradition, who also painted landscapes in a picturesque idiom that has obvious Dutch connections. What a number of his early French and Italian subjects show is that he quickly acquired an influence from Claude-Joseph Vernet. Although Vernet's Italianate landscapes were popular with English collectors from the 1740s,[8] there is nothing in Marlow's work before he went abroad to suggest that he had taken any notice of them: but in the paintings he did after 1766 and in some of the drawings which date from his travels in 1765–6 there are clear references to the French painter. The question they raise, especially the drawings, is exactly when and where Marlow encountered Vernet's work. Almost certainly the answer must be at the Salon exhibition in Paris of 1765, in which Vernet was represented by no fewer than 25 paintings covering the whole range of his *oeuvre* from Italian landscapes, tranquil coastal scenes and French views to dramatic sea-pieces. The Salon exhibition usually opened on 25 August, the king's name day, and the influence which appears in Marlow's work must be due to his having seen Vernet's paintings in Paris: evidently they captured his imagination, and their impact can be felt in his paintings of continental scenery and the coastal views which, from 1766 onwards, figure prominently in his repertoire. The influence of a painting such as Vernet's *View of Nogent-sur-Seine* (Berlin, Staatliche Museen Preussischer Kulturbesitz, Nationalgalerie), one of the 1765 exhibits, is clearly apparent in several of Marlow's pictures — not only compositionally, in the way he frequently made use of the structural devices that occur in the French artist's work, but also in terms of the mood invoked. An often repeated view of *Villeneuve-lès-Avignon* (Fig. 1), for instance, clearly depends on Vernet's example, just as Marlow's paintings of Mediterranean coastal scenes often reproduce ideas derived from the same source. The transforming power of Vernet's inspiration served as an important factor in Marlow's response to the scenery of France and Italy, and some of the success he enjoyed after he returned to England in 1766 can be attributed to the fashionable appeal of Vernet's work among British collectors of the period.

---

[8] See P. Conisbee, *Claude-Joseph Vernet* (London, 1976).

FIG. 1. William Marlow, *Villeneuve-lès-Avignon*. Oil on canvas, *c.* 1775–80. City Museum and Art Gallery, Bristol.

Marlow's response to the pictures he must have seen by Vernet in Paris visually documents an aspect of Grand Tour taste in general, and its influence on English landscape in particular, that so far has received relatively little attention. The Salon exhibitions were seen by many British travellers, and among artists especially there would have been a particular interest. Marlow's case suggests that the topic could have an important bearing on our perception of how English artists' and patrons' ideas of what constituted the 'typical' Grand Tour landscape were mediated through their knowledge of contemporary French painting, and British critical and artistic responses to the Salon exhibitions would be a subject worth investigating more fully.

The primary purpose of Marlow's tour was, of course, to assemble a body of material which he could exploit when he returned by taking orders from patrons who wanted souvenirs of their travels (and, one suspects, from those who may not have made the Grand Tour but by showing off the right pictures could claim the cultural credibility that travel conferred). It would also provide him with the means to practise independently of actual commissions, since there was a ready sale for such pictures through public exhibitions and through the auction rooms. As Christie's records show, Marlow quite regularly used the sale-room as a retail outlet. Whereas before 1765 he took on commissions that required travel around the country to paint country-house portraits and English picturesque subjects in addition to his London views, after 1766 he seems to have taken on very little work of the kind, and when he did it was of a rather higher status than before in terms of patronage. The only views of country houses he did after returning from Italy were one of Chatsworth and four of Castle Howard, and other than London views there are no new British subjects (apart from a few scenes around Twickenham where he had a lease on the manor house). This suggests that the strategy of developing as a specialist in Grand Tour subjects led to a much greater independence in the commercial market-place: this was, of course, part of the general process of commodification which was changing the relationship of artists to their public generally at the time,[9] but Marlow's example illustrates especially well how the process worked in one particular type of landscape painting which might be thought of as one where the traditional artist-patron relationship would be more resistant to change. If anything, the opposite is the case: demand was such that pictures of particular places — Lyon, Avignon, Florence and Naples, where Marlow is concerned — could be painted without prior orders and without the risk of their failing to sell.

Altogether, between 1767 and 1796, by which date Marlow had virtually given up painting, he showed 134 pictures at the exhibitions of the Society of Artists and the Royal Academy. Of these, 82 (or nearly two-thirds) are specifically identified in the catalogues as of French or Italian subjects; another

---

[9] For the changing circumstances of painting as a profession in eighteenth-century England, see D. Solkin, *Painting for Money* (London, 1994).

nineteen are simply described generically (as, for example, 'A Landscape', 'A Sea View', 'A Moonlight'), with the remainder being of English scenes. The unidentified subjects almost certainly included a significant proportion of compositions in the general 'Grand Tour' category, so continental scenes may have accounted for a total of something close to three-quarters of his exhibited work. A similar calculation for his output as a whole over the same 30·years would result in a very comparable, or possibly even higher, proportion of French and Italian pictures relative to English subjects. What Marlow's output shows very clearly is how the Grand Tour 'souvenir' transformed the market for landscape paintings in England in the second half of the eighteenth century. How he functioned within it becomes apparent from the way he organized his practice and the particular subjects he painted.

The itinerary of his 1765–6 tour can be reconstructed in considerable detail from the many drawings, often quite summary sketches, that he made while travelling.[10] He followed the conventional route through France — from Paris to Chalons, down the Sâone to Lyon, along the Rhône to Avignon and then on to Nîmes and Marseille, to sail probably to Livorno. The sequence of his journey in Italy is less clear, but in the time he was there he visited most of the principal sites and cities between Florence, Rome and Naples; on his way back he crossed through the Alps, but there are no drawings to suggest that he toured elsewhere on the Continent. When he returned to London he worked up from his sketches a series of outline pen and ink compositional drawings for pictures, which he seems to have kept in an album from which prospective clients could order finished versions in either watercolours or oils. For the first five years he was back he showed only foreign subjects in the Society of Artists exhibitions, using the opportunity to advertise himself and stimulate demand. A particular feature of these early years was the number of French scenes he exhibited, presumably to carve out for himself a particular part of the market in Grand Tour views. The number of repetitions he made of them show that they proved especially successful, and in two cases, his pictures of Lyon and of Avignon (Figs 1 and 2), there are more than two dozen finished versions in oils and watercolour. These are subjects that Marlow seems to have made peculiarly his own, and generally his French views along the Sâone, Rhône and in the south, at Nîmes, constitute a particularly distinctive contribution to the Grand Tour theme — no other painter at the time produced as many. One reason for their appeal lay in the classical antiquities they include — the ruins of the Roman bridge at Avignon set against the ancient palace of the popes formed a conjunction of two symbols of transience which expressed the kind of association that charged such scenes with

---

[10] A large group of Marlow's French and Italian sketches were sold at Christie's, 14 July 1987, lot 30 (Ypres, Paris, Auxerre, Corbeille, Macon, Chalons, Avignon, Nîmes; Florence, Rome, Naples, Pozzuoli, Posilippo, Terracina). There are others in the Oppé Collection, recently acquired by the Tate Gallery, London, in the Victoria and Albert Museum, London, and the Yale Center for British Art, New Haven.

FIG. 2. William Marlow, *Lyons, with the Chateau of Pierre Encise.* Watercolour, *c.* 1775–80. Formerly Anthony Reed, London (1984).

FIG. 3. William Marlow, *Nimes from the Tour Magne.* Watercolour, c. 1770. (Courtesy of the Yale Center for British Art, Paul Mellon Collection (New Haven))

moral, as well as historical, meaning for the British traveller; or the various antiquities in and around Nîmes, such as the Pont du Gard, the Tour Magne overlooking the city (Fig. 3) and the Amphitheatre, all of which Marlow painted several times. He continued to show French subjects into the 1790s, and versions of his two most often repeated compositions of Avignon and Lyon recur at more regular intervals than any other subjects in his *oeuvre*. Only his paintings of Naples and its environs are, as a group, more numerous than the French pictures he produced.

For Italian subjects there was more competition, and this must explain the particular concentrations that occur in his *oeuvre*. While the overall range of what he painted is predictable enough — most of the principal sites and picturesque scenery admired by the Grand Tourists are to be found — the pattern that emerges is again one that reflects an artist consciously developing his own space within the market. Although he made many drawings in Rome, for example, there are very few finished paintings and watercolours of what might be regarded the standard iconography for the city. Only two subjects are repeated: one is a view of *The River Tiber with the Castel Sant'Angelo and St Peter's*, which was commonplace with almost every topographical artist who visited Rome, and certainly in prints one of the commonest and most familiar Roman scenes represented in the eighteenth century;[11] the other is a far more original picture of which there is a watercolour and oil, the latter exhibited in 1783 as *A Back View of St. Peter's, Rome* (Fig. 4).[12] Like the majority of Marlow's few other Roman views, it is an unusual composition, with no obvious English precedent. As a subject, Rome was a crowded field, with too many Italian and other English painters supplying what the Grand Tourists wanted for Marlow to make much impact. For the same reason he seldom painted the sort of picturesque views of antique remains that proliferated in the work of other artists: a couple of untraced exhibition watercolours of remains in the Forum, another of the Pantheon, which has not come to light, and a single oil painting of the Tomb of Cecilia Metella are his only examples of what was one of the major genres in Grand Tour painting.

Instead, Marlow concentrated his attention on Italian subjects where there were fewer competitors, at least among English painters working in London in the 1770s and 1780s. The two largest groups of pictures he produced were of Florence and of the coastal scenery in the area of Naples. In his paintings of places like Posilippo, Borgo di Chiaia, and the villas and remains around the shores of the Bay of Baiae, Marlow unites a combination of picturesque scenery and sensitivity that achieves perhaps his most original interpretation of the Italian landscape, and in a way that raises his treatment of the Grand Tour

---

[11] W.Kroenig, 'Storia di una veduta di Roma', *Bolletino d'Arte* 57 (1972), 165–99.

[12] The view is taken from the Via Aurelia Antica, looking towards the Vatican Walls. Christie's, New York, 12 January 1996, lot 13; for the watercolour version, see J. Egerton, *English Watercolour Painting* (Oxford, 1979), pl. 8.

FIG. 4. William Marlow, *A Back View of St. Peter's, Rome*. Oil on canvas, 1783. Private collection. *(Photograph courtesy of Christie's Images Ltd. 1999)*

souvenir to a different level of sensibility. Nowhere else to the same degree did he respond so evocatively to the associational and poetic responses which contemporary travel literature and travellers' own accounts express. They are also among Marlow's most Vernet-inspired pictures, with artfully arranged local accents supplied by fisherfolk and shipping, in obvious imitation of their French source, adding to their appeal. As well as Vernet's own pictures of Neapolitan coastal scenery, Marlow also must have seen paintings by the Italian Carlo Bonavia, who was active in Naples between 1751 and 1788, producing views which also evidently are modelled on Vernet's example.[13]

To judge from the number of Italian and French landscapes Marlow painted from the 1760s to the 1780s, he must have been among the most successful artists earning a living principally from Grand Tour subjects. There is also the evidence supplied by contemporary references, such as the observation made by the painter Thomas Jones, in his *Memoirs* for 1769, who recalled that when he was first setting out on his own career Marlow was one of the artists 'in full possession of (the) landscape business'.[14] Later, Edward Garvey, another painter who, like Jones, went to Italy and produced a good many Grand Tour landscapes, told the diarist and Royal Academy Secretary Joseph Farington that when he had first arrived in London from Ireland in the 1760s he found Richard Wilson and Marlow very popular, and that '... Marlow's work captivated him so much that ... he thought that as a Young Man he would rather be Marlow than Wilson'.[15] In 1782 the author of *An Essay on Landscape Painting*, published anonymously in London, listed Marlow among the 'six most eminent landscape painters of our country'.[16] By then, however, other artists were already taking his place and there were many more painters showing Italian landscapes at the Royal Academy and Society of Artists. The more subtle watercolours of painters like Cozens and John 'Warwick' Smith, and the intenser vision of an artist such as Joseph Wright of Derby, were preferred to Marlow's more limited, view painter's, approach.

On at least two occasions, however, Marlow was more innovative in his choice and treatment of subject: he was the first painter in England to exhibit two of the subjects with which an emerging romantic spirit in British landscape painting is often associated. These were his paintings of *An Eruption of Mount*

---

[13] For Bonavia, see *In the Shadow of Vesuvius. Views of Naples from Baroque to Romanticism 1631–1830* (London, 1990), 115–16 (illustrations 52–6). The same catalogue has an essay by L. Stainton, '"Classic ground": British artists in Naples in the 18th and 19th centuries', pp. 23–9, in which, however, Marlow's contribution as the first English painter to depict Neapolitan subjects in large numbers is not mentioned.

[14] A.P. Oppé, 'The memoirs of Thomas Jones', *Walpole Society* 32 (1951), 20.

[15] J. Farington, *Diary*, 14 February 1804.

[16] Anonymous (attributed to J. Holden Pott), *An Essay on Landscape Painting. With Remarks General and Critical on the Different Schools and Masters, Ancient and Modern* (London 1782), 65.

Vesuvius, at Naples,[17] shown at the Society of Artists twice in 1768 (once in the regular annual summer exhibition, and again in a special display arranged for the King of Denmark's visit to London later that year) and also in 1773, and a picture of *A Waterfall on the Alps*, exhibited in 1773. The first Vesuvius painting (Fig. 5), obviously influenced by Vernet's earlier treatments of the volcano by night, precedes by several years Joseph Wright of Derby's paintings of the theme. At the 1768 exhibition its novelty understandably attracted critical attention, one reviewer writing of it ecstatically in terms emotionally charged with romantically sublime sensibility: 'A dreadful scene! but so elegant is the execution of this admirable performance, that while we look with pleasure on its beauties, we cannot help getting into the belief that we are indeed on the spot, and really beholding an eruption of that terrible volcano'.[18]

Marlow was almost certainly in Naples to witness the activity of Vesuvius, described by Sir William Hamilton in *Campi phlegraei*, which began in November 1765 and continued intermittently over the next few months. Very probably, indeed, he was there with Hamilton, who had bought Marlow's work before leaving England for Naples in 1764.[19] Even more dramatically spectacular than the 1768 picture is Marlow's later scene of intrepid tourists clambering among the rocks and sulphurous exhalations at the volcano's summit, a painting for long attributed to Vernet's follower Jacques-Antoine Volaire who rather specialized in Vesuvian scenes (Fig. 6).[20] Few paintings by Marlow come so close to conveying the actual experience of one of the Grand Tour's most exhilarating excitements. There is a description of it in a letter to the painter Ozias Humphry which attempts to explain its impact: 'a most beautiful production of the kind ... the Criticqual Remarks on it was just (fine, only go and see it & if you approach within three yards of it does it not scorch you)'.[21]

The other painting that does something similar is the Alpine waterfall, another scene which was no less novel in the context of exhibition English landscape paintings in the early 1770s (Fig. 7). The composition, known from a watercolour version,[22] reveals that Marlow was one of the first English painters to give expression to the rugged grandeur of sublime mountain scenery in his

---

[17] Private collection, formerly Paul Mellon Collection (as Joseph Wright of Derby); Washington, National Gallery of Art, *A Selection of Paintings from the Collection of Mr and Mrs Paul Mellon* 1969, no. 6 (then with Stanley Moss and Company of New York, 1979).

[18] *Critical Observations on the Pictures which are now Exhibiting ... by the Society of Artists of Great Britain* (London, 1768), 95.

[19] K. Sloan, '"Picture-mad in virtu-land": Sir William Hamilton's collections of paintings', in I. Jenkins and K. Sloan (eds), *Vases and Volcanoes. Sir William Hamilton and his Collection* (exhibition catalogue, British Museum, London, 1996), 80.

[20] Liverpool, Walker Art Gallery, attributed to J.A. Volaire. Marlow returned to the subject again in 1795, exhibiting *An Eruption of Mount Vesuvius* at the Royal Academy in that year.

[21] Letter from Henry Spicer to Ozias Humphry, 9 January 1774, Royal Academy (London), Humphry Correspondence HU/2/2.

[22] Yale Center for British Art (Paul Mellon Collection), New Haven. Marlow previously exhibited an Alpine subject in 1769 at the Society of Artists (*A Part of the Lake on the Top of Mount Cenis*).

FIG. 5. William Marlow, *An Eruption of Mount Vesuvius*. Oil on canvas, 1768. Formerly Stanley Moss and Company, New York.

FIG. 6. William Marlow, *Mount Vesuvius in Eruption*. Oil on canvas, 1773. *(Courtesy of the Board of Trustees of the National Museums and Galleries on Merseyside (Walker Art Gallery, Liverpool))*

FIG. 7. William Marlow, *A Waterfall in the Alps*. Watercolour, *c.* 1773.
(Courtesy of the Yale Center for British Art, Paul Mellon Collection (New Haven))

work, and as with the Vesuvius pictures it displays an interest in the more 'terrible' aspect of nature that foreshadows later romantic painting. The tiny carriage toiling its way between towering precipices must have struck a chord in many returned Grand Tourists' memories. From the experience of crossing through the Alps in the north to witnessing the spectacle of Vesuvius erupting in the south, William Marlow's Italian subjects, like his French ones, demonstrate the importance of the Grand Tour to the development of landscape and topographical painting in England in the later eighteenth century, and also how important it was for an artist to acquire 'a few foreign graces and airs' to succeed in the intensely, and intensifyingly, competitive arena of London's art market.[23]

---

[23] His last Grand Tour paintings to be exhibited, three Italian subjects (Tivoli, a coastal scene of somewhere near Naples and Vesuvius erupting), were shown at the Royal Academy in 1795. In the same year Marlow produced a set of six etchings of picturesque 'Views in Italy' (one each of Florence and Civitavecchia, and four entitled *Views near Naples* of villas and ruins along the coast). By then the war which had broken out with France in 1794 had brought a temporary end to travel, but by publishing the etchings when he did, Marlow may have hoped that, for a public recently deprived of access to Italy, they would stimulate a renewed demand for Grand Tour subjects. For the etchings and related paintings, see M. Liversidge, 'Six etchings by William Marlow', *Burlington Magazine* 122 (1980), 547–53.

6

Sir John Soane's Grand Tour:
Its Impact On His Architecture
And His Collections

DAVID WATKIN

There is probably no other British eighteenth-century architect for whom the Grand Tour was more important than it was for Soane.[1] Thanks to the rich holdings of the Soane Museum, there is also probably more visual material recording his involvement with Italy than is the case with any other British architect. Soane's intensive 27-month stay in Italy, in 1778–80, was an experience which coloured his entire career, culturally and emotionally. Indeed, he celebrated 18 March every year as the anniversary of the day on which he had set out for Rome from London in 1778, at the age of 24. He never returned to Italy, but referred to his experiences there constantly, especially in the lectures he gave at the Royal Academy, where he was appointed Professor of Architecture in 1806. Indeed, his entire lecture course could be interpreted as an attempt to recreate for his students the lessons he had learnt in Italy. For example, he exhibited a drawing made for him by Henry Parke of one of his pupils perched precariously on a ladder, attempting to measure one of the sumptuous Corinthian capitals of the Temple of Castor and Pollux in the Forum. This demonstrated his belief that 'art cannot go beyond the Corinthian order'.[2]

Another of the lessons which he believed we could learn from Rome was that modern civilization had not yet been able to match the quality and, in particular, the sheer scale of ancient buildings, a point he demonstrated in his lectures by a drawing of the Colosseum and of John Wood's Circus in Bath of 1754 (Fig. 1), drawn to the same scale so that the Roman building towers over

---

[1] The best account of Soane's Grand Tour is P. du Prey's Ph.D. thesis, *John Soane's Education 1753–80* (Princeton University, 1972; New York, 1977).

[2] Lecture II. See D. Watkin, *Sir John Soane: Enlightenment Thought and the Royal Academy Lectures* (Cambridge 1996), 509. As Professor Andrew Wallace-Hadrill pointed out to me, Parke's drawing of the temple shows it with the entablature returned over the end capital, which was not the case in the actual building.

Fig. 1. Comparative elevations of the Colosseum, Rome, and the Circus, Bath. Illustration to Soane's Royal Academy lectures (Sir John Soane's Museum). *(By courtesy of the Trustees of Sir John Soane's Museum)*

the modern one. The Grand Tour was also important to Soane because, as the son of a bricklayer — about which he always had a chip on his shoulder —, he benefited from the fact that the English class system was temporarily forgotten in Italy, where there were easy relations between patrons and architects. Soane seems to have been entirely happy in Italy for the only time in his life. 'Oh it was a bright day', he wrote in a poem about his time, 'it flew on wings of down'.[3] It was important because it was here that, with the social barriers down, he was able to meet members of the upper classes and nobility, many of whom were to become valuable clients, and, it must be said, friends, on his return to England. Though not well educated and not a good draughtsman — the drawings illustrated in this paper are by his pupils, not him — he got on immediately with English patrons and connoisseurs in Italy.

TEACHERS AND PATRONS

The careers of the two architects who most influenced Soane as a young man, Sir William Chambers and the brilliantly inventive George Dance, had both been profoundly influenced by their own lengthy Grand Tours. In this respect, Chambers and Dance were powerful role models for Soane and will have given him much useful advice and information about what to see in Italy. From 1768 to 1772, Soane was in the office of Dance, who had been in Italy (from 1759 to 1764), where he had won the Gold Medal of the Ducal Academy at Parma in 1763 with his design for a Public Gallery. These designs, of which Soane obtained copies and which he admired for the rest of his life, were still on display in the Parma Academy a few years later, when they were seen by Lady Miller, who praised them lavishly in her *Letters from Italy* (1776). It can be no coincidence that in 1778 Soane took this guidebook with him from London to Italy, where it became his constant companion during his travels. It seems likely that he was introduced to it by George Dance, whose enormous library influenced Soane's activities as a bibliophile and book-collector.

As a student at the Royal Academy from 1771, Soane came under the powerful influence of Sir William Chambers, particularly in his francophile tastes and his passion for Rome and antiquity. The reason why Soane was able to indulge in a Grand Tour at all was that, as a student at the Royal Academy, he won the coveted Gold Medal in December 1776 with his design for a Triumphal Bridge, an essentially Roman design reaching back to the designs of students at the French Academy in Rome in the 1740s.

Soane set out from London on 18 March 1778 with the first six-monthly payment of £30 from the Royal Academy, arriving in Rome, via Genoa, on 2 May 1778 after six weeks' travel. He made a slow social start in Rome in the late spring and summer of 1778, but made a catch in September that year by meeting

[3] J. Soane, *Memoirs of the Professional Life of an Architect* (London, 1835), 195.

the Bishop of Derry, then in the course of his third lengthy Grand Tour. A charming portrait by Hugh Hamilton shows the Bishop with his grand-daughter in the *giardino inglese* of the Villa Borghese with the Borghese altar, which he tried to buy, and in the background the Temple of Aesculapius designed by Antonio Asprucci, whose son, Mario, he subsequently employed. The Bishop, who was to become Earl of Bristol in December 1779, seems to have made Soane a special protégé of his in the autumn of 1778, giving him a copy of Palladio's *I quattro libri* in October. The connection with the Bishop was to be vitally important to Soane for establishing the network of patronage on which his career rested. These patrons included Philip Yorke, a friend of the Bishop, who arrived in Rome in mid-October 1778. Yorke was the grandson of the former Vice Chancellor, 1st Earl of Hardwicke, and was making his Grand Tour at the expense of his uncle, the wealthy 2nd Earl. Yorke became a friend and important future patron of Soane. Even more significantly, it was through the Bishop that Soane met Thomas Pitt (who arrived in Rome in December 1778), a nephew of the great Earl of Chatham, the elder William Pitt, who had died on 11 May 1778. When news of the death of Chatham, a friend and idol of the Bishop, arrived in Rome in May, Soane designed a mausoleum for him and began a life-long friendship with Thomas Pitt, whose first cousin, William Pitt the younger, was prime minister from 1783. Soane was to be indebted for many important commissions to William Pitt, not least that for the Bank of England.

In designing a mausoleum for the Earl of Chatham, Soane was, as often, following in the footsteps of Chambers, who, in Rome, had designed a mausoleum for Frederick, Prince of Wales, when news of his death reached Rome in 1751, just as news of Chatham's death was to reach Soane. Another imaginative product of this moment in Rome was the plan Soane made for what he called a British Senate House, inspired by the neo-antique thermal planning of Marie-Joseph Peyre, to which he had evidently been introduced by Chambers at the Royal Academy. He subsequently explained that the design was produced 'in the gay morning of youthful fancy ... [by a] mind animated by contemplation of the majestic Ruins of the sublime Works of Imperial Rome'.[4] It is a measure of the impact of Rome on Soane's entire career that, 50 years later, he was still preoccupied with monumental designs for a British Senate House, or Houses of Parliament.

ROME AND THE IMPORTANCE OF PIRANESI

We know that Soane and Thomas Hardwick made measured drawings of seven famous monuments in Rome in May and June 1778,[5] a process in which they were especially concerned with planning. The buildings, both ancient and

---

[4] J. Soane, *Designs for Public and Private Buildings* (London, 1828), 23.
[5] See P. du Prey, 'Soane and Hardwick in Rome', *Architectural History* 15 (1972).

modern, included, on 19 June, the so-called Temple of Minerva Medica, illustrated by Piranesi. Using ladders, they mounted to the top of the dome, measuring the height with a plumb line. It was the kind of vaulted, centrally-planned space, its dome divided by ten radiating ribs, which appealed greatly to Soane and his master, George Dance, but part of the dome fell in 1828 and was later damaged by lightning. Acquiring the name Temple of Minerva Medica in the seventeenth century, it is today believed to be a banqueting pavilion or reception hall. Other buildings in Rome measured by Soane and Hardwick, both ancient and modern, included Sant'Agnese fuori le mura, Santa Maria Maggiore, Santa Maria degli Angeli, the Pantheon and the Temple of Vesta. Soane also made measured drawings of the so-called Temple of Vesta, or the Sibyl, at Tivoli, which, for him, was the perfect example of the Corinthian order. The temple, of which he bought a cork model in Rome by Altieri, remained a passion for him throughout his career. The Bishop of Derry even asked him to erect a copy of it at Downhill, the house he built in Ireland, while Soane acquired casts of its order, which he used in the design of the Tivoli corner at the Bank of England, and illustrated it frequently in his Royal Academy lectures.

On his visit to Rome we know that he had, for guidance, a letter which his master at the Royal Academy, William Chambers, had written to his pupil Edward Stevens when he set off for Rome in 1774. The letter, Soane's copy of which he kept all his life, is of fundamental importance for showing the extent to which architects such as Chambers, commonly described by modern architectural historians as 'neo-classical', could urge their pupils to study 'Baroque' architects such as Bernini. Soane's response to Bernini, like that of the French architect, Charles de Wailly, a friend of William Chambers, was in harmony with the interest in Picturesque planning and in the handling of light which were central to the preoccupation with nature in eighteenth-century architectural aesthetics. Though urging his pupils to study antiquity, Chambers also stressed that they should:

> work in the same quarry with Michelangelo, Vignola, Peruzzi and Palladio. Form if you can a style of your own in which endeavour to avoid the faults and blend the perfections of all. Observe well the works of the celebrated Bernini, at once an able architect, painter, and sculptor; see how well they are conducted, how artfully he took advantage of circumstances, and sometimes made even the faults of his situations contribute towards the perfection of his work; his compositions are not in the sublime style of antiquity but they are always ingenious, graceful and full of effect. Nicola Salvi, though he had no general principles to guide him, sometimes fortunately hit upon the right, as appears by parts of his fountain of Trevi.

Soane subsequently had illustrations made for his Royal Academy lectures of many of the buildings Chambers had recommended him to visit, including

Bernini's Scala Regia which inspired the Scala Regia built by Soane for George IV at the House of Lords in 1822–3. The image he showed of Salvi's Trevi Fountain was a drawing actually made by Chambers and Pécheux. Chambers also encouraged his pupils to make contact with Piranesi.[6] Soane wisely took this advice and met the Venetian architect before his death on 9 November 1778. The appearance of the youthful Soane, recorded in a portrait painted by Christopher Hunneman, at this time in Rome, contrasts with the great Nollekens bust of Piranesi in his maturity. Piranesi was so taken with the young architect that he gave him four engravings from his *Vedute di Roma*: the Pantheon, the Tomb of Cecilia Metella, and the Arches of Constantine and of Septimius Severus. These feature today in the Picture Room at the Soane Museum. Soane was also familiar with Piranesi's celebrated neo-Egyptian wall decorations in the English Coffee House in the Piazza di Spagna, the meeting place of the English community in Rome, for he used it as his postal address while in the city. Soane subsequently bought copies of virtually all of Piranesi's engravings, contained in over eighteen folio volumes. He also bought as many as twenty paintings by Clérisseau, the drawing master in Rome of both Chambers and Adam.

In a further tribute to Chambers, Soane said rather charmingly that his garden buildings at Kew gave us some sense of the range of styles deployed in a landscape setting by Hadrian's architects in his villa at Tivoli.[7] The Serapaeum at Tivoli, with its strange ribbed vaulting, powerfully recorded by Piranesi, was influential on Soane, as in the domed saloon he designed at Wimpole in 1792 for Philip Yorke. However, we should also remember that Yorke regarded the Cappella Corsini in San Giovanni in Laterano, designed by Galilei in 1734, as the greatest modern work. He commissioned Soane to make this drawing of it in July 1779, so its forms may also lie behind the Wimpole saloon and, eventually, behind the Cenotaph to Pitt which Soane built at the National Debt Redemption Office.

A child of the Picturesque, Soane was also struck by the great gardens of Renaissance and Baroque Rome, most of which have disappeared since his day. He drew the Villa Madama by Raphael and, for his Royal Academy lectures, had an attractive view made of the aviaries in the gardens of the Villa Farnese on the Palatine, based on a plate in Falda. These were similar to the aviary at the Villa Borghese by Rainaldi of 1617–19. We might compare them with Soane's reconstruction of the aviary described by Varro, as a circular peripteral temple over a pool housing birds and used as a banqueting house. This is based on Soane's sketches of its reconstruction by Montfaucon in his *L'antiquité expliquée,* itself based on Pirro Ligorio.

---

[6] Soane Museum Private Correspondence, i.c.7.1.
[7] Lecture IX. See Watkin, *Soane, Enlightenment Thought* (above, n. 2), 623. The parallel had been drawn by Chambers himself in his *Designs of Chinese Buildings* (1757), [ii].

TRAVELLING IN ITALY

Soane and the Bishop of Derry left Rome to winter in Naples, with Thomas Pitt and others, on 23 December 1778, Soane spending two months with the Bishop. In Naples, Soane will have been intrigued by the church of San Paolo Maggiore, its entrance front incorporating part of the Roman temple of Castor and·Pollux. This church, right in the centre of Naples so that no one can miss it, had already been described and illustrated by Palladio,[8] as well as studied by Inigo Jones[9] and Lord Burlington, while the columnar screen in Soane's Lothbury Courtyard at the Bank of England, seemingly the survival of some antique building, was a distant echo of the Neapolitan church. On Christmas Day 1778, Soane and the Bishop explored the site of the Villa of Lucullus near Terracina, Soane designing a triclinium inspired by this source for the Bishop at Downhill, his seat in Ireland.

Soane sketched at Pompeii on at least three occasions, sometimes with Thomas Pitt. These were exciting times because the most important excavations took place in the 1770s, their drama well-captured in Francesco Piranesi's engravings. On 5 January 1779 Soane drew the Temple of Isis, a fascinating example of the Roman Egyptianizing style, which had been excavated in 1764–6. Soane was also impressed by the Via delle Tombe at Pompeii, which he later illustrated in his Royal Academy lectures as an example for the modern age of how to bury great men and heroes at the entrance to cities, as an example of civic virtue, rather than unhygienically in crowded churches in the middle of towns. He also observed the use of colour and painting in decorative interiors, even bringing back a piece of stucco coloured in what we call Pompeiian red. He used this as a model for interior colour in his own house in Lincoln's Inn Fields from 1792. Pompeii meant much to him: as well as the scrap of stucco he bought back 'a piece of cinder from Vesuvius', also still in the Museum. He had climbed Vesuvius on 20 January 1779 and made a number of journeys with the Bishop, a keen vulcanologist, to study volcanic features. He later bought a large cork model of Pompeii and was given fragments of moulding and pavement from the city by a friend.

Soane visited the important sixth-century BC Doric temples at Paestum on 30 January 1779 with Philip Yorke, and again on 15 February, when he drew them, though he was no great draughtsman, and described them as 'exceedingly rude. Grecian Doric but not the elegant taste ... of stone formed by petrification'. It seems that in Naples early in 1779 Soane met Rowland Burdon, of whom he became a close friend and occasional business associate for 58 years. In the spring of 1779, Burdon organized a party to visit Sicily and Malta with Soane and other friends who were eventually to promote his career, including John

[8] A. Palladio, *I quattro libri* (Venice, 1570), iv, ch. xxiv.
[9] See E. Chaney, 'Inigo Jones in Naples', in J. Bold and E. Chaney (eds), *English Architecture Public and Private: Essays for Kerry Downes* (London and Rio Grande, 1993), 31–54.

Patteson, John Stuart of Allanbank and Henry Greswold Lewis. They delayed
their journey to see the Holy Week ceremonies in Rome, for though the
Protestant English objected to Roman Catholic doctrine, they always adored the
rich ceremonial. They began the week-long sea journey to Palermo on 21 April
1779. From Palermo they set off on 7 May for Segesta and then Trapani,
Agrigento and Selinunte, later visiting the other side of the island, where Soane
visited Taormina, doubtless seeing the great theatre, by 9 June 1779.

The amazing incomplete temple at Segesta brings Doric alive, since it
retains the stone blocks which would have been shaven off once the temple was
complete but which were used during construction to secure hauling tackle. The
temple is set in stunning mountainous scenery which Soane saw as
complementing the architecture. As a result, he disapproved of attempts to imitate
Grecian temples as garden buildings in the very different green, moist and modest
landscapes of England, as Athenian Stuart's Doric temple at Shugborough.
However, Soane attempted a simple echo in a barn at Malvern Hall for Henry
Greswold Lewis, who had visited Segesta with him.

In mid-August 1779 Soane and Rowland Burdon travelled to Parma, where
Soane discovered that the Gold Medal of the Ducal Academy there for 1780 was
for a design for a *castello d'acqua*. He resolved to enter this in emulation of his
master George Dance, who, as we have seen, had entered the competition
successfully in 1763, but instead sent to the Academy on 9 May 1780 a design for
a Triumphal Bridge in partial fulfilment of the conventional *morceau de
réception*. The Doric forms of Paestum and Segesta had influenced him so much
that this design was a remodelling in the Greek Doric style of his Gold Medal
Triumphal Bridge design of 1776. Greek Doric designs were still a great novelty
and the Parma Academy accordingly awarded him a diploma of honorary
membership.[10]

Soane's understanding of Italian culture was also enlarged by studying a
range of Renaissance, seventeenth-, and eighteenth-century buildings. Visiting
Verona in 1779, he welcomed the vigour of Sanmicheli's buildings in contrast to
the purity of Palladio. He later had drawings made of them for his lectures,
including the Cappella dei Pellegrini at San Bernadino and the Porta Palio, both
in Verona, writing, 'They exhibit such boldness of execution and originality of
invention as has seldom been surpassed'.[11] In Rome, he not only admired Bernini
for skilfully creating the Scala Regia on an awkward site, but also Peruzzi's
similar skill in placing the Palazzo Massimi on a curved street. In praising
Peruzzi for 'making an unfavourable situation contribute to the beauty of the
design',[12] he will have been thinking of the occasions in his own career when he
had been confronted with similar problems.

[10] Du Prey, *John Soane's Education* (above, n. 1), 188.
[11] Lecture V. See Watkin, *Soane, Enlightenment Thought* (above, n. 2), 560.
[12] Watkin, *Soane, Enlightenment Thought* (above, n. 2), 559.

Two spectacular but strikingly contrasted modern villas impressed Soane particularly: the Villa Albani in Rome, which will be discussed below, and the Villa Palagonia at Bagheria, near Palermo, which he visited on his Sicilian tour in May 1779. The Baroque Villa Palagonia, with its convex and concave façades, had been built in 1705 from designs by Tommaso Napoli, but had been eccentrically altered for a later Prince of Palagonia, who redecorated the interiors and added the grotesque figures lining the approach walls. Speaking in 1817 of the illogicalities of Pompeiian wall-decoration, Soane complained: 'But all these instances of bad taste are nothing to the palace at Bagaria near Palermo'.[13] He proceeded to quote at length from the account in Brydone's *A Tour through Sicily and Malta* (1776), a book which he had taken with him on his visit to the villa with Rowland Burdon in 1779. In 1819, preparing his Royal Academy lectures, he relied on Burdon to jog his memory of the distant days of their Grand Tour, writing to him for information about the 'monster-making Prince at the Bagaria'. Soane complained that 'The inside is as whimsical and fantastical as the out. The ceilings are composed of large looking glasses joined together ... The windows are composed of glass of different colours'. However, it is impossible not to be reminded of the similar effects in Soane's own work, particularly his Breakfast Room in Lincoln's Inn Fields, adorned with both mirrors in the ceiling and stained glass.

THE VILLA ALBANI

Soane studied carefully the planning and decoration of the prestigious Villa Albani (Torlonia from 1866), built on the Via Salaria from designs by Carlo Marchionni in 1755–62 for Cardinal Alessandro Albani, 'the Hadrian of the eighteenth century'.[14] Piranesi published engravings of it soon after its completion, and may have introduced it to Soane.[15] Built to house the Cardinal's antique marbles and other works of art, it is really a gallery or museum rather than a villa. Indeed, it was made a centre of archaeological study by Albani's librarian, Winckelmann, who much influenced its decoration and arrangement. Winckelmann had been murdered ten years before Soane's visit, but Soane could have met the ageing Cardinal Albani, who died in 1779.

Soane made plans of the villa and drawings of the principal first-floor *salone* with marble-lined walls encrusted with antique sculpture and bas-reliefs. Further sculpture was displayed in mirror-lined wall niches: 'Glass behind the figure', as Soane noted on his drawing. He must also have admired the two 'Greek' tempietti which Marchionni added on to the east and west wings of the villa, the

---

[13] Watkin, *Soane, Enlightenment Thought* (above, n. 2), 350–1.

[14] See H. Beck and P.C. Bohl (eds), *Forschungen zur Villa Albani: Antike Kunst und die Epoche der Aufklärung* (Berlin, 1982).

[15] For a first attempt at relating Pitzhanger to the Villa Albani, see D. Watkin, 'Soane's concept of the villa', in D. Arnold (ed.), *The Georgian Villa* (Stroud, 1996), 94–104.

western originally with a caryatid portico leading into the gardens, which were laid out by Antonio Nolli. At the end of the gardens was the semicircular *Canopus*, or coffee house, decorated by Clérisseau and perhaps recalling the *Canopus* which Soane had seen in Hadrian's Villa at Tivoli. Soane will also have seen the tempietto, an aviary built dramatically as a ruin on one side of Cardinal Albani's gardens.

The elaborate recreation of an ancient Roman bath complex at the end of the south wing of the Villa Albani was recorded by Soane in a careful plan (Fig. 2). It influenced subsequent bath-rooms which he proposed in 1783–4 at Malvern Hall, Warwickshire, for Henry Greswold Lewis, and at Taverham Hall, Norfolk. Soane's numerous designs for *un castello d'acqua decorato d'una pubblica fontana* for the prize competition of the Parma Academy in 1780 also showed influence from the Villa Albani. The great hemicycles in Soane's designs, made with help from Thomas Pitt, recall the *Canopus* at the Villa Albani, while his fountains supported by atlantes also echo the fountain at the Villa Albani, which was engraved by Piranesi and incorporated antique granite telamons brought from the Villa Negroni. Soane subsequently praised this fountain in his Royal Academy lectures as an example of the correct (that is, load-bearing) use of caryatids: 'If caryatids or Persians are admitted in modern works', he asserted, 'it must be ... as Cardinal Albani did at his villa near Rome, where four antique male statues supported a fountain'.[16]

Related to the *castello d'acqua* are designs for fantastic stables and kennels which Soane made in Rome as part of a villa, or casino, for the Bishop of Derry. From this and from his related design for a temple-villa, he learned not to copy literally from the antique in modern villa design, a fault which he believed accounted for templar houses such as Wilkins's Grange Park, Hampshire (1805–9). Succeeding to the Earldom of Bristol on 22 December 1779, the Bishop of Derry inherited Ickworth in Suffolk. In January 1780 he asked Soane to build a mansion for him there. Three years before, he had actually bought for incorporation at Downhill figural panels from three rooms of an antique Roman town-house of the Hadrianic period, which had been discovered in 1777, buried in the grounds of the Villa Negroni (formerly Montalto).[17] Their excavation is recorded in a remarkable painting by Thomas Jones, produced in the atmosphere of excitement which the event inspired.[18] The Bishop eventually gave the grand

---

[16] Lecture III. See Watkin, *Soane, Enlightenment Thought* (above, n. 2), 519. Winckelmann, in his *Monumenti antichi inediti* [1767], vol. II (Rome, 1821), which Soane owned, had pointed out the significance of the giant bearded telamons of granite which formed this fountain; see p. 269.

[17] The Villa Montalto, which changed its name to Negroni after 1696 on its purchase by Cardinal Gianfrancesco Negroni, was built on the Esquiline Hill in 1579 for Sixtus V by Domenico Fontana as the first major monument on one of the hills of Rome since antiquity. Its great collection was dispersed in 1786 and the villa was subsequently demolished for the Stazione Termini.

[18] See A. Wilton and I. Bignamini (eds), *Grand Tour: the Lure of Italy in the Eighteenth Century* (exhibition catalogue, Tate Gallery, London, 1996), no. 173.

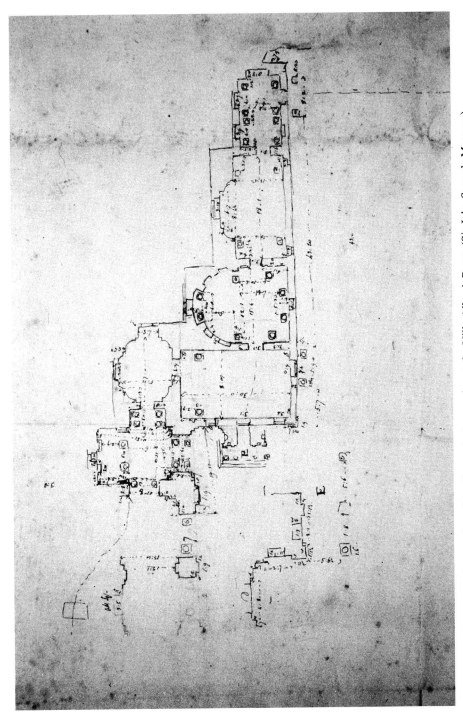

FIG. 2. Soane, plan of the Roman bath complex at the Villa Albani, Rome (Sir John Soane's Museum).
(By courtesy of the Trustees of Sir John Soane's Museum)

commission for Ickworth to Mario Asprucci and Francis Sandys, and not to
Soane, but it is highly probable that Soane visited the Villa Negroni because his
friend Thomas Hardwick had made drawings there recording the frescoes in
1777. Soane also acquired the hand-coloured engravings by Camillo Buti and
Angelo Campanella of the frescoes, which the Bishop allowed to be published.[19]

In the end, it was Soane, not the Bishop, who created interiors inspired by
the now lost Negroni frescoes. His Front Parlour at Pitzhanger Manor, Ealing,
echoes plates I and III from Buti's record.[20] In 1811 Basevi made a large copy of
the central panel of Buti's plate III of Room C in the Negroni house for exhibit in
Soane's Royal Academy lectures. Soane displayed eight of Buti's engravings,
framed and glazed, in the Breakfast Room at 13 Lincoln's Inn Fields, and
probably also used them as an inspiration for the design and colouring of the
adjacent Dining Room and Library.

PITZHANGER AND THE INFLUENCE OF THE VILLA ALBANI

Pitzhanger Manor (Fig. 3) suggests that the memory of Soane's Italian journey,
and of the Villas Albani and Negroni in particular, never left him. In a manuscript
of 1813, he noted that Pitzhanger was 'intended to give some faint idea of an
Italian villa ... [for] in like manner in the fronts of Italian villas we see an
immense quantity of ancient remains of sculpture and architectural fragments'.
He explained that the visitor to Pitzhanger 'might suppose that its builder was
possessed of a number of detached pieces of ornament, such as eagles and
wreaths, demiboys and foliage, columns and statues, pedestals and acroters &c.,
and that ... [his aim was] a desire to preserve them from ruin, or to form a
building to give a faint idea of an Italian villa'. Soane concluded that, 'this
building may thus be considered as a picture, a sort of portrait'.[21] The story of his
life, one might say, and of his attachment to Italy.

Pitzhanger recalls the Villa Albani by the way in which its front is encrusted
with casts of antique fragments in Rome, including eagles within wreaths (Fig. 4)
from the bas-relief in the portico of the church of Santi Apostoli, of which he
exhibited a cast at Lincoln's Inn Fields. These eagles, which we now know came
from the Forum of Trajan,[22] noted for the grandeur of its conception as an
expression of imperial power, had appealed to Piranesi as a compelling image of
ancient Roman authority. These wreathed eagles had not been significantly

---

[19] The twelve plates, based on paintings of the frescoes by Anton Raphael Mengs and his
brother-in-law, were published slowly between 1778 and 1802. Eight of those acquired by Soane
were inscribed 'G. Dance', suggesting once more the closeness of Soane and his master.
[20] H. Joyce, 'The ancient frescoes from the Villa Negroni and their influence in the eighteenth
and nineteenth centuries', *Art Bulletin* 65 (September 1983), 438.
[21] Soane Museum, AL Soane Case 170, ff. 134–135.
[22] See J.E. Packer, *The Forum of Trajan in Rome: a Study of the Monuments*, 3 vols
(California, 1997).

FIG. 3. Soane, Pitzhanger Manor, Middlesex, *c.* 1800. Entrance front

echoed by previous architects, but appear prominently in the frontispieces to two of Piranesi's books, *Della magnificenza ed architettura dei Romani* (1761) and *Vasi, candelabri, cippi, sarcofagi, tripodi, lucerne ed ornamenti antichi* (1778) (Fig. 5). Soane may have based the entire design of his eagle plaques at Pitzhanger on Piranesi's engraving in the *Vasi*, for they incorporate the flowing ribbons which do not feature on the cast which Soane owned. The columnar façade of Pitzhanger, echoing in disposition a triumphal arch, was originally to have featured roundels of the chariots of the Sun and Moon, after Thomas Banks's terracottas of the famous medallions on the short sides of the Arch of Constantine. In the executed design Soane transferred these roundels to the entrance vestibule. Pitzhanger also featured roundels in the attic incorporating images of the lion statues at the Villa Medici. Near the garden front of the Villa Albani is, today, a large free-standing version of the Medici lion, of which Soane also exhibited a cast at 13 Lincoln's Inn Fields. In addition, Soane incorporated ornaments inspired by the pedestals of the candelabra in the so-called Temple of Bacchus (Mausoleum of Santa Costanza), a building which, in the eighteenth century, could be seen from the gardens of the Villa Albani.[23]

FIG. 4. Soane, Pitzhanger Manor, Middlesex, *c.* 1800. Panel with wreathed eagle.

The decorative or architectural peppering of façades with sculptural fragments and casts, as at the Villa Albani, was not, of course, an eighteenth-century invention but was familiar in the Renaissance, as at the house in Florence of the Mannerist painter Federico Zuccaro. It is instructive to compare Soane's lecture illustration of Zuccaro's house with an interior at the Soane Museum. There are other examples at the Villa Medici, and in the well-known Palazzo Mattei as arranged in *c.* 1610 by Carlo Maderno to stress the ancestry back to ancient Rome of the Mattei family. Soane also made a ground-plan of the Capitoline Museum where, on the first floor, he would have seen rooms with architectural fragments concreted into the four walls. But it was probably

---

[23] See Watkin, 'Soane's concept of the villa' (above, n. 15), 168, n. 31.

Piranesi's dramatic representations of assemblies of antique fragments which really lay behind Soane's display technique, as in the Dome in which he managed to three-dimensionalize Piranesi's flat engravings.

FIG. 5. Giovanni Battista Piranesi, *Vasi, candelabri, cippi, sarcofagi, tripodi, lucerne ed ornamenti antichi* (1778), frontispiece to vol. II.

The four Erechtheion caryatids which surmount the free-standing Ionic columns on the entrance front of Pitzhanger also echoed the caryatid portico on the western tempietto at the Villa Albani. It is not always realized that three of those at the Villa Albani were genuine antique figures discovered in 1766 in Rome during excavations at the site of the so-called House of the Caryatids, the Triopion of Herodes Atticus (AD 103–77), the Greek politician, author and patron.[24] Two further caryatids from this *villa suburbana* on the Via Appia, near the Porta San Sebastiano, had already been discovered in the sixteenth century by Pope Sixtus V (1585–90), who took them to the Villa Montalto (later Negroni), where they remained until 1784. One of these is now in the Vatican,[25] the other was bought in 1786 by Charles Townley, who displayed it in his celebrated gallery in Park Street. It is now in the British Museum.[26]

---

[24] P.C. Bohl (ed.), *Forschungen zur Villa Albani: Katalog der Antiken Bildwerke*, 4 vols (Berlin, 1989–94), II (1990), 90–6.

[25] Braccio Nuovo, no. 47. See E. Schmidt, *Geschichte der Karyatide: Funktion und Bedeutung der Menschlichen Trägern und Stützfigur in der Baukunst* (Würzburg, 1982), 99.

[26] No. 1746. See B.F. Cook, *The Townley Marbles* (London, 1985), 38.

Piranesi published a striking reconstruction of the portico of which he assumed the Villa Albani caryatids had formed part in a plate dedicated to Henry Hope in his *Vasi* (Fig. 6).[27] One of the caryatids bears an inscription on the back in Greek, giving the names of the artists, Kriton and Nikolaos. Charles Townley reported that opinion in Rome was that Piranesi's reconstruction was entirely fanciful. In common with much of the collection at the Villa Albani, the caryatids were taken to Paris by Napoleon in 1795, but were recorded *in situ* by Percier and Fontaine in their account of the villa in *Choix des plus célèbres maisons de plaisance de Rome et de ces environs* (1809), a work which Soane owned. The caryatids were returned in 1815 and are today displayed in the *Atrio della Cariatide* at the Villa, their place in the tempietto being taken by columns.

Graecophile Romans such as Hadrian had occasionally incorporated caryatids inspired by those on the Erechtheion into buildings such as the *Canopus* at Hadrian's Villa at Tivoli.[28] However, they rarely featured in post-antique architecture before the eighteenth century, when one of their first uses was in the Villa Albani. Sharing, with Hadrian, a belief in the superiority of Greek over Roman architecture, Soane will have welcomed these Athenian resonances, which he echoed at Pitzhanger. The pediment of the caryatid tempietto at the Villa Albani is crowned with a fertility-cult statue of the 'many-breasted' Diana of Ephesus. Originally housed within the portico, it had been placed on the pediment by the time of Percier and Fontaine. Once again there is a Soane connection, for in 1801 he bought an important ancient Roman marble version of this statue which, illustrated in Montfaucon's *Antiquité expliquée* (1719), was probably the one recorded in the grounds of the Villa Giulia, Rome, in the sixteenth century.

Another parallel at Pitzhanger with the Villa Albani is Soane's creation of elaborate Roman ruins in the garden (Fig. 7). These are similar in conception and even in detail to the artificial ruin at the Villa Albani which, modelled on the temple at Clitumnus, incorporated antique architectural remains. Here, again, there is a neat link with Soane, for he had visited Clitumnus in August 1779 and had made a beautiful drawing of the celebrated temple which was remade from earlier antique fragments in the fourth or fifth century. Shortly after, he sent a copy of his drawing to Lady Miller, in the hope of persuading her to erect a copy of the temple in England.

SOANE AS COLLECTOR

The first ancient marbles Soane bought were at the Bessborough Sale in 1801, including a statue of Aesculapius, which had been in the collection of Cardinal

---

[27] A third caryatid, holding a wreath in her right hand, was recorded by Piranesi as having been taken to the Palazzo Mattei.

[28] See E.E. Schmidt, 'Die Kopien der Erechtheionkoren', *Antike Plastik* 13 (1973).

FIG. 6. Giovanni Battista Piranesi, portico of Herodes Atticus, Rome
(*Vasi, candelabri, cippi, sarcofagi, tripodi, lucerne ed ornamenti antichi* (1778)).

Polignac and was a Roman second-century version of a Greek original. At this sale Soane also bought the famous Diana or Artemis of Ephesus mentioned above. (The pendant objects are now thought to be testicles not breasts.) This celebrated cult statue was also a favourite with Piranesi, who had grotesquely envisaged it as the model for the body of a clock which he published in his *Diverse maniere*, in which book the statue also appears in multiple form on the title page. In the same book, plate 63 is of a table made for Cardinal Rezzonico which includes an urn with winged griffins. Soane bought this at the Mendip sale in 1802, and he put it with other urns in the library at Pitzhanger in niches over bookcases, the round vases on top of square cineraria, as in Piranesi. To complete the funereal effect, Soane created a groined ceiling based on an engraving of a tomb by Santi Bartoli copied in Montfaucon's *Antiquité expliquée*.

FIG. 7. Soane, Pitzhanger Manor, Middlesex, *c.* 1800. Artificial ruins. *(By courtesy of the Trustees of Sir John Soane's Museum)*

Further links with the Roman world of Piranesi, which Soane had entered, was the rectangular cinerary urn in the Soane Museum, of which Piranesi had included a plate in his *Vasi*. Said to have been found at Siena, it was restored by Cavaceppi before featuring in Piranesi's own museum or show-room in the Palazzo Tomati near the Spanish Steps. Another object from Piranesi's collection which Soane acquired was the dolphin capital which Piranesi illustrated in his

Della magnificenza.[29] Piranesi claimed to have found it in a vineyard by the Porta Salaria, near the Villa Albani.

Other important Roman pieces in Soane's collection included the pilaster capital from the attic of the Pantheon, which he acquired in 1823; a further six from the Townley collection are in the British Museum. Of equal interest were the Holland-Tatham marbles, assembled in Rome in 1794–6 by Tatham for Henry Holland to use as models for decoration and ornament. Dating from the Empire, they came from Rome and the imperial villas. Soane acquired them, perhaps in 1816, arranging them in his Study in 1816 and 1822. In addition, Soane liked to acquire objects already assembled by architects he admired, beginning with casts brought from Italy by James Playfair, which he purchased in 1795. From Robert Adam's collection he acquired a Roman Egyptianizing palm capital, a variant of one in the Capitoline Museum, and the side of a sarcophagus carved with a scene depicting *the Abduction of Persephone* which had been in Cardinal Sforza's collection in the mid-sixteenth century. He owned plaster casts of the beautiful Capitoline *Endymion* and one of the Apollo *Belvedere*, made in 1718 for Lord Burlington, which he placed at the centre of the Soane Museum. Enjoying the resonances which ancient objects acquire as they pass from one civilization and century to another, Soane will have been proud to acquire objects owned or commissioned by men with great names in the history of European civilization: Sforza, Polignac, Borghese, Burlington, Robert Adam, William Beckford and dozens more. Here was a way in which Soane, the brick-layer's son, could legitimize himself.[30]

His Grand Tour was important to him because it also helped to raise him up and establish himself in numerous ways, socially, educationally and culturally, as well as to influence directly many of his designs, particularly those of his own houses. The very activity of collecting to which he was so passionately attached was, itself, part of the way of life of the Grand Tour: indeed, Soane continued collecting to within weeks of his death, at the age of 83, in 1837. The collection which he housed in the Soane Museum was, as I have suggested, a three-dimensional record of his Grand Tour; for he was always trying to recreate the heady days of his Italian stay, where, at the Villa Albani, he first saw a museum masquerading as a house.

---

[29] See J. Wilton-Ely, 'Soane and Piranesi', in *Late Georgian Classicism* (*Georgian Group Symposium, 1988*), 45–57.

[30] In this process, Soane was following a pattern familiar in ancient Rome itself, where the rising middle class expressed its new status by the acquisition of sculpture and works of art. See A. Wallace-Hadrill, *Houses and Society in Pompeii and Herculaneum* (Princeton, 1994), 183–6.

THE FEMALE ASPECT

7

Sir William Hamilton's 'Pantomime Mistress': Emma Hamilton And Her Attitudes

LORI-ANN TOUCHETTE

> The environs of Naples are truly Classic Ground, I have visited Lake Avernus, have been in the Elysian fields, in the Baths of Nero, & in the Tomb of Virgil. I have also descended upwards of 100' into the Crater of Vesuvius, & saw the astonishing effects of the destruction of the Village of Torre del Greco ... I have been at Herculaneum & Pompeii & the Museum at Portici, & saw Lady Hamilton's Attitudes, & made several drawings from the King of Naples' Collection at Capo de Monte.[1]

Thus, the history painter William Artaud describes his trip to Naples in May of 1796; his sketchbook of the journey includes a visual record of Lady Hamilton's performance (Fig. 1). As this excerpt from his letter reveals, the attitudes of Emma Hamilton were as much a part of the southern part of the Grand Tour in the late eighteenth century as the ruins of Pompeii and Herculaneum (Fig. 2).[2] Travellers' letters and diaries abound with descriptions of the mimetic power of 'Sir William Hamilton's Pantomime mistress', as coined by Horace Walpole.[3] But what was the relationship between the attitudes and their setting within the

---

[1] I. Jenkins and K. Sloan (eds), *Vases and Volcanoes. Sir William Hamilton and his Collection* (exhibition catalogue, British Museum, London, 1996), 261, no. 161, quoting from A.C. Sewter, *The Life, Works and Letters of William Artaud 1763–1823* (M.A. thesis, Manchester, 1952), 115.

[2] The most recent treatment of the attitudes appears in Jenkins and Sloan, *Vases and Volcanoes* (above, n. 1), esp. pp. 252–61. Emma's performances also figure in the recent biography by F. Fraser, *Beloved Emma: the Life of Emma Lady Hamilton* (London, 1986), and in the article by G. Chazal, 'Les "Attitudes" de Lady Hamilton', *Gazette des Beaux-Arts* 94 (Dec. 1979), 219–26. As noted in *Vases and Volcanoes*, the fullest discussion remains that of K.G. Holmström in her monograph, *Monodrama, Attitudes, Tableaux Vivants. Studies on some Trends of Theatrical Fashion 1770–1815* (Stockholm, 1967).

[3] Walpole's letter to Mary Berry, 17 August 1791, published in W.S. Lewis (ed.), *The Yale Edition of Horace Walpole's Correspondence* XI (New Haven, London, 1944), 237–8. The full quotation is as follows: 'on Mrs Hart, Sir W. Hamilton's pantomime mistress — or wife, who acts all the antique statues in an Indian shawl. I have not seen her yet, so am no judge, but people are mad about her wonderful expression, which I do not conceive, so few antiques [sic] statues having any expression at all — nor being designed to have it'.

FIG. 1. William Artaud (1763–1823), *Sketches of Lady Hamilton's Attitudes* (1796). British
Museum, Prints and Drawings 1973-12-8-85 (7). *(© The British Museum;*
reproduced courtesy of The British Museum)

landscape of a new-found knowledge of the ancient world as revealed in the
excavations of the Campania region?[4] Can we posit a direct connection between
the ancient world or 'Classic Ground', which Artaud centres in Naples, and
Emma Hamilton's performances? How did Sir William Hamilton serve not only
as the 'Pygmalion to Emma's Galatea',[5] but also as an intermediary between the
classical tradition and the court of Naples and beyond in the late eighteenth
century?

This paper will locate the origins of Emma Hamilton's attitudes within the
cultural milieu of late eighteenth-century Naples, a culture whose fascination
with the classical past was fuelled by the recent discoveries at Pompeii and
Herculaneum. Rather than reading the attitudes as indicative of the general
interest in pantomime in the period, it will be argued that they developed in
response to specific images and finds from these ancient sites, set against the
backdrop of ancient literary sources on pantomime. Specifically, an image of

---

[4] Excavations at Herculaneum commenced in 1738; work at Pompeii began ten years later.
[5] Jenkins and Sloan, *Vases and Volcanoes* (above, n. 1), 253.

FIG. 2. Pietro Antonio Novelli (1729–1804), *Attitudes of Lady Hamilton* (1791). National Gallery of Art, Washington D.C., 1988.14.1. (© *Board of Trustees, National Gallery of Art, Washington; courtesy of the National Gallery of Art, Washington*)

Emma Hamilton 'dancing the Tarantella' by William Lock, which echoes the representation of a pair of so-called 'Herculaneum dancers', will be discussed. The publication of the ancient image in *Le antichità di Ercolano esposte* was accompanied by a commentary relating the dance depicted to pantomime as detailed in the work of the second-century AD essayist, Lucian. A comparison between the basic characteristics of ancient pantomime as set out in the Greek and Latin sources and contemporary descriptions of Emma's attitudes will serve to demonstrate the strong dependence of Emma's performances on the ancient form; at the same time, divergences from ancient pantomime will be explored as expressions of Emma's particular strengths and weaknesses. I should say that my approach to this subject is conditioned by my training as a classicist and ancient art historian; at the same time, I have attempted to restrict my evidence of the ancient sources to material that was known in the eighteenth century.

THE ATTITUDES AND ANCIENT IMAGES

From contemporary records it is clear that Emma's attitudes were viewed as a 'completely new and singular experience'.[6] The earliest and most complete description is to be found in Goethe's *Italian Journey* in the entry for 16 March 1787:

> Sir William Hamilton, who resides here as ambassador from England, has at length, after his long love of art, and long study, discovered the most perfect of nature and art in a beautiful woman. She lives with him, an English woman of about 20 years old. She is very handsome, and of a beautiful figure. The old knight has made for her a Greek costume, which becomes her extremely. Dressed in this, and letting her hair loose, and taking a couple of shawls, she exhibits every position, variety of posture, expression, and look, so that at last the spectator almost fancies it is a dream. One beholds here in perfection, in movement, in ravishing variety, all that the greatest of artists have rejoined to be able to produce. Standing, sitting, kneeling, lying down; grave or sad, playful, exulting, resplendent, wanton, menacing, anxious — all mental states follow rapidly one after the other. With wonderful taste she suits the folding of her veil to each expression, and with the same handkerchief makes every kind of head-dress. The old knight holds the light for her, and enters into the exhibition with all his soul. He thinks he can discern a resemblance to all the most famous antiques, all the beautiful profiles on the Sicilian coinage — aye of the Apollo Belvedere itself. This much at any rate is certain — the entertainment is unique. We spent two evenings on it with thorough enjoyment.[7]

---

[6] Holmström, *Monodrama* (above, n. 2), 126.

[7] Translation from A.J.W. Morrison and C. Nisbet, *Goethe's Travels in Italy* (London, 1892).

The consensus of the many spectators who followed after Goethe was that Emma's performances represented a novel art form. Thus, Lord Charlemont declares that Emma's attitudes had 'found out some new pleasure for mankind'.[8] This aspect of changing an experience we thought was familiar to us into something new was also noted by the early nineteenth-century writer Hammarsköld: 'Attitudes constitute the art of representing plastic works of art by mimic means, gestures and draping, and transforming their local and existing life into a successive temporal one'.[9] We might compare this definition with an account describing the attitudes of Emma by Conte della Torre di Rezzonico from 1789:

> she single-handedly created a living gallery of statues and paintings. I have never seen anything more fluid and graceful, more sublime and heroic; the English Aspasia knows well how to assume every part; thus at one moment I was admiring in her the constancy of Sophonisba in taking the cup of poison ... at another the desperation of Gabriella de Vergy, on discovering the heart of her warrior lover still beating in the fatal vase; afterwards, changing countenance at a stroke, she fled, like the Virgilian Galatea who wishes to be seen among the willow after she has thrown the apple to the shepherd, or else she has cast herself down like that drunken Bacchante extending an arm to a lewd Satyr.[10]

Conte della Torre di Rezzonico is not the only spectator who refers to Emma's attitudes as the equivalent of an entire gallery of ancient images.[11] It is striking, however, that the visual record of her performances, as preserved in the drawings and engravings of Novelli, Rehberg and others, does not allow for the precise correlation between ancient statues, vases and wall paintings and the poses struck by Emma (Fig. 3).[12] For example, although Jaffé suggests that, much like Wedgwood, Emma 'too could use the engraved plates [of the publications of Sir William's collection] as a pattern book when devising her Attitudes',[13] the search for a close comparison between the two is futile. Similarly

---

[8] In B. Fothergill, *William Hamilton: Envoy Extraordinary* (London, 1969), 249. Lady Elizabeth Foster added her own assessment: 'every one was perfect — everything she did was just and beautiful'.

[9] L. Hammarsköld, *Utkast till de bildande konsternas historia i föreläsningar* (Stockholm, 1817), 357, quoted in Holmström, *Monodrama* (above, n. 2), 119.

[10] Translation from Jenkins and Sloan, *Vases and Volcanoes* (above, n. 1), 260. For the original text, see F. Mocchetti (ed.), *Opere del Cavaliere Carlo Gastone, Conte della Torre Rezzonico* VII: *Giornale del viaggio di Napoli negli anni 1789 e 1790* (Como, 1819), 247–8.

[11] For example, Fraser, *Beloved Emma* (above, n. 2), 271.

[12] For example, Jenkins and Sloan, *Vases and Volcanoes* (above, n. 1), 258–9, no. 159 (Novelli); 260, no. 160 (Rehberg); 261, no. 161 (Artaud). All twelve plates from Rehberg's publication of his drawings in engravings by Tommaso Piroli are reproduced in R. Wendorf, *Emma Hamilton's Attitudes by Frederick Rehberg* (Cambridge, Mass., 1990).

[13] P. Jaffé, *Lady Hamilton in Relation to the Art of her Time* (exhibition catalogue, London, 1972), 55.

FIG. 3. Tommaso Piroli (1750–1824) after Frederick Rehberg (1758–1835), *Drawings Faithfully
Copied from Nature at Naples and with Permission Dedicated to the Right Honourable Sir
William Hamilton* (1794). British Museum, Prints and Drawings 1873-8-9-133.
(© *The British Museum; reproduced courtesy of The British Museum*)

unprofitable is any attempt to find prototypes of the attitudes in the numerous
volumes of ancient sculpture published by Cavaceppi, Montfaucon and others,
volumes which we know were to be found in Sir William's library.[14] Rather, we
should keep in mind the comments of Comtesse de Boigne in the memoirs of her
visit to Naples in 1792: 'It is in this way that she [Emma] was inspired by
ancient statues, and that without slavish imitation, she recalled them to the poetic
imagination of the Italians through a type of improvisation in action'.[15]

---

[14] B. Cavaceppi, *Raccolta d'antiche statue* (Rome, 1768–72); B. de Montfaucon, *L'antiquité
expliquée et représentée en figures* I–XV (Paris, 1719); 2nd revised edition, I–X (Paris, 1722);
XI–XV (Paris, 1724). For details of these and other books in Sir William's library, see *Catalogue
of the Very Choice and Extremely Valuable Library of Books ... the Property of the Late Sir
William Hamilton ... Which Will be Sold at Auction by Mr. Christie on Thursday, 8th of June,
1809, and Two Following Days* (London, 1809), esp. p. 26, nos. 94 and 97, for the works
mentioned here.
[15] M.C. Nicoullaud, *Mémoires de la Comtesse de Boigne* I (1781–1814) (Paris, 1907) 114:
'C'est ainsi qu'elle s'inspirait des statues antiques, et que, sans les copier servilement, elle les
rappelait aux imaginations poétiques des Italiens par une espèce d'improvisation en action'.

We must return to Conte della Torre di Rezzonico for the only direct references drawn between known ancient images and Emma's attitudes:

> I observed with great delight that just as the Greeks learnt to preserve the beauty of their females' faces even when expressing tears or pain, equally the new Campraspe when adopting an attitude of pain never lost her beauty, and even when occasionally opening her eyes round in fright, did not seem to act, but imitated to perfection now the *Medusa* of Rondanini and of Strozzi, now the *Marys at the Sepulchre* of Annibale Carracci.[16]

It is of interest that the ancient images that he chooses are detached heads, on a marble relief and gem respectively. We might compare the *Medusa* of Rondanini, mentioned by Rezzonico, with the Fury in the *Orestes and Iphigenia* of Tischbein.[17] In this painting, Emma served as the model not only for Iphigenia and Orestes, but also for the Furies in the background. The connection to the attitudes is made explicit in a diary entry of Tischbein:[18]

> The face of Lady Hamilton remained always beautiful, as it was; yet with the slightest movement, say of her upper lip, she was able to express contempt which made her beauty fade away. I have painted the face of Iphigenia as faithfully as possible from hers, without taking away anything or adding to it. As I was painting Lord Hamilton came in and gave her a letter announcing the death of a friend. She was so taken by pain and grief that she burst into violent movements. But in sorrow, crying with her arms over her head, falling and lamenting over her friend, then over herself, all the Attitudes she took were for a painter well worth seeing.

Although Tischbein uses the term 'Attitudes' here, Emma is not 'acting', but responding to the news of the death of a friend. The recognizability of the attitudes is an issue to which I shall return. For the moment it will suffice to note that the eighteenth-century audience was intent on identifying the characters portrayed in ancient statuary, vases and wall paintings. Historical and mythological scenes were reconstructed as a means of reading the ancient images. Many of these identifications have since been rejected. For example, d'Hancarville labelled his drawing after a vase painting in Hamilton's first vase collection 'The Argive poetess Telesilla rallying the women of Argos to defend their city against the marauding Spartans'; modern scholars identify the subject

---

[16] Translation from Jenkins and Sloan, *Vases and Volcanoes* (above, n. 1), 258–9; original text in Mocchetti, *Rezzonico* (above, n. 10), 246–7.

[17] N. Spinosa *et al.*, *Civiltà del '700 a Napoli 1734–1799* (exhibition catalogue, Florence, 1979), I, 320, no. 176. Signed and dated on the altar: W. Tischbein f. / Napoli 1788. According to the catalogue entry, Landsberger first recognized the resemblance to the Rondanini *Medusa*.

[18] Quoted in S.F. Rossen and S.L. Caroselli (eds), *The Golden Age of Naples: Art and Civilisation under the Bourbons 1734–1805* (Detroit, 1981), I, 176–7, no. 64.

as a generic scene showing three women.[19] In a similar fashion, the restoration of ancient statuary included the addition of attributes that could transform generic fragmentary statues into representations of specific mythological or historical figures. A Roman copy of the Diskobolos of Myron demonstrates the phenomenon. Excavated at Ostia Antica by Gavin Hamilton, the torso was transformed into the Greek hero, Diomedes, virtually made to order by Cavaceppi to suit the iconographic requirements of the patron.[20]

EMMA BECOMES AN (ART) OBJECT

Like Greek statuary, the attitudes of Emma Hamilton spawned many imitations, inspired by first-hand knowledge of the performances themselves or at second remove from the correspondence and verbal accounts of travellers on the Grand Tour, as well as the publication of the engravings of Rehberg (in 1794) and others.[21] Literary works of the period, such as those of Goethe (*Luciane in Die Wahlverwandschaften*) and of Madame de Staël (*Corinne*), included heroines/anti-heroines who performed 'pantomimic Attitudes and dances' modelled after those of Emma or her imitators.

Rather than looking at the later life of the attitudes, I would like to concentrate on the origin of this art form. Contemporaries of Emma wove the origins of the attitudes into concocted tales of her early life. These apocryphal narratives have irrevocably distorted the reality of Emma Hart's early life. Immorality is the connection between them; Emma is identified first as a prostitute, and later as a model, posing as Hygeia in Dr Graham's Temple of Health and finally as a nude life model in the Royal Academy. According to Sir James Bland Burges, writing in about 1791: 'This Miss Hart, on her first coming from the country, set out as a common Prostitute in Hedge Lane. Being very handsome she was engaged by the Committee of the Royal Academy to exhibit herself naked as a model for the young Designers'.[22] Thomas Rowlandson's *Lady H******* Attitudes*, probably of the same year,[23] shows a

---

[19] See Jenkins and Sloan, *Vases and Volcanoes* (above, n. 1), 152–3, fig. 66; 158–9, no. 35.

[20] On this statue, see S. Howard, *Antiquity Restored. Essays on the Afterlife of the Antique* (Vienna, 1990), 70–7. The letter from Gavin Hamilton to Lord Shelbourne concerning the Diomedes is also reproduced in C.A. Picòn, *Bartolomeo Cavaceppi: Eighteenth-century Restoration of Ancient Marble Sculpture from English Private Collections* (London, 1983), 24.

[21] This subject is treated fully in Holmström, *Monodrama* (above, n. 2), 140ff. On the use of Rehberg's sketchbook as pattern-books for amateur artists, see Jenkins and Sloan, *Vases and Volcanoes* (above, n. 1), 260–1, no. 160. Rehberg's drawings — *Drawings Faithfully Copied from Nature at Naples and with Permission Dedicated to the Right Honourable Sir William Hamilton* — are most easily accessible in Wendorf, *Emma Hamilton's Attitudes* (above, n. 12*)*.

[22] Fitzwilliam Museum, Percival Bequest MSS. In Jaffé, *Lady Hamilton* (above, n. 13)*,* 71, no. 91. See also Fothergill, *William Hamilton* (above, n. 8), 217.

[23] See Jenkins and Sloan, *Vases and Volcanoes* (above n. 1), 302–3, no. 192: 'This print was most likely the source of an unsubstantiated tradition that Emma Hart once modelled for the life class at the Royal Academy'.

naked Emma, in a pose recalling the Kauffman portrait celebrating her marriage to Sir William. As for the performance of the attitudes, Hamilton draws back the drapery to expose Emma to the artist's view. Classical statues cavort in the background.

For a less scurrilous and indeed verifiable tale of Emma Hart as a model we must turn to the period of her life as the mistress of Charles Greville and her introduction to George Romney. Holmström conceives the development of the attitudes as the joint production of George Romney and William Hamilton:

> It was in Romney's studio that Emma Hart learnt to pose, to control and develop her talent for mimoplastic expression and to handle draperies in the antique style. It can scarcely be doubted that the circumstance that Lady Hamilton's talent developed into something more than a source of inspiration for a prominent painter is something for which Sir William Hamilton must be given the credit. It was entirely due to him that the poses of the gifted model became a free scenic form ... His great passion was geological and archaeological research, and, above all, the collection of objects of art. When he took over his nephew Greville's young mistress, he saw himself above all as making a valuable acquisition to his exquisite collection of art.[24]

Thus, Hamilton on the eve of Emma's arrival in Naples wrote to Greville: '[t]he prospect of possessing so delightfull an object under my roof certainly causes in me some pleasing sensations'.[25] Lady Palmerston's letter to her brother Benjamin Mee (16 January 1793) suggests that this view of Emma as an addition to Hamilton's collection was prevalent at the time. She writes: 'Sir William perfectly idolises her and I do not wonder he is proud of so magnificent a marble, belonging so entirely to himself'.[26] Just three years later, the *Morning Herald* was to take up the theme again, this time with an ironic tone. After describing Emma at length, the text continues: 'Such, after ransacking Herculaneum and Pompeia, for thirty-eight years, is the Chief curiosity, with which the celebrated *antiquarian* Sir William Hamilton, has returned to his native country'.[27]

And yet the impetus behind the development of the attitudes must extend beyond this 'objectivization' of Emma and reside in William Hamilton's desire to mould Emma to satisfy the requirements of her new role as ambassadress. As we shall see, the specific form of the performances was particularly well suited

---

[24] Holmström, *Monodrama* (above, n. 2), 136–7.

[25] A. Morrison, *Catalogue of the Collection of Autograph Letters and Historical Documents Formed between 1865 and 1882 by A. Morrison. The Hamilton and Nelson Papers* I: nos. 1–302; II: nos. 302–1067 (London 1893–4), combined and annotated by A.W. Thibideau, esp. I, no. 149.

[26] B. Connell, *Portrait of a Whig Peer (2nd Viscount Palmerston)* (London, 1957), 276, in Jaffé, *Lady Hamilton* (above, n. 13), 50.

[27] J. Russell, *Nelson and the Hamiltons* (Middlesex, 1969), 211.

to the expression of Emma's strengths, while at the same time it allowed for the diminution of her weaknesses. That Sir William was the creator of the art form is revealed by Emma herself in an early letter (August to December 1787):

> And Greville it is true that the[y] have all got it in their heads I am like the Virgin, and the[y] do come to beg favours of me. Last night their was two preists come to our house, and Sir William made me put the shawl over my head, and look up, and the preist burst into tears and kist my feet and said 'God had sent me a purpose'. Now as I have such a use of shawls, and mine is wore out, Sir William is miserable. For I stand in Attitudes with them on me.[28]

The source of Sir William's inspiration, however, remains open to discussion. Fraser follows the interpretation of Isaac Gerning, a German writer who travelled to Naples in 1796, who suggests that an incorrect restoration spawned the attitudes, almost by chance.[29] Fraser continues:

> It is easy to imagine Sir William tut-tutting over some Pallas from Herculaneum, and gestering towards the offending arm. Emma says, Like this, you mean?; and strikes the appropriate attitude and correct position. Sir William is bemused by her likeness to the Pallas and asks her to play the part of Andromeda. He did not need to know Ovid's Pygmalion to see that Emma's impersonation was inspired. Let us then assume that he coached her to a point where she could flow from one attitude to another ... Is this a wholly unprecedented species of drama, as all accounts would lead us to believe? Not entirely. In 1778, some cousins of Sir William's, the Cathart sisters, had seen a show called 'Pygmalion', in which a 'statue' came to life and sang and danced.

But it is the uniqueness of Gerning's story that warrants caution. No other witness to the attitudes, and there were many, mentions this connection.[30] Nor is Fraser completely correct in her association of the attitudes with the 'living statue' of *Pygmalion*. Although Horace Walpole disparagingly refers to Emma as Sir William's 'Gallery of Statues',[31] Emma's performances went far beyond contemporary theatrical productions, such as *Pygamalion*.

---

[28] Morrison, *The Hamilton and Nelson Papers* (above, n. 25), I, no. 168.
  [29] Fraser, *Beloved Emma* (above, n. 2), 122–3; see I. Gerning, *Reise durch Oesterreich und Italien* (Frankfurt, 1802), I, 291.
  [30] Compare the case of the connection with the 'Herculaneum dancers' posited below, which is mentioned in several contemporary accounts of the attitudes and reflected in contemporary literature.
  [31] Lewis, *Horace Walpole's Correspondence* (above, n. 3), XI, 249.

DRAMATIC AND VISUAL ART IN THE ATTITUDES

Holmström's interpretation of the attitudes places them within the context of contemporary theatrical performance. She denies the validity of Goethe's attribution of their source to Neapolitan *tableaux vivants*, and does not propose a direct connection with contemporary English theatre. At best, she says, 'we must confine ourselves to a reference to the general interest of the time in pantomime'.[32] The attitudes' divorce from contemporary theatre cannot have been complete, however. The catalogue of Sir William's books included a twelve-volume set on English theatre.[33] According to Jaffé, sets of drawings such as those of Rehberg were always associated with actresses and theatre; he also cites Romney's interest in theatre.[34]

The challenge is whether we can trace the origins of the attitudes more precisely or must restrict ourselves, *pace* Holmström, to a reference to a general interest in pantomime in the eighteenth century. Four treatises on the subject of ancient mime and pantomime were published in the course of the century. The 1710s saw the production of the treatments of Calliachi and Ferrari; the volumes of Boulenger de Rivery and of Ficoroni date to 1752 and 1754 respectively.[35] What I hope to demonstrate is that there is clear evidence for a knowledge of ancient pantomime on William Hamilton's part which extends beyond a superficial acquaintance and which can be tied directly to ancient sources on the subject. It is noteworthy that Hamilton received a classical education at Westminster School in the years 1739 to 1745.[36] Unlike Romney, who 'could read neither Latin nor Greek, and therefore had to rely on his more classically educated friends for suggestions of classical scenes suitable for pictorial expression',[37] Hamilton had direct access to the classical texts. Examination of Sir William's library allows us to proceed beyond vague comments on the connection between Emma's performances and pantomime. As Fraser suggests: 'Juvenal wrote on pantomime, and Sir William probably read him; Noverre, a celebrated ballet master, read in the library of Sir William's friend Garrick a mass of literature on pantomime in 1760. All of these, no doubt, contributed to

---

[32] Holmström, *Monodrama* (above, n. 2), 136.

[33] *Catalogue of the Very Choice and Extremely Valuable Library of Books* (above, n. 14), 22, no. 51.

[34] Jaffé, *Lady Hamilton* (above, n. 13), 36–9.

[35] N. Calliachi, *De Ludis Scenicis Mimorum: & Pantomimorum Syntagma Posthumum, Quod e Tenebris Erutum Recensit* (Patavii, 1713); O. Ferrari, *De Pantomimis et Mimis: Dissertatio* (Wolfebuttelii, 1714); F. Ficoroni, *Dissertatio de Larvis Scenicis et Figuris Comicis Antiquorum Romanorum; et ex Italica in Latinam Linguam Versa* (Rome, 1754); C.-F.-F. Boulenger de Rivery, *Recherches historiques et critiques sur quelques anciens spectacles, et particulierement sur les mimes et sur les pantomimes* (Paris, 1752).

[36] See R. Ackermann, *The History of the Colleges of Winchester, Eton and Westminster* (London, 1816), for basic information on public schools in this period.

[37] Jaffé, *Lady Hamilton* (above, n. 13), 14, no. 6.

Sir William's conception of the Attitudes'.[38] In fact, Sir William owned the work of Ficoroni devoted to ancient pantomime and mime; and his library contained copies of several of the ancient texts associated with the theatre.[39]

For the visual derivation of the attitudes, however, we must turn to the Naples area and the excavations at Pompeii. Among the best-known images after the antique of eighteenth-century Europe are the so-called 'Herculaneum dancers' (Fig. 4). In a letter of 1764, Winckelmann described them as the best pictures in the Museo d'Ercolano.[40] Images of the dancers graced porcelain dinner services, furniture and the wall paintings in the 'Etruscan' rooms of places as diverse as the palaces of the King of Naples and the country houses of English gentlemen. Gonzàlez-Palacios attributes the veritable explosion in interest in this material to the efforts of Sir William and Hackert, as well as to the publication of *Le antichità di Ercolano esposte,* the lavish publication of the antiquities excavated at Herculaneum and Pompeii produced for the King of Naples by the Accademia Ercolanese in the years from 1757 to 1792.[41]

That the 'Herculaneum dancers' were neither from Herculaneum nor, most probably, were they dancers is yet another example of how classical antiquity was received and restated to satisfy the needs of the eighteenth century. The wall paintings were excavated in the Villa of Cicero on the Via dei Sepulchri in Pompeii in 1749.[42] They were first reproduced in volumes I (1757) and III (1762) of *Le antichità di Ercolano esposte.* The central images were detached from the wall; the removal of their framing elements has made possible the reconstruction of the original form of the wall with the central 'dancers' framed within fantastic golden architecture of the Third Style of Pompeiian wall painting.[43]

Emma Hamilton has often been seen as the reincarnation of these 'dancers'. In particular, scholars have pointed to the earlier form of the attitudes which

---

[38] Fraser, *Beloved Emma* (above, n. 2), 124.

[39] *Catalogue of the Very Choice and Extremely Valuable Library of Books* (above, n. 14), 25, no. 84.

[40] J.J. Winckelmann, *Notizie ... al Sig. E. Füessly* (1764). The original text reads: 'le miglior pitture del Museo sono quelle ritrovate a Pompeia e queste pitture sono le Danzatrice, insieme ai Centauri maschi e femmine' [1830–33 edition, VII (1831), 265]; quoted in Spinosa *et al., Civiltà* (above, n. 17), 73.

[41] For example, Jaffé, *Lady Hamilton* (above, n. 13), 34–6, nos. 40–3. This material is fully treated in Spinosa *et al., Civiltà* (above, n. 17); see esp. A. Gonzàlez-Palacios, 'Le arti decorative e l'arredamento alla corte di Napoli: 1734–1805', 76–8; also, 'La real fabbrica della porcellana di Napoli', 126. For specific examples; in porcelain: 131, no. 365; 140, no. 377b; 330–9, nos. 2, 7, 9, 13, 15, 16 ; in furniture: 190, pl. 12, 210–11, no. 457.

[42] The wall paintings are now in the Museo Nazionale, Naples: *Le collezione del Museo Nazionale di Napoli* (Naples, 1989), 140, no. 127, inv. 9297 for the series in which three single female figures flank a central group with two women. Four panels with Centaur couples (no. 128, inv. 9133) come from the same villa. Another series with four draped females (no. 126, inv. 9295) does not appear in the excavation reports for 1749, but seems to come from the villa as well. The three groups are treated in Spinosa *et al., Civiltà* (above, n. 17), 72–3, no. 326a–c.

[43] F.L. Bastet and M. de Vos, *Il terzo stile pompeiano* (Rome, 1979), 70, no. 38, pl. 35. The wall paintings are dated to *c.* AD 40.

FIG. 4. *Herculaneum Dancers (Le antichità di Ercolano esposte* I (1752), pl. 17).

Emma is said to have performed within a black box framed in gold.[44] Goethe describes the apparatus in his entry for 27 May 1787:

> I was next struck by a box standing upright, open in front, painted black inside and encased in the most splendid golden frame. There was room enough in the interior for a human body to stand upright, and in agreement with this fact we learned the use to which it was put. The lover of art and of women, not content with seeing the beautiful figure he had made his own as a mobile statue, wanted, furthermore, to gratify his taste by beholding her as a bright inimitable picture, and had therefore, on various occasions, set her in this golden frame, her bright varied dress showing to advantage against the dark background; the whole got up in the style of the antique pictures of Pompeii, sometimes, however, of more modern works. The epoch of such exhibitions seemed, however, to be over. The apparatus, too, was heavy to remove and to set up in a proper light; we were not therefore, to be indulged with so pretty a spectacle.

It is generally accepted that the box was discarded and, with it, the relationship between the attitudes and the 'Herculaneum dancers'. Holmström has suggested that:

---

[44] For example, Holmström, *Monodrama* (above, n. 2), 138–9; Jaffé, *Lady Hamilton* (above, n. 13), 35; Spinosa *et al.*, *Civiltà* (above, n. 17), 38, 73.

A more probable reason is that Sir William had tired of his living pictures, which from an aesthetic point of view were of little merit and which by no means did justice to the artistic talents of the beautiful model; he therefore trained Emma to appear instead in moving, or rather shifting, pictures, thereby introducing a new genre on the borderline between pictorial art and theatre.[45]

And yet, the connection between the attitudes and the 'Herculaneum dancers' endured beyond the 'de-framing' of Emma. In Madame de Staël's description of the attitudes of Corinne, modelled on those of Emma, her heroine is said to call to mind these 'dancers'.[46] The drawing by William Lock of 1791 is also perhaps best interpreted within the context of the 'Herculaneum dancers' (Fig. 5).[47] The title, *Emma, Lady Hamilton Dancing the Tarantella*, was attached already to the drawing on its acquisition by the British Museum in 1906. The image does not, however, match descriptions of the tarantella. In his treatise on this dance, Goethe notes that two girls with castanets danced while a third accompanied them with a tambourine.[48] A visual record is preserved in the painting of *Peasants dancing at Posillipo* by Pietro Fabris.[49] Mariano Bovi's version of Lock's drawing is entitled more simply *The two sisters* in a catalogue of 1802; another edition is lettered below the image 'Grace is in all their steps &c. Milton'.[50] Contemporary descriptions of Emma dancing the tarantella are not detailed enough to provide comparison with these images.[51]

Both in text and in image, Emma often brought the notion of Grace to mind. Walpole wrote: 'Her Attitudes were a whole theatre of grace and various expressions'.[52] Or alternatively, in the words of William Lock the elder, 'All the Statues & Pictures I have seen were in grace so inferior to Her, as scarce to

---

[45] Holmström, *Monodrama* (above, n. 2), 139.

[46] See Chloe Chard's essay in this volume, Chapter 8, p. 156, for the relevant quotation from *Corinne*.

[47] See also Jenkins and Soane, *Vases and Volcanoes* (above, n. 1), 254–6, text for no. 156

[48] W.Goethe, *Viaggio in Italia* (trans. A. Tomei) (Rome 1905), 374.

[49] Jenkins and Soane, *Vases and Volcanoes* (above, n. 1), 246–7, no. 148.

[50] Jenkins and Soane, *Vases and Volcanoes* (above, n. 1), 256, no. 157, (dating from 1796). Walter Sichel, Emma's biographer, had a copy of the same image inscribed in pencil 'Lady Hamilton'. For illustration, see also plate opposite 109.

[51] See Fraser, *Beloved Emma* (above, n. 2), for several descriptions of Lady Hamilton dancing the tarantella. Esp. p. 150, D'Espinchal's account of Emma dancing the tarantella, from E. D'Hauterire (ed.), *Comte J.T. D'Espinchal, Journal d'Emigration* (Paris, 1912), 88–9. Again, Fraser, pp. 176–7, quoting from Lady Malmesbury's journal, 11 January 1792: Lady Malmesbury admired Emma's attitudes, thinking them beyond 'the most graceful statues or pictures'. She also saw Emma dance the tempestuous tarantella — 'beautiful to a degree'. She added an etymological note: 'It is not what the spider (tarantula) makes people dance without a master but the dance of Tarentum (Taranto), and the most lively thing possible'. Again from Fraser, p. 272, Mrs Trench's diary: 'After I went, Mr. Elliot told me she acted Nina intolerably ill, and danced the Tarantola'.

[52] Lewis, *Horace Walpole's Correspondence* (above, n. 3), XI, 340. Walpole, after having seen Emma, to Mary Berry, 23 August 1791.

Fig. 5. William Lock (1767–1847), *Emma, Lady Hamilton, Dancing the Tarantella* (1791). British Museum, Prints and Drawings 1906-7-19-4. *(© The British Museum; reproduced courtesy of The British Museum)*

deserve a look'.[53] The doubling or tripling of images of Emma serves as a record of the fluidity of her movement, in some ways comparable to the Novelli sketches of her attitudes.[54] Perhaps the best known example is the triple portrait of Emma as the three muses (*c.* 1789–90) by the Irish artist, Hugh Douglas Hamilton.[55] Double images are preserved in the works of Dominique Vivant Denon (1791).[56]

---

[53] Compare the tone of this later description of Emma in the *Morning Herald*: 'Her Ladyship is in her 49th year, rather taller than the common height, still displaying a superior graceful animation of figure, now a little on the wane, from too great a propensity to the *en bon point*. Her attitudinarian graces, so varying in their style, and captivating in their effect, are declining also, under this unfortunate personal extension' quoted in Russell, *Nelson and the Hamiltons* (above, n. 27), 211. See also, Jenkins and Sloan, *Vases and Volcanoes* (above, n. 1), 272–3, no. 171.

[54] See Jenkins and Sloan, *Vases and Volcanoes* (above, n. 1), 258–9, no. 159.

[55] It is worth noting that Hugh Douglas Hamilton owned a copy of the first few volumes of *Le antichità di Ercolano esposte*; see Jenkins and Sloan, *Vases and Volcanoes* (above, n. 1), 262–3, no. 162 — the engravings after the wall paintings are known to have influenced his work.

[56] Chazal, 'Les "Attitudes"' (above, n. 2), 224, fig. 11.

Moreover, according to Conte della Torre di Rezzonico, one of the attitudes acted by Emma was 'the Graces'.[57]

Comparison of Lock's image of the dancing Emma and her 'sister' with the sole example in the 'Herculaneum dancers' series in which the dancers are paired is illuminating (Fig. 4), since the relationship between the visual records is more precise than usually found in the representations of the attitudes. The text that accompanies the publication of this image in *Le antichità di Ercolano esposte* refers first to the relationship between the dance shown and the contemporary *contra-dansa*.[58] It continues with specific details from the essay on the dance by the second-century AD writer, Lucian, which preserves the fullest account of the ancient form of pantomime. The descriptive text of the image of another 'dancer' identifies the subject by analogy with the themes of ancient pantomime artists.[59] The texts are striking for their precise discussion of the minute issues of costume and head-dress, and their attempt to correlate the antique images with contemporary ancient sources. It is noteworthy that William Hamilton, from the time of his arrival in Naples, was involved in the publication of the antiquities from Herculaneum and must have known the text that accompanied these images of the 'Herculaneum dancers'. Two sets of the volumes on Herculaneum, including the ones on the wall paintings, were included in the sale of Sir William's library.[60]

Sir William's interest in pantomime may also have been stimulated by an event that occurred shortly after his arrival in Naples in 1764. Under the direction of Bernardo Tanucci, excavations in the Campania region had turned their focus on Pompeii. Present at the uncovering of the Temple of Isis, Sir William was fascinated by the well-preserved state of the temple and the potential for interpreting the wall painting and sculpture within its context.[61] In 1775, he presented a paper before the Society of Antiquaries in London that included a discussion of the discovery of the temple[62] and an image of the excavations by Pietro Fabris was also included in the *Campi phlegraei* publication of 1776.[63] One of the sculptural finds from the temple was a herm statue of an actor.[64] The inscription names him as C. Norbanus Sorix and notes

---

[57] Mocchetti, *Rezzonico* (above, n. 10), 247.

[58] *Le antichità di Ercolano esposte*, 8 vols (Naples, 1757–92) I, 93–5, no. 5, pl. 17. 'In questa prima si veggono due ballatrici, che rappresentano una graziosa svolta, solita a praticarsi nella nostra contradanza.'

[59] *Le antichità di Ercolano esposte* III, 141–3, no. 5, pl. 28.

[60] *Catalogue of the Very Choice and Extremely Valuable Library of Books* (above, n. 14), 28, nos. 129–31.

[61] See Jenkins and Sloan, *Vases and Volcanoes* (above, n. 1), 28–9, 42–3.

[62] Published in *Archaeologia* 4 (1777), 160–75, esp. p. 173.

[63] Jenkins and Sloan, *Vases and Volcanoes* (above, n. 1), 42, fig. 14.

[64] *Alla ricerca di Iside: analisi, studi e restauri dell'Iseo pompeiano nel Museo di Napoli* (Rome 1992), 67–8, no. 3.1.

that he was a 'secundarus', a second actor or assistant to the pantomime actor.[65] If my conjecture is correct, Sir William's interest in pantomime was born in precisely the same year as Emma Hamilton herself — she who was to become his own living pantomime artist.

ANCIENT PANTOMIME AS THE MODEL FOR THE ATTITUDES

Turning to the conjunction between the art of ancient pantomime — as described in the text of Lucian and other ancient writers — and the eye-witness accounts of Emma Hamilton's attitudes, some striking points can be made. For example, Libanios (AD 314–93) characterized pantomime in this way: 'with its genre pictures it is their [the people's] museum of art'.[66] We might recall the statement of Mrs Trench that Emma presented 'in succession the best statues and paintings extant'.[67] As noted above, it is near impossible to recognize specific works of art in the attitudes, yet the ancient texts on pantomime may point us in the correct direction. According to Lucian: 'she [pantomime] has not kept away from painting and sculpture, but manifestly copies above all else the rhythm that is in them, so that neither Phidias nor Apelles seems at all superior to her'.[68]

Ancient pantomime was performed by solo artists and should not be confused with mime acted by a troupe of actors.[69] Its introduction is traditionally dated to 22 BC in Rome; pantomime continued to be popular through the sixth century AD, despite arousing the ire of the Church Fathers. The audience's focus was on a single silent figure who played out a large repertoire of characters aided by drapery and masks, as well as a chorus and musicians.

I would like to examine in turn the various elements of the pantomime in relation to Emma's attitudes. Lucian's account reveals that 'the themes of tragedy are common to both [dance and pantomime], and there is no difference between those of the one and those of the other, except that the themes of the dance are more varied and more unhackneyed, and they contain countless

---

[65] Lucian, *Works* (trans. A.M. Harmon), vol. 5, *The Dance* (London and Cambridge, Mass. 1936, second edition 1955), chapters 68 and 83. (All references in Lucian are to chapters, not pages.) Emma sometimes used a secondary actor. See, for example, the account of Comtesse de Boigne quoted in Holmström, *Monodrama* (above, n. 2), 113–14. Vigée-Lebrun also described the participation of a girl in the recreation of a scene recalling one of the groups from Poussin's *Rape of the Sabines* (Holmström, 117).

[66] Libanios, *Pro Saltatoribus*.

[67] Fraser, *Beloved Emma* (above, n. 2), 271.

[68] Lucian, *The Dance* (above, n. 65), 35.

[69] The standard works on ancient pantomime remain M. Kokolakis, *Pantomimus and the treatise ΠΕΡΙ ΟΡΧΗΣΕΩΣ* (Athens, 1959) and M. Bonaria (ed.), *I mimi romani* (Rome, 1965). More recently, see also F. Dupont, *L'acteur-roi ou le théâtre dans la Rome antique* (Paris, 1985), 389–98; K. Neiiendam, *The Art of Acting in Antiquity. Iconographical Studies in Classical, Hellenistic and Byzantine Theatre* (Copenhagen, 1992); E. Simon, *The Ancient Theatre* (London, 1982), 36.

vicissitudes'.[70] Emma's performances too focus on the tragic. Mythological and historical figures, Iphigenia, Cleopatra, Medea, Niobe, Ariadne, Sophonisba and Agrippina, are joined by the genre figures of the Greek god of tragedy, Bacchantes, Nymphs and Muses.

Emma's use of multiple shawls and her flowing hair, remarked upon in all the accounts, parallels that of the cloak by the pantomime artist. To quote from Mrs Trench again: 'She [Emma] disposes the shawls so as to form Grecian, Turkish and other drapery, as well as a variety of turbans. Her arrangement of the turbans is absolute sleight of hand, she does it so quickly, so easily and so well'.[71] The emphasis on the beauty of bodily form of the actor/artist and the descriptions of Emma are also analogous.

Like that of Emma Hamilton, the novelty of the pantomime artist rested in his ability to call to mind an entire cast of characters in fluid, shifting tableaux. We might recall the accounts of Goethe and Conte della Torre di Rezzonico quoted above. In Lucian's account, this characteristic is described thus:

> In general, the dancer undertakes to present and enact characters and emotions, introducing now a lover and now an angry person, one man afflicted with madness, another with grief, and all this within fixed bounds. Indeed the most surprising part of it is that within the selfsame day at one moment we are shown Athamas in a frenzy, at another Ino in terror; presently the same person is Atreus, and after a while, Thyestes; then Aegisthus, or Aerope; yet they are all but a single man.[72]

Alternatively, Cassiodorus writes in *c.* AD 537 that 'The same body portrays Hercules and Venus, it displays a woman in a man, it creates a king and a soldier, it renders an old man and a young: you could thus imagine that in one man there were many, differentiated by such a variety of impersonation'.[73]

The most marked trait of the art of ancient pantomime is the silence of the actor. Lucian writes that 'in the words of the Delphic oracle, whosoever beholds dancing must be able to understand the mute and hear the silent dancer'.[74] The closed mouth of his mask visually articulates the silence of the pantomime artist; an invisible chorus of voices sings the accompaniment to his dance. Again, from Lucian, we are told that 'His mask is most beautiful, and suited to the drama that forms the theme; its mouth is not wide open, as with tragedy and comedy, but closed, for he has many people who do the shouting in his stead'.[75] Here,

[70] Lucian, *The Dance* (above, n. 65), 31.
[71] In Fraser, *Beloved Emma* (above, n. 2), 271.
[72] Lucian, *The Dance* (above, n. 65), 67.
[73] The *Variae* of Marcus Aurelius Cassiodorus Senator (trans. with notes and introduction by S.J.B. Barnish) (Liverpool, 1992), esp. 4.51. 9.
[74] Lucian, *The Dance* (above, n. 65), 62.
[75] Lucian, *The Dance* (above, n. 65), 29–30.

however, the attitudes diverge from the ancient form in two ways — the absence of the mask, and the lack of musical accompaniment —, though Lucian does recount an incident in which a pantomime artist performs with neither music nor a chorus. In response to the criticism of Demetrius the Cynic that the dancer was a mere adjunct to the music, the pantomime artist Paris challenged the philosopher to watch his performance before he passed judgement on the ·art form:

> He promised indeed to perform for him without flute or songs. This is what he did ... in such as wise that Demetrius was delighted beyond measure with what was taking place and paid the highest possible tribute to the dancer; he raised his voice and shouted at the top of his lungs 'I hear the story that you are acting, I do not just see it; you seem to me to be talking with your very hands!'[76]

This tale is paralleled in the case of the attitudes by the audiences who cry out the identity of the figures portrayed as they are recognized. Thus, Comtesse de Boigne recounts her participation as a young girl in one performance of Emma Hamilton.[77] Two vignettes were acted out in turn; the audience responded with exuberant cries of 'Bravo la Medea', 'Viva la Niobe' as the image changed aspect.

The muteness of the pantomime was retained in the attitudes, however, and served to diminish what could be viewed as the most obvious weakness of Emma Hamilton, her social background. A single episode recorded in the memoirs of Lady Holland is illustrative. 'Just as she was lying down, with her head reclining on an Etruscan vase to represent a water-nymph, she exclaimed in her provincial dialect: "Doun't be afeared Sir Willum, I'll not crack your joug". I turned away disgusted.'[78] Emma has broken the spell of the attitudes by speaking, and the response of the audience is swift and cruel.

Emma's strength seems to have rested in her ability to represent a wide range of emotions, while never deviating from classical beauty. Hayley's description of her reads: 'Her features like the language of Shakespeare, could exhibit all the feelings of nature and all the gradations of every passion, with a most fascinating truth, and felicity of expression'.[79] The mask of the pantomime

---

[76] Lucian, *The Dance* (above, n. 65), 63.

[77] 'Les applaudissements passionnés des spectateurs artistes se firent entendre avec exclamations de: 'Bravo la Medea! Puis m'attirant à elle, me serrant sur son sein en ayant l'air de me disputer à la colère de ciel, elle arracha aux mêmes voix le cri de: 'Viva la Niobe'!', quoted in Holmström, *Monodrama* (above, n. 2), 113–14. See also Chloe Chard, Chapter 8 in this volume, n. 14.

[78] Earl of Ilchester (ed.), *Journal of Elizabeth, Lady Holland* I (London, 1908), 243, in Jaffé, *Lady Hamilton* (above, n. 13), 38, no. 45.

[79] Jenkins and Sloan, *Vases and Volcanoes* (above, n. 1), 175. Hayley continues: 'Her peculiar force, and variations of feeling, countenance and gesture, inspirited and ennobled the productions of his art'.

FIG. 6. Raphael Morghen (1758–1833) after Angelica Kauffman, *Lady Hamilton as the Comic Muse* (1791). British Museum, Prints and Drawings 1843-5-13-1009.
(© The British Museum; reproduced courtesy of The British Museum)

artist would never have suited Emma, because it would have veiled both her natural talent and her great beauty. And yet, it is fascinating that Sir William chose to celebrate his second marriage with a conventional image of his new bride as the Comic Muse, Thalia, the mask of Comedy placed above her head (Fig. 6).[80] Angelica Kauffman's portrait is inscribed in Latin: 'The beautiful Thalia, whom the Greeks painted, has been recreated more beautiful in Latium'. It may have been Emma herself who had suggested the choice to Sir William. In an early letter (18 January 1787) she relates the response to her of the English banker, Mr Hart: 'for he says he never saw the tragick and comick muse blended so happily together'.[81]

---

[80] Jenkins and Sloan, *Vases and Volcanoes* (above, n. 1), 272–3, no. 171, an engraving by Raphael Morghen after the Kauffman painting.

[81] Morrison, *The Hamilton and Nelson Papers* (above, n. 25), I, no. 163.

And yet, Emma was not a mere instrument, trained to perfection by Sir William. She appears to have taken an active part in developing the attitudes. A book entitled *Moeurs, coutumes des Romains* was inscribed by Emma 'Given to Lady Hamilton by her dear friend the Queen of Naples at Caserta 1794'.[82] According to Sir James Bland Burges, while in Naples Emma 'improved her skill in Attitudes by the study of antique figures, from which she learned a variety of the most voluptuous and indecent poses'.[83]

* * *

Let us conclude with a more positive description of the attitudes. On the 23 December 1800, Emma gave a public performance. She was eight months pregnant at the time and contemporary caricatures of her in her expanded state echo the harshness of Lady Holland's comments.[84] But the review of her performance as Agrippina in the *Gentleman's Magazine* of April 1801 is wildly complimentary:[85]

> Lady Hamilton appeared in the character of Agrippina, bearing the ashes of Germanicus in a golden urn, as she presented them before the Roman people, with the design of exciting them to avenge the death of her husband, who, having been declared joint Emperor by Tiberius, fell a victim to his envy, and is supposed to have been poisoned by his order, at the head of the forces which he was leading against the rebellious Armenians. Lady Hamilton displayed with truth and energy every gesture, attitude, and expression of countenance that could be conceived in Agrippina herself, best calculated to have moved the passions of the Romans on behalf of their favourite general. The action of her head, of her hands, and arms in the various positions of the urn; in her manner of presenting it before the Romans, or of holding it up to the Gods in the act of Supplication, was most classically graceful. Every change of dress, principally of the head, to suit the different situations in which she successively presented herself, was performed instantaneously with the most perfect ease, and without retiring or scarcely turning aside a moment from the spectators. In the last scene of this most beautiful piece of pantomime, she appeared with a young lady of the company, who was to impersonate a daughter. Her action in this part

---

[82] Jaffé, *Lady Hamilton* (above, n. 13), 55, no. 70.

[83] Fothergill, *William Hamilton* (above, n. 8), 249.

[84] A single example will suffice: Isaac Cruickshank's etching entitled *A Mansion House Treat — or Smoking Attitudes* (see Jenkins and Sloan, *Vases and Volcanoes* (above, n. 1), 229, no. 188). Emma appears beside Lord Nelson in a pose immortalized in plate 6 of Rehberg's drawings (Jenkins and Sloan, *Vases and Volcanoes* (above, n. 1), 260–1, no. 160). See also the 'expanded' version of 1807, tentatively attributed to James Gillray (*Vases and Volcanoes*, 303, no. 193). The bubble above Emma's head in the Cruickshank etching reads: *Pho the old man's pipe is allways out, but yours burns with full vigour.*

[85] Jaffé, *Lady Hamilton* (above, n. 13), 71–2, no. 92.

was natural and just and so pathetically addressed to the spectators as to draw tears from several of the company. It may be questioned whether this scene, without theatrical assistance of other characters and appropriate circumstances, could possibly be represented with more effect.

Emma's attitudes had reached the pinnacle of their performance. Following the lead of a famed ancient pantomime artist of the time of Nero, she presented only one attitude. Sir William's early conception of the attitudes, based on his knowledge of the antiquities of Pompeii and Herculaneum and his reading of the ancient sources, combined with Emma's study of ancient statuary and costume was rewarded with the lavish praise of the *Gentlemen's Magazine*. Like ancient pantomime, her performance 'charms the eyes and makes them wide awake, and it rouses the mind to respond to every detail of its performance'.[86]

Yet the attitudes would have been unthinkable outside their geographic and historical setting — an art form inspired by and created from a precise revealed past, experienced within a world in which the idea of the past made present was paramount. In the third volume of his publication of Sir William's vase collection, Baron d'Hancarville writes: 'Antiquity is a vast country separated from our own by a long interval of time'.[87] Travellers on the Grand Tour remark again and again on the immediacy of the past observable through contemporary custom in Italy. Thus, Richard Payne Knight described his journey through Southern Italy to Sicily as an exercise in 'history and morality, that is, an investigation of ancient remains and modern manners'.[88]

The new excavations undertaken in the Naples area in the mid to late eighteenth century produced many remarkable 'ancient remains'. In the response to these finds we can identify different strands of interest. Clearly the 'treasure hunt' aspect was important, and in many ways a collection like Sir William's was informed by this passionate desire for objects of beauty and value. Concomitant with this is the educative aspect, a desire to classify and order the evidence in a proto-scientific manner, to find a pattern amongst what must have initially seemed to be chaotic heaps of evidence coming to light. Sir William's sobriquet, 'Pliny the Elder', underlines his approach to the material culture of the past and present. Present at the excavations in Pompeii, he delivered a lecture on the finds before the Society of Antiquaries in London. Like his 'namesake', Sir William's interests extended to the natural world; he followed Pliny's lead in recording first-hand the various eruptions of Vesuvius of his day.

---

[86] Lucian, *The Dance* (above, n. 65), 85.

[87] *Antiquité Etrusques, Grecques et Romaine, tirées du cabinet de M. William Hamilton, envoyé extraordinaire et plénipotentiare de S.M. Britannique en Cour de Naples* (Naples 1766–67) III, 3. See also Jenkins and Sloan, *Vases and Volcanoes* (above, n. 1), 40–64, esp. pp. 40–2.

[88] M. Clarke and N. Penny (eds), *The Arrogant Connoisseur: Richard Payne Knight 1751–1824* (exhibition catalogue, Manchester, 1982), 20.

The classical past was revealed not only through the excavations, but also, as I have shown, through the ancient texts collected by Sir William in his library, alongside contemporary works on the performance arts and pantomime. From his scholarly interest in all things classical he was able to evoke the ancient world through his creation of the attitudes. Although we have no specific evidence, such as diary or journal entries, which openly link the development of the attitudes with what he knew of past dramatic art from his books, it is not difficult to imagine in Sir William a mind so thoroughly imbued with the images — both historical and mythological — of the classical past, that perhaps even unconsciously he was able to connect the past with the present in his presentation of Emma.

The attitudes were indeed a specific response by Sir William to the stimulus of ancient sites and ancient art, both literary and visual; and they stand as a bridge between the performance of pantomime in the ancient world and the interest in the genre in the eighteenth century. The double image of the 'Herculaneum dancers' articulates this interrelationship quite precisely. The find of the wall painting led the commentator on the image to ancient texts on pantomime, which in turn inspired Sir William, like an eighteenth-century Pygmalion, to fashion Emma as the embodiment of both the visual and textual traditions. Finally, William Lock's drawing of Emma, with its echo of the 'Herculaneum dancers', captures the creative moment as the ancient wall painting is transformed into the living flesh of Emma herself. Again, past and present become inseparable.

The attitudes seem at first to have the silent static quality of poses, as if taken, even if not literally taken — as I have shown —, from the excavated vases, wall paintings and statuary. But the flowing, changing aspect of the performance, as one pose was succeeded by another, underlines the imposition of a sequence, a structure, on the multiplicity of images. That the attitudes appeared so effortless and graceful to the audience was clearly due to the personal skills of the performer. We are left to speculate on the precise interplay of roles of Sir William and Emma herself within the context of the attitudes; to assume that he was acting as her 'puppet master' is to take an over simplistic view. To see Emma as the prime mover, however appealing an idea it might be to the modern mind, is clearly far from accurate. It is somewhere between these two extremes, in the interesting 'grey area' of their collaboration, that the truth about the genesis of the attitudes lies.

Yet not only is this aspect of creativity important; as we have seen, the performances themselves reinforced Emma's role as art object. Even as her behaviour with Lord Nelson subjected her husband to ridicule, Emma continued to be the centrepiece of Sir William's collection of exquisite art objects. Many of the paintings, ancient vases and sculptures had been sold, but Emma remained as a monument to Hamilton's intimate knowledge of classical antiquities and of ancient sources on theatrical performance. As in Lucian's description of

Pantheia, the consort of Lucius Verus, Emma was a woman who is 'a composite of all the most beautiful statues of the ancient world in both body and soul'.[89]

---

[89] Lucian, *Works* (trans. A.M. Harmon), vol. 4, *On Portraiture* (London and Cambridge, Mass. 1925, second edition 1955).

8

Comedy, Antiquity, The Feminine And The Foreign: Emma Hamilton And Corinne

CHLOE CHARD

LANGUOR AND ANIMATION IN NAPLES

The painter Elisabeth Vigée-Lebrun, in Naples in 1790, embarks on a description of the Comtesse Skawronska, wife of the Russian ambassador in that city, and niece of Potemkin:

> *Son bonheur était de vivre étendue sur un canapé, enveloppée d'une grande pelisse noire et sans corset. Sa belle-mère faisait venir de Paris pour elle des caisses remplies des plus charmantes parures que faisait alors mademoiselle Bertin, marchande de modes de la reine Marie-Antoinette. Je ne crois pas que la comtesse en ait jamais ouvert une seule, et quand sa belle-mère lui témoignait le désir de la voir porter les charmantes robes, les charmantes coiffures que ces caisses renfermaient, elle répondait nonchalamment: A quoi bon? pour qui? pour quoi? Elle me fit la même réponse quand elle me montra son écrin, un des plus riches qu'on puisse voir: il contenait des diamants énormes que lui avait donnés Potemkin, et que je n'ai jamais vus sur elle. Je me souviens qu'elle m'a conté que, pour s'endormir, elle avait une esclave sous son lit, qui lui racontait tous les soirs la même histoire.*[1]

Vigée-Lebrun begins work on a portrait of the Comtesse, but just as the second sitting has come to an end, 'le chevalier Sir William Hamilton, ambassadeur d'Angleterre à Naples' arrives, and asks her to paint 'une superbe femme qu'il me présenta: c'était madame Harte, sa maîtresse, qui ne tarda pas à devenir lady Hamilton, et que sa beauté a rendue célèbre'. The artist describes Emma in terms that place her in sharp contrast to the Russian ambassadress:

---

[1] *Souvenirs de Madame Vigée Le Brun*, 2 vols (Paris, 1891); first published in 1835–7; I, 191–2.

*Je peignis madame Harte en bacchante couchée au bord de la mer,
et tenant une coupe à la main. Sa belle figure était fort animée et
contrastait complétement avec celle de la comtesse; elle avait une
quantité énorme de beaux cheveux châtains qui pouvaient la couvrir
entiérement, et ainsi en bacchante, ses cheveux épars, elle était
admirable* (Fig. 1).[2]

FIG. 1. Elisabeth Vigée-Lebrun, *Emma Hamilton as a Bacchante* (1790). Oil on canvas, 134.6 ×
157.5 cm. Private collection.

The two women, compared to each other in this way, as rival sights of Naples,
exemplify, respectively, the two traits of character that northern European travel
writings regularly attribute to the Neapolitans themselves — and to the
inhabitants of the warm South in general: the qualities that Germaine de Staël, in
her novel *Corinne: ou, l'Italie* (1807) terms 'la mollesse et la vivacité du Midi'.[3]
In Vigée-Lebrun's descriptions, the alignment of the women with the topography
in which they find themselves is never entirely explicit, although the reference to
posing Emma as a bacchante beside the sea defines her as a woman whose
beauty can readily be naturalized as part of the aesthetic delights of the warm

---

[2] *Souvenirs de Madame Vigée Le Brun* (above, n. 1), I, 193.
[3] Germaine de Staël, *Corinne: ou, l'Italie* (ed. C. Herrmann), 2 vols (Paris, 1979), I, 97 (book IV,
chapter 3).

South.[4] The Earl of Minto, however, in a culminatory twist at the end of an extended description, directly identifies a point of resemblance between Lady Hamilton and 'the other ladies of Naples':

> She is the most extraordinary compound I ever beheld. Her person is nothing short of monstrous for its enormity, and is growing every day. She tries hard to think size advantageous to her beauty, but is not easy about it. Her face is beautiful; she is all Nature, and yet all Art; that is to say, her manners are perfectly unpolished, of course very easy, though not with the ease of good breeding, but of a barmaid; excessively good-humoured and wishing to please and be admired by all ages and sorts of persons that come in her way ... With men her language and conversation are exaggerations of anything I ever heard anywhere; and I was wonderfully struck with these inveterate remains of her origin, though the impression was very much weakened by seeing the other ladies of Naples.[5]

This quality of exaggeration, which Lord Minto attributes to Emma by reference to her size as well as to her behaviour, has often been seen as a source of the comic: it is the exaggerated form in which the Comtesse Skawronska displays another attribute of the Neapolitans, taking their famous indolence to the point of positive social aberrancy, that renders her, too, potentially amusing. Exaggeration, in both cases, neatly fits Henri Bergson's category of the naivety that fails or refuses to recognize the established norms and limits of social behaviour, or to worry about the judgement of others: in *Laughter: an Essay on the Meaning of the Comic*, Bergson suggests that 'a comic character is generally comic in proportion to his ignorance of himself', and argues that we laugh at the inflexibility manifested by those who fail to adapt to social expectation.[6]

Naivety of this kind — an unreflective pursuit of individual inclination, which ignores the rules internalized by more worldly members of society — is often attributed to the Neapolitans themselves: in Samuel Sharp's *Letters from Italy* (1766), for example, the traveller describes a monk, preaching at the Largo del Castello in the city, who is 'mortified and provoked' to find that the Punch in a puppet-show attracts more attention than he does. The monk takes dramatic

---

[4] For an account of bacchantes as figures whose 'heathenish rites' survive in southern Italy, in the form of the dance known as the 'Tarantella', or 'Tarantata', see Henry Swinburne, *Travels in the Two Sicilies in the Years 1777, 1778, 1779, and 1780*, 2 vols (London, 1783–5), I, 391–3. Swinburne describes the 'Tarantati' as 'exact copies of the ancient priestesses of Bacchus', and comments: 'The orgies of that God, whose worship, under various symbols, was more widely spread over the globe than that of any other divinity, were, no doubt, performed with energy and enthusiasm by the lively inhabitants of this warm climate' (I, 392, 392–3). Sydney, Lady Morgan, emphasizes the ease with which Emma can be made to assume a place within the setting of the coastal areas around Naples by terming her a 'Syren' (*Italy*, third edition, 3 vols; London, 1821; first published in 1821, III, 230).

[5] The Countess of Minto (ed.), *Life and Letters of Sir Gilbert Elliot, First Earl of Minto, from 1751 to 1806*, 3 vols (London, 1874), II, 364–5.

[6] H. Bergson, *Laughter: an Essay on the Meaning of the Comic* (translated by C. Brereton and F. Rothwell) (London, 1911), 16.

action: 'with a mixture of rage and religion he held up the crucifix, and called aloud, *Ecco il vero Pulcinello; —* "Here is the true Punchinello, — come here , — come here!"'[7] Vigée-Lebrun, watching the festival of 'la madone de l'Arca' with the Hamiltons, bursts out laughing when a woman comes forward to scold the Virgin Mary furiously, holding the Madonna responsible for the fact that her husband mistreats her.[8]

Moments of laughter such as this are, in fact, relatively rare in travel writing of the late eighteenth and early nineteenth centuries. Laughter is often regarded with suspicion, as too easy and superficial a response, which suggests that the traveller may not have paused long enough to observe the topography of the foreign, and grasp the character of the forms of alterity that it presents to view. Hester Piozzi, writing to her daughter from Pisa, identifies a category of inadequate travellers whose proclivity for 'tittering' proclaims their disinclination to confront any form of cultural difference: 'We have been living of late much like the Travellers Ld Chesterfield talks of, who keep all together — and tittering at the Natives when they *see* them — do nothing but *Huzza for old England'*.[9]

Northern European travellers in Italy, however, are often eager to laugh at Emma — an anomalous figure, since she is on the one hand a traveller herself, who has come to the warm South from colder, northerly climes, and, on the other hand, a woman who has transmuted into one of the tourist attractions of Naples, and has therefore merged herself with the topography of the foreign. Travellers who transmute into spectacle are often defined as comic; commentaries that register amusement at such figures present them as risking the consequences of the inexorable social rule that moving from the position of subject of observation to that of object entails a dramatic loss of authority and dignity. Travel writings are full of complaints about English travellers who make spectacles of themselves on the Grand Tour — on the model of 'the young Æneas' in the fourth Book of Pope's *Dunciad* (1743), whose transformation is introduced through an effect of sudden bathos:

> Intrepid then, o'er seas and lands he flew:
> Europe he saw, and Europe saw him too.[10]

---

[7] *Letters from Italy, Describing the Customs of Manners of that Country, in the Years 1765, and 1766*, second edition (London, 1767; first published in 1766), 183–4.

[8] *Souvenirs de Madame Vigée Le Brun* (above, n. 1), I, 219, 220.

[9] E.A. Bloom and L.D. Bloom (eds), *The Piozzi Letters: Correspondence of Hester Lynch Piozzi, 1784–1821 (Formerly Mrs. Thrale)*, 3 vols (Newark, 1989–1993), I, 165; Piozzi refers to an essay by Philip Dormer Stanhope, 4th Earl of Chesterfield, in *The World* 29 (19 July 1753).

[10] Lines 293–4; J. Butt (ed.), *The Poems of Alexander Pope*, 11 vols (London and New Haven, 1961–9), V — J. Sutherland (ed.), *The Dunciad* (1963), 373. A female traveller on this model is described, for example, in 'A family continental tour, and its results', published anonymously in *Blackwood's Magazine* 46 (285) (July 1839), 56–65: the daughter of an English family on their travels has, it is observed, 'begun to abandon herself to that latitudinarian "insouciance" of manners and conduct by which our fair countrywomen so frequently astonish foreigners' (59).

At the same time, travellers who cross over from the side of the spectator to that of the spectacle are frequently defined as sites of enthralment, inviting the traveller to abandon his or her stance of amused detachment, and gaze in fascination or wonder; the same propensity to exaggeration is, in such cases, often perceived as the source both of the fascination and of the amusement. John Moore, in his *View of Society and Manners in Italy*, describes a visit to Lady Mary Wortley Montagu's son Edward in Venice, during which Montagu, by his determination to adopt and champion all Turkish customs, seems consciously to proclaim his own spectacular status: he sits 'on a cushion on the floor, with his legs crossed in the Turkish fashion', and perfumes his beard with the steam from 'some aromatic gums', which are 'burnt in a little silver vessel'. Despite some dismissive remarks on this exhibition of self-conscious exoticism, Moore devotes nearly eight pages to the visit.[11] Emma Hamilton, like Edward Wortley Montagu, is described as exciting curiosity, wonder and enthralment, as well as inducing mockery. By examining the aspects of Emma that are seen as enthralling, it is possible to begin to chart some of the elements of the effect that she produces, as one of the sights of Naples, which allow the traveller, however fascinated, to regain a position of detachment, and to perceive her as incipiently comic.

One source of Emma's power to enthral is her dramatic life story — her rise from extremely humble beginnings to a social position as the wife of the British ambassador at Naples, received at the Neapolitan court, and living on friendly, intimate terms with Queen Maria Carolina: as Vigée-Lebrun exclaims, in fascination: 'La vie de lady Hamilton est un roman'.[12] (It is her status as a woman who assumes an equivalence to the heroines of fiction that I take as my justification for referring to her by her first name only, rather than adopting the usual convention of using both names or the surname alone.) Emma is invested with yet greater fascination, however, by her ability to change expression rapidly and run through different passions and poses: an ability manifested in her 'attitudes', witnessed by a number of northern European travellers to Naples.

These attitudes provide Emma with a means of actively forging her own continuities with the topography of the warm South. They evoke the Italian past, both classical and Christian, and so supply the travellers who watch them with a means of accomplishing one of the tasks that they regularly set themselves when engaged in translating the topography of the Grand Tour into discourse: the task of transmuting historical time into personal time. Vigée-Lebrun describes 'ce talent d'un nouveau genre':

> *Rien n'était plus curieux en effet que la faculté qu'avait acquise*
> *lady Hamilton de donner subitement à tous ses traits l'expression de*

---

[11] John Moore, *View of Society and Manners in Italy*, second edition, 2 vols (London, 1781), I, 31.

[12] *Souvenirs de Madame Vigée Le Brun* (above, n. 1), I, 194.

la douleur ou de la joie, et de se poser merveilleusement pour
représenter des personnages divers. L'œil animé, les cheveux épars,
elle vous montrait une bacchante délicieuse, puis tout à coup son
visage exprimait la douleur, et l'on voyait une Madeleine repentante
admirable.[13]

REVIVING THE PAST

Emma, then, in Vigée-Lebrun's description, is not merely seen as animated in
her manner, but is invested with a power to reanimate — and revive — the
classical past, in the tableau of the bacchante, and, in that of Mary Magdalene,
the Christian past. Most other contemporary accounts place their primary
emphasis on her power to revive classical antiquity. The Comtesse de Boigne,
citing the transition from Medea to Niobe in the course of her explanation of the
attitudes (she herself, she says, was the young girl who played the part of the
victim in both), comments: 'C'est ainsi qu'elle s'inspirait des statues antiques, et
que, sans les copier servilement, elle les rappelait aux imaginations poétiques des
Italiens par une espèce d'improvisation en action' (Fig. 2).[14]

Women are placed in various forms of affiliation with antiquity during this
period, and often supply metaphors for a revival of the antique past, or for a
resurgence of life alongside a recognition of the remoteness of the ancient world.
Such metaphors invoke an assumption that the feminine, when it fuses with
antiquity, allows the ancient past to be transported more easily into an intimate,
private domain of individual feeling. One rhetorical option that allows female
figures to assume this role is to introduce a narrative of a visit to a monument
that bears the trace of an ancient female presence — such as the Tomb of Cecilia
Metella (Fig. 3) or the Fountain of Egeria. Byron, for example, in his account of
the first of these monuments in Canto IV of *Childe Harold's Pilgrimage*, begins
by explaining at great length how little classical scholarship can tell us about the
woman whom it commemorates, but then declares that he has forged a close
relationship both with Cecilia Metella and with the ancient past:

> I know not why — but standing thus by thee
> It seems as if I had thine inmate known,
> Thou tomb! and other days come back on me
> With recollected music ...[15]

---

[13] *Souvenirs de Madame Vigée Le Brun* (above, n. 1), I, 194, 195–6.

[14] Charlotte-Louise-Eléonore-Adelaide de Boigne, *Mémoires de la Comtesse de Boigne* (ed. C.
Nicoullaud), 4 vols (Paris, 1907), I, 115. See also Lori-Ann Touchette, Chapter 7 in this volume,
n. 77.

[15] Stanza 104, lines 1–4; *Complete Poetical Works* (ed. J.J. McGann), 7 vols (Oxford, 1980–
92), II, 159. For the account of the Fountain of Egeria in the same poem, see Canto IV, Stanzas
116–120; *Complete Poetical Works*, II, 163–4. Late eighteenth- and early nineteenth-century
accounts of visits to the Tomb of Cecilia Metella are examined in greater detail in my essay 'The

FIG. 2. *Emma Hamilton as Medea, or as Niobe* (detail), plate XII in Frederick Rehberg, *Drawings Faithfully Copied from Nature at Naples and with Permission Dedicated to the Right Honourable Sir William Hamilton* (1794). Drawn by Rehberg and engraved by Tommaso Piroli, 26.9 × 20.8 cm.

Another option is to tell the story of a visit to an ancient site at which a woman makes her appearance. Charles Dupaty, for example, in an account of a 'dîner champêtre' with friends in the Temple of the Sibyl at Tivoli (Fig. 4), describes 'l'arrivée imprévue d'une charmante Tivolienne ... qui rougissait de nos sourires et de nos regards'.[16] At Terracina, Sydney, Lady Morgan, is struck by 'a lovely creature' who 'touched my arm playfully with a myrtle branch, and begged, with the smile of a young Sibyl, to accompany us, being, she said, a good "*cicerone per gli antiquità*"'.[17] Lamartine, in a long 'note additionnelle' to his *Dernier chant du pèlerinage d'Harold* (a continuation of Byron's *Childe Harold's Pilgrimage*), relates the story of a visit to Pompeii, during which he walks up a

road to ruin: ghosts, moonlight and weeds', in C. Edwards (ed.), *Roman Presences: Receptions of Rome in European Culture, 1789–1945* (Cambridge, 1999), 125–39.

[16] *Lettres sur l'Italie en 1785,* 2 vols (Rome, 1788), I, 257, 256.

[17] *Italy*, third edition, 3 vols (London, 1821), III, 137.

Sepolcro di Cecilia Metella & Tombeau de Cecilie Metelle

FIG. 3. *Sepolcro di Cecilia Metella/Tombeau de Cecilie Metelle*, engraving in Carlo Fea, *Descrizione di Roma e de' contorni ... abbellite delle piu interessanti vedute*, 3 vols (Rome, 1822). 7.25 × 11.15 cm.

Tempio della Sibilla in Tivoli / Temple de la Sibylle a Tivoli

FIG. 4. *Tempio della Sibilla in Tivoli/Temple de la Sibylle a Tivoli*, engraving in Carlo Fea, *Descrizione di Roma e de' contorni ... abbellite delle più interessanti vedute*, 3 vols (Rome, 1822). 7.1 × 11.1 cm.

street newly cleared of ashes, preceded by three young girls: 'Elles resemblaient à trois beaux songes de vie égarés dans les régions de la mort. Une seule âme comme la leur repeuplerait un grand sépulchre'. He comes across some archaeological diggers, and their director hands him a pick and asks him to make the first symbolic move to clear the earth. The poet hands the pick to the three young girls instead, and at their weak attempts to use it the sand runs away like water. Lamartine is enchanted by the spectacle:

> *Leurs longs cheveux se renversaient sur leurs fronts et leur voilaient le visage; la sueur d'un jour d'été roulait en larges perles sur leurs joues, un peu hâlées par le soleil d'Italie; quand elles relevaient leurs fronts en secouant leurs tresses, on croyait voir dans cette exhumation charmante un jeu ou une allégorie vivante, semblable à ces allégories ingénieuses inventées ou déifiées par l'antiquité.*[18]

He declares, however, that this spectacle is 'ni une allégorie ni un jeu' — the revival of the past goes beyond mere allegory:

> *La cendre en s'ébranlant découvrit successivement à nos regards une porte, une cour, un bassin orné de mosaïque, des statuettes admirablement bien conservées dans leur moule de poussière, des instruments de musique, et des peintures sur les murs aussi vives de couleurs que si le pinceau n'était point encore séché. C'était l'art sous toutes les formes, ressuscité par la beauté, et retrouvant à la fois son soleil dans le ciel, et son culte dans les jeux de trois jeunes femmes.*[19]

A further option, in investing the feminine with a power to revive antiquity, is to note the resemblance of a woman to antique sculpture, or to portray women as aligning themselves with antique art in various kinds of performance. Emma Hamilton is not the only woman who is described as invoking the antique in the context of quasi-threatrical performances. In an early chapter of de Staël's *Corinne* the eponymous heroine, at a ball in Rome, dances the tarantella, a 'tambour de basque' (tambourine) in her hand. Like Emma, she takes her inspiration from a distant past:

> *Corinne connaissoit si bien toutes les attitudes que représentent les peintres et les sculpteurs antiques, que, par un léger mouvement de ses bras, en plaçant son tambour de basque tantôt au-dessus de sa tête, tantôt en avant avec une de ses mains, tandis que l'autre parcouroit les grelots avec une incroyable dextérité, elle rappeloit les danseuses d'Herculaneum, et faisoit naître successivement une foule d'idées nouvelles, pour le dessin et la peinture.*[20]

---

[18] A. de Lamartine, *Nouvelles méditations poétiques avec commentaires* (Paris, 1892), 298.
[19] Lamartine, *Nouvelles méditations poétiques* (above, n. 18), 298.
[20] De Staël, *Corinne* (above, n. 3), I, 141 (book V, chapter 1).

The suggestion of a power of revival and reanimation is reinforced by a hyperbolic account of Corinne's extraordinarily animating effect on the musicians and the rest of her audience: 'je ne sais quelle joie passionnée, et quelle sensibilité d'imagination électrisoit à la fois tous les témoins de cette danse magique, et les transportoit dans une existence idéale, où l'on rêve un bonheur qui n'est pas de ce monde'.[21]

Earlier in the narrative, the relation between the antique and the contemporary within the figure of Corinne is defined more precisely. She makes her first appearance when Oswald, Lord Nelvil, a Scotsman on the Grand Tour, arrives in Rome just as she is to be crowned on the Capitol in recognition of her talents as an *improvvisatrice*. She arrives on a chariot of antique construction, dressed in the manner of Domenichino's *Sybil*, and is described as tall, 'mais un peu forte, à la manière des statues grecques'. The narrator emphasizes her ability to combine the antique with the mundanely contemporary: 'elle donnoit à la fois l'idée d'une prêtresse d'Apollon, qui s'avançoit vers le temple du Soleil, et d'une femme parfaitement simple dans les rapports habituels de la vie'.[22]

Corinne's fusion of past with present is accomplished, then, from the start, by an identification with ancient sibyls — an identification that is explored further when she and Lord Nelvil visit her 'maison de campagne' at Tivoli, and, later, when she gives one of her improvisations at Miseno, near Naples (Fig. 5). She is assigned as her theme, on this occasion, 'les souvenirs que ces lieux retraçoient', and swiftly includes the Cumaean Sibyl among the figures whose memories endure here. Corinne soon becomes so completely absorbed in these memories that she is 'tout à coup saisie par un attendrissement irrésistible: elle considéra ces lieux enchanteurs, cette soirée enivrante'. After a pause in the improvisation, she muses sadly on the destiny that pursues exalted minds, and mentions the Sibyl as a woman whose genius brings pain and sorrow in its wake:

> *Que vouloient dire les anciens, quand ils parloient de la destinée*
> *avec tant de terreur? Que peut-elle, cette destinée, sur les êtres*
> *vulgaires et paisibles? Ils suivent les saisons, ils parcourent*
> *docilement le cours habituel de la vie. Mais la prêtresse qui rendoit*
> *les oracles se sentoit agitée par une puissance cruelle.*[23]

As though to emphasize that she too is 'agitée par une puissance cruelle', Corinne concludes her performance by fainting; she concludes, in other words, with a dramatic physical affirmation of her identification with the ancient woman of inspiration.[24]

---

[21] De Staël, *Corinne* (above, n. 3), I, 141 (book V, chapter 1).

[22] De Staël, *Corinne* (above, n. 3), I, 45 (for the reference to the painting), 46 (book II, chapter 1).

[23] De Staël, *Corinne* (above, n. 3), II, 72, ('La ville de Cumes, l'antre de la Sibylle, le temple d'Apollon, étoient sur cette hauteur'), 75, 76 (book XIII, chapter 4).

[24] De Staël, *Corinne* (above, n. 3), II, 76 (book XIII, chapter 4).

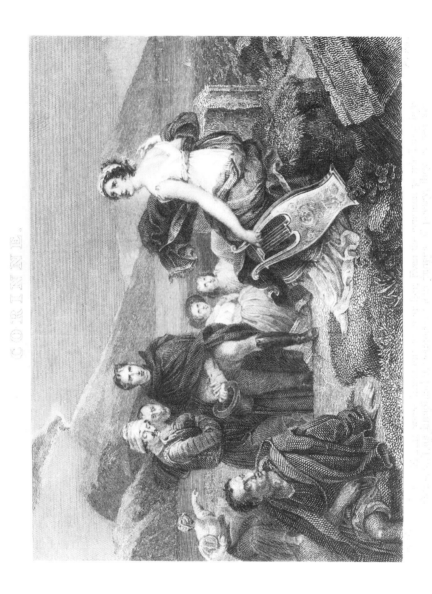

FIG. 5. *Corinne*. Engraving after François Gérard, *Corinne Improvisant au Cap Misène* (1822). British Museum, Prints and Drawings 1870-7-9-826. (© *The British Museum; reproduced courtesy of The British Museum*)

WOMEN PROCLAIM THEMSELVES AS DIFFERENT FROM ANTIQUITIES

The power of women to revive the ancient past, as portrayed in travel writing, is dependent not only on the ease with which femininity is elided with antiquity, but also on a recognition that there is a distinction between the two: a recognition, in other words, that women are different from ruins and antiquities because they are full of life and antiquities are not. De Staël's account of Corinne dancing the tarantella implies that the heroine's ability to inspire artists with new ideas might go beyond that of the paintings at Herculaneum, despite her resemblance to them. An Australian successor to Emma, 'La Milo', or 'The Modern Milo', Pansy Montague, arouses disappointment, when performing her own 'silent and static representations of ancient statues' in London in 1906, by failing to supply the animation — the power to imbue the art of the past with unaccustomed life — that her audiences had expected. Anita Callaway's account of her in *Heritage: the National Women's Art Book*, quotes an English newspaper as complaining, on behalf of her audience:

> What did they see? A series of statues, cold, white statues, for all the world like the statues that they neglect every day of their lives when they pass the National Gallery. A very nice, strictly correct, highly educational exhibition, which may be cordially recommended to teachers, parents and guardians.[25]

In some descriptions of women who resemble or imitate antiquities, on the other hand, the animation necessary to the process of revival is presented as overstepping the limits that the task of reanimating the past requires — in other words, is seen as so irrepressible that, far from affirming continuity and fusion, it prompts a sharp awareness of the difference between the woman and the works of art that she evokes. In commentaries on Emma Hamilton, such a recognition of the difference between the feminine and the antique is registered especially strongly. Far from viewing Emma as evoking the antique within the everyday, in the manner of Corinne on the Capitol, travellers describe her as inducing a sense of extreme disjunction between the antique and the mundanely contemporary. Almost all the accounts of her attitudes, and of the talent for evoking figures from ancient history and myth that she displays within them, note the astonishing discontinuity between this talent and her everyday social behaviour. The Comtesse de Boigne remarks: 'Hors cet instinct pour les arts, rien n'étais plus vulgaire et plus commun que lady Hamilton. Lorsqu'elle quittait la tunique antique pour porter le costume ordinaire, elle perdait toute distinction'.[26] Vigée-Lebrun, too, notes how ordinary Emma appears in everyday clothing.[27]

---

[25] J. Kerr (ed.), *Heritage: the National Women's Art Book* (Sydney, 1995), 219.
[26] *Mémoires de la Comtesse de Boigne* (above, n. 14), I, 115.
[27] *Souvenirs de Madame Vigée Le Brun* (above, n. 1), I, 198.

The Earl of Minto approaches this discontinuity from the opposite direction:

> We had the *attitudes* a night or two ago by candlelight; they come
> up to my expectations fully, which is saying everything. They set
> Lady Hamilton in a very different light from any I had seen her in
> before; nothing about her, neither her conversation, her manners, nor
> figure announce the very refined taste which she discovers in this
> performance, besides the extraordinary talent that is necessary for
> the execution.[28]

As the next half-sentence emphasizes, such a disjunction between elevated
artistic aspiration and vulgar manners supplies the crucial precondition for an
effect of comic incongruity: as though uneasy at voicing such rapture in the
performances of this 'extraordinary compound', Lord Minto swiftly introduces a
note of bathos: 'and besides all this, says Sir *Willum*, "she makes my apple-
pies"'.[29] De Boigne, more self-consciously, analyses the danger of such a
moment of bathos that the genre itself invites: 'D'autres ont cherché à imiter le
talent de lady Hamilton, je ne crois pas qu'on y ait réussi. C'est une de ces
choses où il n'y a qu'un pas du sublime au ridicule'.[30]

Another woman of the same time who is seen as inviting effects of bathos,
by aligning herself with the elevated domain of the antique, but displaying the
ebullience of a living woman in her social behaviour, is Paolina Borghese,
Napoleon's sister, renowned — among other things — for the fact that she posed
for Canova's neo-classical sculpture of *Venus*. James Galiffe, in *Italy and its
Inhabitants* (1820), defines this sculpture as the site of a split between the ideal
and the bathetic, and between antiquity and the conventions of everyday life,
through a narrative (repeated by Thomas Love Peacock in *Crotchet Castle*)
which suggests that, in the traveller's view, different rules might apply to
goddesses and to women: 'One of Canova's best statues is said to be that of
Buonaparte's youngest sister, Princess Borghese, who sat naked for it; and who
replied to an English lady who asked how she could bear to do so, that "there
was a very good fire in the room!"'.[31]

Such abrupt disjunctions between the antique and the contemporary social
world are established, in travel writing, not only in the context of women such as
Paolina and Emma — travellers who transmute into sights for other travellers to
gaze at — but also in the context of ancient monuments. Charles Dupaty
describes himself in the Colosseum, meditating on the work of time, when

---

[28] *Life and Letters of Sir Gilbert Elliot, First Earl of Minto* (above, n. 5), II, 365–6.
[29] *Life and Letters of Sir Gilbert Elliot, First Earl of Minto* (above, n. 5), II, 366; an editor's
note by the Countess of Minto explains: 'Lady Hamilton's manner of pronouncing her husband's
christian name'.
[30] *Mémoires de la Comtesse de Boigne* (above, n. 14), I, 113.
[31] *Italy and its Inhabitants: an Account of a Tour in that Country in 1816 and 1817*, 2 vols
(London, 1820), I, 254–5. See Thomas Love Peacock, *Nightmare Abbey, Crotchet Castle* (ed. R.
Wright) (Harmondsworth, 1969; *Crotchet Castle* was first published in 1831), 189.

suddenly, 'à travers les dernières lueurs du jour, et ces premières ombres du soir, mêlées ensemble', he sees a young woman. 'Elle étoit belle!', he exclaims, 'elle étoit vêtue avec grace! Ses cheveux et ses vêtements étoient mollement agités par un vent frais'. Instead of fusing with the pleasures of the antique, however, like the woman who appears in the Temple of the Sibyl at Tivoli to serve Dupaty and his friends with food, this young woman blots out antiquity altogether: 'Le Colisée disparut', says Dupaty abruptly.[32]

Similar reminders of a discontinuity between the antique and the feminine are issued, amid repeated expectations of a fusion between the two categories, in a much later work, which takes up a number of the themes of late eighteenth- and early nineteenth-century travel writing: Freud's essay 'Delusions and dreams in Jensen's *Gradiva*' (1907). The novella by Wilhelm Jensen that this essay analyses, *Gradiva: ein Pompejanisches Phantasiestück* (1903), tells the story of Norbert Hanold, a young archaeologist living in a German university town, who 'had surrendered his interest in life in exchange for an interest in the remains of classical antiquity'. He is, however, attracted to a bas-relief that he has seen in a museum of antiquities in Rome. The relief represents a young girl, 'with her flowing dress a little pulled up so as to reveal her sandalled feet', stepping forward in an 'unusual and peculiarly charming' manner. He calls her 'Gradiva': 'the girl who steps along'. In a dream that fills him with terror, he sees her buried in ashes in Pompeii on the day of the eruption of Vesuvius in AD 79, and he forms a conviction that this has in fact been her fate. He decides to make 'a spring-time journey to Italy', and his researches soon present him with a pretext for such a journey. Moving restlessly on from Rome to Naples, he goes to Pompeii, partly in order to avoid the swarms of honeymoon couples whom he meets on his travels, with whom he feels completely out of sympathy. At 'the 'hot and holy' mid-day hour, which the ancients regarded as the hour of ghosts, he sees the Gradiva of the relief; in the series of events that follow, this figure is finally revealed to be not a ghost, as Hanold at first thinks, but a living woman, whom he has known well in the days before 'archaeology took hold of him and left him with an interest only in women of marble and bronze'.[33]

Freud, in his remarks on Hanold, discerns an incipient comedy in the plot of a return of repressed sexuality within the very domain in which it appears most incongruous: the domain of scholarly enquiry and intellectual speculation, which provides the context for Hanold's speculations about the ancient past. He emphasizes the strong basis in popular belief for the conviction that scholarship and erotic life are utterly distinct: 'Mathematics enjoys the greatest reputation as a diversion from sexuality. This had been the very advice to which Jean-Jacques

---

[32] *Lettres sur l'Italie* (above, n. 16), II, 64, 65.

[33] S. Freud, 'Delusions and dreams in Jensen's *Gradiva*', in *The Pelican Freud Library* (translated under the general editorship of James Strachey), Vol. XIV (ed. A. Dickson), 27–118; 36, 37, 39, 42, 59.

Rousseau was obliged to listen from a lady who was dissatisfied with him: "*Lascia le donne e studia la matematica!*".[34]

The comic incongruity between the two domains is emphasized especially strongly when the narrative indicates that women of flesh and blood may not always understand that Hanold is scrutinizing them as ghosts or antiquities. The supposed ghost of Gradiva reacts with some amazement when he decides to determine whether or not she *is* a ghost by suddenly swatting a fly on her hand. Earlier in the story, Hanold's fascination with the bas-relief leads him to scrutinize the feet of women in the streets: 'an activity which brought him some angry, and some encouraging, glances from those who came under his observation; "but he was aware of neither the one nor the other"'.[35]

DISJUNCTIONS AND CONTINUITIES

For Hanold — and, more briefly, for the reader — Gradiva assumes a spectral role in the contemporary world: 'ni présente ni absente "en chair et en os", ni visible ni invisible', as Derrida has described her in his essay *Mal d'archive*.[36] Once she herself realizes that the archaeologist is confusing the personal with the historical, however, she leads him — gradually — to a realization of this confusion, by playing a game with him, and acting the part of a ghost that he has assigned to her. She is, in other words, staging a performance that, in its self-conscious contrivance, can be aligned with the games and allegories that, Lamartine insists, do not in fact structure his own experience of revival of the ancient past at Pompeii.

Corinne, on the other hand, is presented as utterly eschewing the artifice of games and allegories. In her performances, she is described as utterly absorbed by the themes on which she improvises — as in the account of her moment of *attendrissement* and her fainting fit at Miseno. At the Capitol, too, in her initial performance, she is described as shy and nervous before she is given her topic; once the cry of 'La gloire et le bonheur de l'Italie' is heard around her, however, she feels herself 'déjà saisie, déjà soutenue par son talent' and 'animée par l'amour de son pays'.[37]

As these moments of emotional identification might suggest, Corinne defines her art as natural rather than artificial. Early in the novel, she describes improvisation as specific to Italy, and as one aspect of 'la libéralité de la nature' in that country: when Sicilian boatmen improvise verses, she says, 'on diroit que le souffle pur du ciel et de la mer agit sur l'imagination des hommes, comme le

---

[34] 'Delusions and dreams' (above, n. 33), 61.
[35] 'Delusions and dreams' (above, n. 33), 52, 38.
[36] J. Derrida, *Mal d'archive: une impression freudienne* (Paris, 1995), 132.
[37] De Staël, *Corinne* (above, n. 3), I, 52 (book II, chapter 3).

vent sur les harpes éoliennes, et que la poésie, comme les accords, est l'écho de la nature'.[38]

At one point in the narrative, Corinne's determination to align herself with nature rather than artifice seems about to waver: in Venice, she decides to adapt her talents to the self-conscious extravagance of a comedy by Gozzi. When dressed as a savage, moreover, in the first act, she manages, in her hair, to combine the wildness required by the part with a care and artistry that testify to 'un vif désir de plaire'. Even amid the cheerful contrivances of this spectacle, however, and amid a sequence of changes of role and costume, she is completely transported by the general mood that it inspires: she approaches comedy not as a means of retreating to a position of detachment, but as a way of achieving a temporary forgetfulness of sorrow: 'elle éprouvait cette sorte d'émotion que cause l'amusement, quand il donne un sentiment vif de l'existence, quand il inspire l'oubli de la destinée, et dégage pour un moment l'esprit de tout lien, comme de tout nuage'.[39]

In her own art of improvisation, Corinne emphasizes, amusement must never extend to mocking laughter; she cites as a necessary precondition for her performances — and those of other *improvvisatrici* and *improvvisatori* — that the spectators should be happy to give themselves up to the spectacle in a spirit of uncritical joy:

> *Une chose me fait encore attacher du prix à notre talent d'improviser, c'est que ce talent seroit presque impossible dans une société disposée à la moquerie; il faut, passez-moi cette expression, il faut la bonhomie du Midi, ou plutôt des pays où l'on aime à s'amuser sans trouver du plaisir à critiquer ce qui amuse, pour que les poètes se risquent à cette périlleuse entreprise. Un sourire railleur suffiroit pour ôter la présence d'esprit nécessaire à une composition subite et non interrompue, il faut que les auditeurs s'animent avec vous, et que leurs applaudissements vous inspirent.*[40]

Corinne's assertion that the art of improvisation would become almost impossible in any context where the audience might assume a stance of amused detachment echoes the view of Hester Piozzi, analysing improvisation with reference to the performances of 'the famous Improvisatore Talassi', in her *Observations and Reflections Made in the Course of a Journey through France, Italy, and Germany* (1789). Piozzi, like Corinne, emphasizes that the crucial precondition for improvisation is the absence of any anticipation of a disjunction between the performer and the spectators:

---

[38] De Staël, *Corinne* (above, n. 3), I, 76 (book III, chapter 3).
[39] De Staël, *Corinne* (above, n. 3), II, 156–7, (book XVI, chapter 1).
[40] De Staël, *Corinne* (above, n. 3), I, 76–7 (book III, chapter 3).

> I have already asserted that the Italians are not a laughing nation: were ridicule to step in among them, many innocent pleasures would soon be lost; and this among the first. For who would risque the making impromptu poems at Paris? *Pour s'attirer persiflage* in every *Coterie comme il faut*? Or in London, at the hazard of being *taken off, and held up for a laughing-stock at every printseller's window?* A man must have good courage in England, before he ventures at diverting a little company by such devices.[41]

It is, she decides, the lack of a spirit of mockery, rather than 'any exclusive privileges or supernatural gifts' on the part of the Italians, that explains why improvisation is specific to Italy: the art is 'among the efforts of those who have learned to refine their *pleasures* without so refining their *ideas* as to be able no longer to hit on any pleasure subtle enough to escape their own power of ridiculing it'.[42] For both Corinne and Piozzi, then, improvisation depends on a situation in which the performer is able to give herself or himself up to the words uttered precisely because the spectators are themselves so happy to identify with the performer.

Emma, in her attitudes, also needs to keep mockery at bay — as de Boigne notes, when remarking on the failure of others to imitate such performances. She is seen as succeeding in this task even by travellers such as Lord Minto, who happily fall in with the figure of the sneering northerner set up by Corinne and Piozzi, and scrutinize her for any characteristics that might invite ridicule. In sharp contrast to Corinne, she achieves the effect of enthralment that precludes mocking laughter not by appeals to nature but by a skilful understanding of artifice; through the elaborately formalized nature of her attitudes, she manages to contain and authenticate the animation that generates such a sense of absurdity on the social scene. Emma deploys the very games and living allegories that, Lamartine and de Staël suggest, revivals of the past can transcend. De Boigne describes an audience enraptured by the game that Emma sets up for them:

> *Un jour elle m'avait placée à genoux devant une urne, les mains jointes dans l'attitude de la prière. Penchée sur moi, elle semblait abîmée dans sa douleur, toutes deux nous étions échevelées. Tout à coup, se redressant et s'éloignant un peu, elle me saisit par les cheveux d'un mouvement si brusque, que je me retournai avec surprise et même un peu d'effroi, ce qui me fit entrer dans l'esprit de mon rôle, car elle brandissait un poignard. Les applaudissements passionnées des spectateurs artistes se firent entendre avec les exclamations de: Bravo la Médéa! Puis m'attirant à elle, me serrant*

---

[41] Hester Piozzi, *Observations and Reflections Made in the Course of a Journey through France, Italy, and Germany*, 2 vols (London, 1789), I, 237, 240. In a footnote, Piozzi translates her own French as 'To draw upon one's self the ridicule of every polite assembly'.

[42] *Observations and Reflections* (above, n. 41), I, 238, 241.

sur son sein en ayant l'air de me disputer à la colère du ciel, elle arracha aux mêmes voix le cri de: Viva la Niobé![43]

Such descriptions, in noting the delight of the audience at solving the puzzle, by matching up the physical and facial expression of Emma Hart herself with the mythical or historical figure whom she represents, ineluctably indicate the importance of the gap between the expressive body and the figure represented — however easily this gap is then overcome. Emma, in other words, resists, at least partially, the fusions and continuities associated with romantic concepts of the symbol, and instead defines herself as an allegorist, drawing on an established store of signs, and directing the audience towards that store of signs in order to solve the puzzles with which she presents them. Whereas Corinne, in dressing as a sibyl and fainting at Miseno, claims a continuity with the inspired female figures of ancient myth, Emma's attitudes retain the discontinuity between the actress and the role that typifies such allegories and games.

The audience is reminded of this discontinuity by Emma's frequent changes of pose. Commentaries always place the greatest possible emphasis on her use of temporal disjunctiveness: as Vigée-Lebrun puts it, 'Elle passait de la douleur à la joie, de la joie à l'effroi, si bien et avec une telle rapidité que nous en fûmes tous ravis'.[44] De Boigne, too, specifically remarks on this power to transform herself: 'Souvent elle variait son attitude et l'expression de sa physionomie. Passant du grave au doux, du plaisant au sévère avant de laisser retomber le schall, dont la chute figurait une espèce d'entr'acte'.[45] Such sequences of discontinuities are in the sharpest possible contrast to Corinne's commitment to fusion: when she appears in the last act of Gozzi's comedy as Queen of the Amazons, the narrator emphasizes above all her power to absorb within her performance a whole range of different passions; the heroine is described as 'cette coquette couronnée, ... mêlant, d'une façon toute merveilleuse, la colère à la plaisanterie, l'insouciance au désir de plaire, et la grâce au despotisme'.[46]

---

[43] *Mémoires de la Comtesse de Boigne* (above, n. 14), I, 114, 115.

[44] *Souvenirs de Madame Vigée Le Brun* (above, n. 1), I, 199.

[45] *Mémoires de la Comtesse de Boigne* (above, n. 14), I, 114.

[46] De Staël, *Corinne* (above, n. 3), II, 157 (book XVI, chapter 2). Germaine de Staël herself, however, often provokes mocking comments from contemporaries on the grounds that she identifies with her heroine, but, in doing so, only draws attention to the gap between them; given the general belief in such an identification, encouraged by the fact that the novelist commissioned from Elisabeth Vigée-Lebrun a portrait of herself as Corinne, at Tivoli (1807–8; Musée d'Art et d'Histoire, Geneva), her descriptions of Corinne are interpreted as ridiculously flattering to herself. See Claudine Herrmann's note on the initial account of the heroine, in *Corinne* (above, n. 1), I, 270–1. I am grateful to Margaret Riordan for pointing out the relevance to my analysis of the mockery that de Staël herself attracts, when I gave a version of this paper at the Department of English Literature at the University of Melbourne, in August 1997.

COMEDY

At the same time, the attitudes, in proclaiming their formalized, allegorical character, render the audience yet more delighted and astonished when the sense of theatrical contrivance is temporarily overcome, and the expressiveness of Emma's face and body seems to enter for a moment into continuity with the figure whom she evokes. The way in which Emma Hamilton's attitudes draw attention to disjunctions rather than continuities, however, directs the attention of travellers all the more sharply to her less adept use of disjunctions in the sphere of everyday life — a context in which obvious contrivance is much more awkward. In her social demeanour, Emma is consistently classified as producing an uncomfortable awareness that she has assumed a role that can hardly come naturally to her. Vigée-Lebrun, describing a visit to Emma in London in 1802, when Lady Hamilton is in mourning for Sir William, explicitly emphasizes the absurdity of her attempts to transfer her acting skills to everyday life:

> Un immense voile noir l'entourait, et elle avait fait couper ses beaux cheveux pour se coiffer à la Titus, ce qui était alors à la mode. Je trouvai cette Andromaque énorme; car elle avait horriblement engraissé. Elle me dit en pleurant qu'elle était bien à plaindre, qu'elle avait perdu dans le chevalier un ami, un père, et qu'elle ne s'en consolerait jamais.[47]

Vigée-Lebrun, registering the comic effect of such a spectacle, uses an idiom that emphasizes the affinity between comedy and artifice: 'J'avoue que sa douleur me fit peu d'impression; car je crus m'apercevoir *qu'elle jouait la comédie*' (emphasis added).[48] Her account of Emma playing Andromaque as comedy — as shameless pretence — delicately suggests that she might be inviting the kind of humorous response that Coleridge defines as an awareness of the finite in relation to the infinite: the sublime grief of a tragic heroine is, in the artist's commentary, juxtaposed with a paltry attempt to observe the social decencies.[49]

In telling this story, Vigée-Lebrun also registers a reaction that both Bergson and Freud have classified as one of the sources of the comic: an

---

[47] *Souvenirs de Madame Vigée Le Brun* (above, n. 1), I, 198.

[48] *Souvenirs de Madame Vigée Le Brun* (above, n. 1), I, 198.

[49] See Coleridge's lecture 'Wit and humour', as summarized by contemporaries in T. Middleton Rayson (ed.), *Coleridge's Miscellaneous Criticism* (London, 1936), 111–30, esp. p. 113: 'Humour is also displayed in the comparison of finite things with those which our imaginations cannot bound; such as make our great appear little and our little great; or, rather, which reduces to a common littleness both the great and the little, when compared with infinity'. (The editor, in a footnote, points out that this sentence is a paraphrase of a passage in Jean Paul Richter's *Vorschule der Asthetik*, section 32.)

economy of feeling and sympathy.[50] In this account and in others, Emma is defined as a figure who invites such an economy in two ways. First, she betrays that she herself never manages to claim the status of a participant in the culture of sensibility, and can therefore hardly be expected to reap the benefits of such a culture. William Beckford explicitly notes that 'she affected sensibility, but felt none'.[51] Secondly, she impresses on those who view her attitudes that she is, among other things, a moving statue, who equivocates uneasily between the domain of the animate — of those who require sympathy — and that of the inanimate.

Unlike Corinne, who absorbs ancient sculpture, spectrally, into her own physical presence, Emma dramatically draws attention to the disjunction between the immobility, permanence and aloofness associated with the art of sculpture and the animation of a living human being. Her attitudes consist of a series of frozen, immobile poses punctuated by movements: de Boigne, describing how she affects the transitions between the poses, affirms, at the same time: 'Mais toujours elle montrait la statue la plus admirablement composée'.[52] Such an opposition between composure and movement is obviously emphasized yet further by the fact that travellers so frequently comment on Emma's animation as a social being. The relation between the two categories assumes particular force of contrast, too, by virtue of the preoccupation that art criticism of the time displays with the very absorptive states that deprive sculpture most strongly of animation. When Horace Walpole assesses 'Sir W. Hamilton's pantomime mistress — or wife, who acts all the antique statues in an Indian shawl', he emphasizes the paradoxical character of the qualities that Emma embodies: 'people are mad about her wonderful expression, which I do not conceive, so few antique statues having any expression at all — nor being designed to have it'.[53]

Moving statues have been defined — in different contexts — as generating comedy and horror — two ways of acknowledging the 'danger and power' with which, Mary Douglas suggests, anomalies of all kinds are necessarily invested.[54] In accounts of Emma Hamilton, the incipient comedy generated by an anomalous combination of the living and the immobile is almost always displaced onto the greater anomaly and incongruity of a woman of low origins and vulgar demeanour who transmutes herself into a work of art, and so aligns herself with

---

[50] See Bergson, *Laughter* (above, n. 6), 4; Freud, 'Jokes and their relation to the unconscious', in *The Pelican Freud Library* (translated under the general editorship of J. Strachey), vol. VI (revised by A. Richards), 295–6.

[51] Quoted in L. Melville [L. S. Benjamin], *The Life and Letters of William Beckford of Fonthill* (London, 1910), 231.

[52] *Mémoires de la Comtesse de Boigne* (above, n. 14), I, 114.

[53] W.S. Lewis (ed.), The Yale Edition of *Horace Walpole's Correspondence*, 40 vols (London, 1937–83), XI, 237–8, 238.

[54] See her *Purity and Danger: an Analysis of the Concepts of Pollution and Taboo* (London, 1966), 94. For a wide-ranging study of the fantasy of a sculpture that moves, speaks, responds or comes to life, see K. Gross, *The Dream of the Moving Statue* (Ithaca and London, 1992).

the ideal. Her role as moving statue none the less supplies two further preconditions for comedy. One comic effect depends on a ribald analogy between her programme of imparting life to the art of sculpture, her ability to reanimate the ancient past, and her power to reanimate her ancient lover. Sculptures, of course, have themselves often been ascribed powers of animation: Anna Jameson, noting the poet Samuel Rogers's fascination with the Venus de' Medici, describes him 'gazing, as if he hoped like another Pygmalion, to animate the statue: or rather perhaps that the statue might animate *him*'.[55] Accounts of Emma's own animation, and her predilection for animating the inanimate, implicitly invite the reader to invest her with similar powers.

A second comic effect is generated by the way in which Emma's role as moving statue echoes and emphasizes another role in which she hovers between the animate and the inanimate: as yet another antiquity in her husband's collection.[56] Walpole observes, in a letter: 'Sir William Hamilton has actually married his gallery of statues'.[57] As a collectible item, Emma is multiplied in the numerous images of her that are produced — images that, in their proliferation, comically exaggerate her husband's propensity to assemble ever greater multiplicities of objects. Vigée-Lebrun notes the shamelessness with which he treats portraits of Emma as possessions to be sold — even one that the artist has drawn in charcoal on the door of his villa beside the sea.[58] Collectible items, however, are often defined as dangerous. Susan Stewart, in *On Longing*, suggests that the otherness of the exotic souvenir 'speaks to the possessor's capacity for otherness; it is the possessor, not the souvenir, which is ultimately the curiosity'. She continues:

> The danger of the souvenir lies in its unfamiliarity, in our difficulty in subjecting it to interpretation. There is always the possibility that reverie's signification will go out of control here, that the object itself will take charge, awakening some dormant capacity for destruction. This appropriation of reverie by the object forms the basis for certain horror stories: 'The Monkey's Paw,' or the ghost stories of M.R. James, for example. In such tales curiosity is replaced by understanding only at the expense of the possessor's well-being.[59]

[55] *Diary of an Ennuyée* (London, 1826), 94.

[56] D.D. Nolta, in 'The body of the collector and the collected body in William Hamilton's Naples', *Eighteenth-Century Studies* 31 (1) (Fall, 1997), 108–14, discusses this aspect of Emma with particular reference to the relation between Emma's attitudes, as depicted in Friedrich Rehberg's engravings, and the decorations on the Greek vases that Hamilton collected (112).

[57] Lewis, *Horace Walpole's Correspondence* (above, n. 53), XI, 249.

[58] *Souvenirs de Madame Vigée Le Brun* (above, n. 1), I, 201, note.

[59] *On Longing: Narratives of the Miniature, the Gigantic, the Souvenir, the Collection* (Durham and London, 1993), 148.

Sir William's 'dormant capacity for destruction' is implicitly acknowledged in his own accounts of his addiction to collecting objects; once this addiction could be seen as seamlessly absorbing the passion of lust in the course of its relentless onward march, contemporaries defined it as a source less of horror than of comedy.[60] The world can hardly wait for the statue to come alive — and remind its purchaser that souvenirs, whether of the antique or the exotic, are often all the more dangerous by virtue of the fact that they are easily acquired.

---

[60] For a useful account of Hamilton's passion for collecting, and of contemporary recognition of the addictive nature of this passion, see K. Sloan, '"Picture-mad in virtu-land": Sir William Hamilton's collections of paintings', in I. Jenkins and K. Sloan (eds), *Vases and Volcanoes: Sir William Hamilton and his Collection* (exhibition catalogue, British Museum, London, 1996), 75–92.

THE CREATION OF A MUSEUM

9

The Gods' Abode: Pius VI
And The Invention Of The Vatican Museum

JEFFREY COLLINS

> The most decisive effect of all works of art is that they carry us back
> to the conditions of the period and of the individuals who created
> them. Standing amid antique statues, one feels as if all the forces of
> Nature were in motion around one.[1]

LARSON AND GAGNERAUX

Several years ago I saw a Far Side cartoon by Gary Larson with the caption 'At
the Vatican's movie theater'. In the image a seated cardinal yells 'down in
front!' at the pope, whose tall mitre is blocking the screen. Larson's joke rests
partly on the cardinal's irreverence and partly on the juxtaposition of His
Holiness and Godzilla. But the humour also depends on the very idea of a
Vatican cinema, an unexpected concession to modernity that challenges our
timeless image of the Church. Larson's cartoon came to mind in front of an
equally arresting image in the exhibition *Grand Tour: the Lure of Italy in the
Eighteenth Century* (Fig. 1). Like Larson's cartoon, Bénigne Gagneraux's large
painting of Pope Pius VI giving King Gustavus III of Sweden a tour of the new
Vatican museum in 1784 foregrounds the collision between epochs and cultures,
as powdered clerics parade past naked pagan gods in soaring rotundas at the
bosom of Western Christendom. Despite his greater decorum, Gagneraux, too,
challenges our received image of the papacy by showcasing the Vatican's latest
and potentially incongruous modernization.

Still, Gagneraux's painting does not surprise us as much as Larson's
cartoon, and this is significant. We are startled by a Vatican cinema but accept a
Vatican museum because of specific historical choices that we have come to take

---

[1] J.W. Goethe, *Italian Journey* [1786–9] (translated by W.H. Auden and E. Mayer) (London,
1962; reprinted by Penguin Classics 1970), 489–90. Here Goethe explains his desire to assemble
plaster casts of the finest antiquities of Rome, so as to be surrounded by their perfection during his
sojourn. For more see *Goethe on Art* (selected, edited and translated by J. Gage) (Berkeley and
Los Angeles, 1980), introduction.

FIG. 1. Bénigne Gagneraux, *Pius VI and Gustav III in the Vatican Museum, January 1, 1784*. National Gallery, Prague (inv. no. O 9025). *(Reproduced courtesy of the Narodni Galerie v Praze)*

for granted. This essay aims to recapture the significance of those choices by focusing on the role of one man — Pius VI (Gianangelo Braschi, 1775–99) — who I believe 'invented' the Vatican Museum we know today. I will argue that his motive was not just personal taste but a wish to capitalize on unprecedented interest in Rome on the part of Enlightened Europe. Inspired by the flood of important visitors to his capital, the ambitious and long-lived Pius VI crafted an artistic showpiece at the Vatican that would resonate with the spirit of the Grand Tour. He spent an enormous proportion of the Church's revenue during his 24-year pontificate on transforming the papal collections into something approaching a modern museum. He radically expanded his predecessor's new sculpture halls, added the Vatican's first painting gallery and print cabinet, and spent some 20,000 scudi to buy the Odescalchi family's coin collection on the eve of the French revolution. It was Pius who completed the Vatican Library's charming Papyrus Room, ornamented its sacred and profane museums, and widened dozens of doorways from the Pio-Clementino to the Sistine Chapel to create a tourist itinerary indelibly linking the papacy with 'classic' art. In short, it was Pius VI who stitched together the recalcitrant fabric of the Vatican and turned an inherited patchwork quilt into a seamless garment.[2]

Although scholars are beginning to talk about the Pio-Clementino, they have paid less attention to its patrons or to its relation to a tourist audience. To examine these issues one must ask three questions: firstly, what constitutes a Vatican 'museum', rather than a collection, and why was one created in the 1770s? Secondly, what determined its character? And, thirdly (a question directly posed by Gagneraux), how did the popes' agendas intersect with the culture of the Grand Tour? On the first point Francis Haskell has argued that the papal museum's very existence was a reaction to tourist greed, the culmination of defensive policies that led to 'the expansion of existing museums and then the building, in stages, of an entirely new and vast one in the Vatican, which soon became the finest of its kind in the world — and it is tempting to look upon its creation as the most beneficial consequence of the Grand Tour'.[3]

---

[2] Pius's artistic patronage is the subject of my forthcoming monograph, *Arsenals of Art*, which considers the museum in this broader context. On the Odescalchi purchase see the Archivio di Stato di Roma, Fondo Camerale II, Antichità e Belle Arti. Pioneering work on the Vatican Museum was done by the late Carlo Pietrangeli, beginning with *Scavi e scoperte di antichità sotto il pontificato di Pio VI* (Rome, 1943); 'Il Museo Clementino Vaticano', *Rendiconti della Pontificia Accademia Romana di Archeologia* 27 (1–2) (1951–2), 87–109; 'I Musei Vaticani al tempo di Pio VI', *Bollettino dei Monumenti, Musei e Gallerie Pontificie* 1 (2) (1959–74), 7–45; and other essays summarized in his *I Musei Vaticani. Cinque secoli di storia* (Rome, 1985).

[3] F. Haskell, preface to A. Wilton and I. Bignamini (eds), *Grand Tour: the Lure of Italy in the Eighteenth Century* (exhibition catalogue, Tate Gallery, London, 1996), 11. On the historical conditions behind the foundation of the museum see also A. Clark, 'The development of the collections and museums of 18th century Rome', *Art Journal* 26 (Winter 1966–7), 136–43; L. Hautecoeur, *Rome et la renaissance de l'antiquité à la fin du XVIIIe siècle* (Paris, 1912); F. Haskell and N. Penny, *Taste and the Antique* (New Haven, 1988), ch. 9.

For Haskell, the Grand Tour catalysed the papal museum by threatening Rome's cultural patrimony. I will argue that, by providing its principal audience, the Grand Tour played an equally important role in shaping its style and message. If so, then both the fact and the form of the Vatican Museum are products of the Grand Tour. Although a thorough discussion of this question demands examination of all of Pius VI's work at the Vatican, I will focus here on two important, but neglected, areas of the Pio-Clementino: the museum's octagonal Sculpture Court and its ten-sided Sala delle Muse.

GODS AND MEN AT THE VATICAN

First I want to set the stage by quoting a nineteenth-century tourist who tells us much about Pius's museological vision. In her 1847 travel memoir, the British actress Fanny Kemble Butler includes a poem she calls 'A Vision of the Vatican'. As Butler stands in the Sistine Chapel she is approached by a radiant apparition who sings:

> Transfigur'd from the gods' abode I come,
> I have been tarrying in their awful home;
> Stand from my path, and give me passage free,
> For yet I breathe of their divinity.
> Jove have I knelt to, solemn and serene,
> And stately Herè, heaven's transcendent queen;
> Apollo's light is on my brow, and fleet,
> As silver-sandall'd Dian's, are my feet;
> Graciously smiling, heavenly Aphrodite
> Hath filled my senses with a vague delight;
> And Pallas, steadfastly beholding me,
> Hath sent me forth in wisdom to be free.[4]

Despite their Victorian hyperbole, Butler's lines summarize a long tradition of tourist responses to the artistic masterpieces in the Vatican. More importantly, her poem reveals Pius's specific and lasting imprint on the papal palace. Although glimpsed in the Sistine Chapel, Butler's speaker is 'transfigured' by her encounter with the pagan gods in the Pio-Clementino, far to the north. 'Transfigured' is an intriguing term, given that Pius had added a copy of Raphael's own *Transfiguration* to the Vatican Pinacoteca, installed between these two poles of the museum.[5] In any case, Butler's phrasing both honours Raphael and presents the Pio-Clementino as a transfiguring site suspended between two worlds, where visitors behold but are also beheld. In this sense,

---

[4] Fanny Kemble Butler, *Year of Consolation* (New York, 1847), II, 155.
[5] On the Vatican painting gallery see C. Pietrangeli, 'La Pinacoteca Vaticana di Pio VI', *Bollettino dei Monumenti, Musei e Gallerie Pontificie* 3 (1982), and forthcoming work by Fabiana Abita, who is studying the Pinacoteca under Pius VI and Pius VII. I thank Christopher Johns for pointing out that Raphael's original canvas did not enter the Vatican collections until after its return from Paris.

Butler's vision is the museum's ideal visitor; from her communion with its masterpieces she takes home not just delight but wisdom.

FIG. 2. Sala delle Muse, Museo Pio-Clementino, begun 1776. Vatican Museums neg. no. xix.27.28. *(Reproduced courtesy of the Vatican Museums)*

Butler's appreciation of the Pio-Clementino's special character can still be recaptured in rooms like the Sala Rotonda or the Sala delle Muse (Fig. 2), which retain much of their original form and represent a major step forward in European museology. For the first time, important classical sculptures were housed in spaces similar to those for which they were made (baths, temples, tombs) and in the ruins of which they were being discovered. While the museum's ground-plans strove for archaeological authenticity (Fig. 3), the materials themselves (mosaic pavements, columns, capitals and decorative details) were being salvaged from ancient buildings. Butler reveals the persuasive possibilities of this totalizing approach, which — to paraphrase Goethe — casts us back to the time and place of the works' original creation. Although the papal museum is related to roughly contemporary collections, such as those of the Villa Albani and Villa Borghese, the Pio-Clementino's wholesale reconstruction of the ancient world inside the Vatican's walls advanced not just Italian neo-classicism but the development of the modern museum.[6]

---

[6] For one discussion of the Pio-Clementino's place in European museology see H. von Steuben, 'Das Museo Pio-Clementino', in *Antikensammlungen im 18. Jahrhundert (Frankfurter Forschungen zur Kunst)* (Berlin, 1981), 149–65.

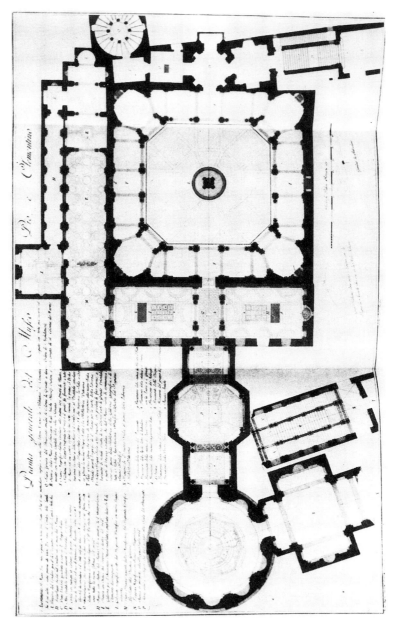

FIG. 3. Plan of the Museo Pio-Clementino engraved after Leandro Ricci, from G.B. Visconti, *Museo Pio-Clementino* vol. 1 (Rome, 1782). The Villa Belvedere lies just north of the octagonal court originally constructed by Bramante, at the top of the plate. The Sala delle Muse extends west towards the Sala Rotonda.

To arrive at the soaring Sala Rotonda, however, we must consider the longer history of art and collecting at the Vatican. The difference between building a museum and embellishing a papal residence must be underlined; Raphael's Stanze, the Sistine Chapel, and even the Vatican Library, are major artistic landmarks but do not constitute a museum per se. Individual popes did expand the papal art holdings, as when Julius II commissioned Bramante to create the octagonal Cortile delle Statue, near the Villa Belvedere, to house the newly-discovered Laocoön, his own Apollo, the Venus Felix, the Cleopatra, the Antinous and other canonical masterpieces that would later anchor the Pio-Clementino.[7] Although Julius is often credited as the founder of the Vatican Museum, his famous courtyard was a private retreat rather than a popular attraction, a recreational dependency attacked by Counter-Reformation pontiffs who sold off pagan sculptures, closed up the niches and reversed the precedent Julius had established in collecting. Because seventeenth-century popes enriched their family's art collections but left little to the Vatican, by 1700 Julius's nascent papal 'museum' was a thing of the past.

It was not until the eighteenth century that papal art collecting was revived seriously. One by one, the popes of this period bought important collections of sculptures, coins or manuscripts and donated them to various Roman institutions, including the Vatican. Some pontiffs even founded 'museums' in the palace, such as Benedict XIV's small Museo Sacro, displaying objects relating to Church history, or Clement XIII's Museo Profano, housing pagan coins, medals, cameos and statuettes in cabinets completed by Pius VI. These early 'museums' were generally single rooms annexed to the Library, a far cry from Pius's neo-classical itinerary. More 'progressive' was the magnificent Capitoline Museum across the city, formed as a result of Clement XII's donation of Cardinal Alessandro Albani's first sculpture collection to the Roman people in the 1730s.[8] But this important model was located at the heart of civic, not papal, Rome, and housed its sculptures in rooms that were classicizing but hardly neo-classical.

The decisive step towards a Vatican museum was taken not by Pius VI but by his immediate predecessor, Clement XIV (Lorenzo Ganganelli, 1769–74), for whom Braschi served as General Treasurer. Sometime in 1770, as Haskell points out, Clement established a museum to house important ancient sculptures that might otherwise leave Rome. Although he first thought of enriching the Capitoline, Clement was persuaded to keep his trophies on papal soil. Because his acquisitions were too large for the Library, he turned to Innocent VII's neglected fifteenth-century Villa Belvedere, just north of Julius's octagonal court

---

[7] J. Ackerman, *The Cortile Belvedere* (Vatican City, 1954); H. Brummer, *The Statue Court in the Vatican Belvedere* (Stockholm, 1970); Haskell and Penny, *Taste* (above, n. 3), ch. 2. The court's entrance bore a quotation from Virgil's *Aeneid* VI: 'Begone, ye uninitiated, begone'.

[8] C. Pietrangeli, 'I Musei Capitolini, prima raccolta pubblica d'Europa', in *Musei e gallerie d'Italia* (1956–7), 22–8; C. Pietrangeli, 'La formazione delle raccolte', *Capitolium* 39 (1964), 209–12.

(Fig. 3).[9] In the first phase of the project, Clement's architect, Alessandro Dori, enclosed the villa's open loggia and replaced doorways with *Serlianas* to create a traditional long gallery lined with statues (Fig. 4). Dori's conservative design retained Pinturicchio's painted landscapes, lunettes and geometric ceiling, copying its design in a colourful pavement. Architecturally, Clement's gallery is indebted to traditional palace planning, while its strong recession, play of colour and light, as well as its sense of abundance, echo the painted galleries of Gianpaolo Panini, fantasies based on Roman collections but far surpassing them in scale. As in Panini's work, stucco faces, scrolls and draperies ornament a crowded rococo ensemble that places putti and saints cheek-by-jowl with ancient statues. Museologically, Clement's gallery resembled the Capitoline in having statues lined up against the walls and busts arranged on shelves in special rooms. In short, the new Vatican museum was designed to compete with existing Roman collections on traditional aristocratic terms.

FIG. 4. Gallery of the Statues, Museo Pio-Clementino, as constructed in the Villa Belvedere
by Alessandro Dori between 1771 and 1772. Vatican Museums neg. no. iv.2.22.
(Reproduced courtesy of the Vatican Museums)

---

[9] On the origin of Clement's museum see Pietrangeli, 'La formazione delle raccolte' (above, n. 8); S. Howard, 'An antiquarian handlist and the beginnings of the Pio Clementino', *Eighteenth-Century Studies* 7 (1) (1973), 40–61; S. Röttgen, 'Das Papyruskabinett von Mengs in der Biblioteca Vaticana. Ein Beitrag zur Idee und Geschichte des Museo Pio Clementino', *Münchner Jahrbuch der Bildenden Kunst* 31 (1980), 189–246. On the villa itself see J. Ackerman, 'The Belvedere as a classical villa', *Journal of the Warburg and Courtauld Institutes* 14 (1951), 70–91; D. Redig de Campos, 'Il Belvedere d'Innocenzo VIII in Vaticano', in *Triplice omaggio a sua Santità Pio XII* (Vatican City, 1958), 289–317; D. Redig de Campos, *I palazzi vaticani* (Bologna, 1967).

FIG. 5. Octagonal Sculpture Court, Museo Pio-Clementino, showing one side of the portico and upper façade added by Michelangelo Simonetti between 1772 and 1774. Vatican Museums neg. no. x.39.18. *(Reproduced courtesy of the Vatican Museums)*

THE OCTAGONAL COURT

The Museo Clementino's second phase corresponded with the replacement of Dori by a younger architect, Michelangelo Simonetti, and marked a shift in the museological paradigm. If the long gallery was essentially modern in inspiration, the continuous portico Clement added to Bramante's octagonal courtyard shows new respect for the precedents set by Julius II and by antique architecture (Fig. 5). Simonetti's lovely portico solved several problems at once. Before Clement's interventions, the courtyard's famous sculptures had been hidden behind ugly wooden shutters, with a hash of unrelated masonry above, a situation repeatedly criticized by foreign visitors. In 1739–40, Charles de Brosses was dismayed by the court's condition, proposing to move the statues to the hallway used for heating the cardinals' food during conclaves. 'Would it not be better', he wrote sarcastically, 'that the cardinals ate cold food and even had a bit of stomach trouble than to leave antique statues in such poor order?'.[10] Simonetti's elegant

---

[10] *Lettres familières écrites d'Italie en 1739 et 1740* (Paris, 1958). The situation was also described by John Galt in his famous account of Benjamin West's visit to the court in 1760: 'The statue then stood in a case, enclosed with doors, which could be opened as to disclose it at once to full view...' (*Works* I, 104).

portico dispensed with the ugly shutters and accentuated the octagonal shape. At the same time, its superimposed arches and pediments pointed like arrows to the major sculptures, just in case visitors had neglected their Lessing or Winckelmann and did not recognize the Apollo Belvedere, the Belvedere Antinous and the Laocoön. These were, after all, the very works that had inspired Winckelmann to rewrite the history of ancient art and found the discipline of art history. With all of Europe clamouring to see them, how could the popes not exploit their prize possessions?

The portico's publicity value was enhanced by careful historical reference. Although Simonetti's stylistic models were modern and even ecclesiastical, the idea of a columnar portico depended on the ancient house or palace, as known from Herculaneum, Pompeii and sites in the Roman Campagna, such as Hadrian's Villa at Tivoli. Continuous peristyles were both a source of important sculptures and an obvious way to evoke an ancient garden at the Vatican — an ambition many scholars trace to Julius himself.[11] Although Simonetti may have been inspired by the expanded role of porticoes at Carlo Marchionni's recent Villa Albani, the Vatican peristyle is far more archaeological; its language is still Renaissance but its *concetto* is ancient, a sheltered, inward-focused walkway ornamented with sculpture, surrounding a domestic garden.[12] At the same time, the court's functional role as a vestibule to Clement's long gallery led its planners to confuse the private peristyle with the more public atrium, another centralized room open above a basin or impluvium. Giambattista Visconti, the museum's curator, called the entire court an impluvium in his dedicatory inscription, a clear evocation of the ancient house. Both the architecture and the accompanying text thus reminded visitors that they were in a space specifically modelled on the classical past.[13]

---

[11] Ackerman, 'Classical villa' (above, n. 9); J. Ackerman, 'Sources of the Renaissance villa', *Acts of the XX International Congress of the History of Art* (Princeton, 1963), 2, 6–18.

[12] On the Villa Albani see articles in E. Debenedetti, (ed.), *Committenze della famiglia Albani. Note sulla Villa Albani Torlonia* (*Studi sul Settecento romano* 1–2) (Rome, 1985) and *Collezionismo e ideologia. Mecenati, artisti e teorici dal classico al neoclassico* (*Studi sul Settecento romano* 7) (Rome, 1991); A. Allroggen-Bedel, 'Die erste Aufstellung der Antiken in der Villa Albani', in *Antikensammlungen im 18. Jahrhundert* (above, n. 6), 119ff. The complex articulation of Simonetti's portico recalls several early eighteenth-century Roman models, including Alessandro Specchi's Michelangelesque portico for Clement XI at the Palazzo dei Conservatori of 1711 and Ferdinando Fuga's more animated portico at Santa Maria Maggiore of 1741–3.

[13] The inscription on the court's western wall reads 'CLEMENS XIIII P.M. / MUSEO / MONUMENTIS VETERUM REFERTO / BIBLIOTHECA / CIMELIIS ET PICTURIS AUCTA / PALATIO SUBSTRUCTIONIS FIRMATO / IMPLUVIUM SIMULACRIS INSIGNE / PORTICU EXORNANDUM CURAVIT / A. MDCCLXXIII PONT. V'. Visconti's draft, with minor variations, can be found in the Biblioteca Apostolica Vaticana, Cod. lat. 10307, f. 112v. Georg Zoega also used the word 'impluvium' to describe the larger Cortile della Pigna in his *De Origine et Usu Obeliscorum* (Rome, 1797).

The portico's third function was to condition the visitor's experience of its contents. Unlike Clement's long gallery, the Villa Albani or most earlier Roman porticoes, Simonetti's peristyle does not provide unified, linear vistas but a series of shifting vignettes. Depending on the viewer's position, its eight domed *gabinetti* either conceal or reveal their occupants and establish intriguing visual dialogues across the central space. More importantly, these *gabinetti* create top-lit chapels or temples that isolate the major sculptures and provide discrete viewing experiences. This role is fundamental. By taking the museum's historic masterpieces out of the fray, these semi-private 'cabinets' encourage the immediate and personal experience of the antique promoted by Winckelmann and diffused by innumerable tourist guidebooks and travel narratives. No visitor could forget Winckelmann's description of Laocoön's noble suffering or Apollo's transcendent beauty. This was by nature a private, ecstatic experience. Here is how Winckelmann described his encounter with the Belvedere Apollo, prior to the portico's construction:

> Before this miracle of art I forget the entire universe and my soul takes on a nobility befitting its dignity. From admiration I pass to ecstasy; I feel my breast dilate and expand as if at the height of prophetic frensy; I am transported to Delos and to the groves of Lycia, places that Apollo honored with his presence; the statue takes on life, as did the beautiful creation of Pygmalion.[14]

Simonetti's sheltered, classical and carefully articulated portico enhances the temporal and spatial disorientation upon which the aesthetic experience depends. On a good day one can still recapture Winckelmann's 'noble simplicity and quiet grandeur' or Goethe's mystical transport by leaving the tour groups behind and stepping into the domed *gabinetti*.

Simonetti's success in creating a Winckelmannian mood depends not only on archaeological reference but on his exploitation of evocative lighting. On the one hand, the domes' central oculi provide the suffused overhead illumination that Montesquieu had recommended in 1729 as ideal for viewing sculpture. Distracting shadows are avoided and the art is revealed to its best advantage.[15] On the other hand, the new portico makes the statues' relative visibility change with atmospheric conditions. Under sunny skies the dim *gabinetti* veil their contents with respect to the court's bright centre, creating a sense of mystery, whereas on overcast days the cabinets seem to glow like beacons. Both effects were recognized and accentuated by contemporary illustrators of the court, who

---

[14] J.J. Winckelmann, *Geschichte der Kunst des Altertums* (Dresden, 1764), 393. For a recent study of Winckelmann see A. Potts, *Flesh and the Ideal: Winckelmann and the Origins of Art History* (New Haven and London, 1994).

[15] C. L. de Secondat, Baron de Montesquieu, 'Voyage en Italie', in *Voyages* (Bordeaux, 1894–6), quoted in G. Consoli, *Il Museo Pio-Clementino. La scena dell'antico in Vaticano* (Rome, 1996), 7.

emphasized the portico's potential for melodrama and surprise. In the case of the Laocoön it is even possible that the new domed setting was meant to recall its dramatic discovery in 1506 in a top-lit, underground room in the so-called Baths of Titus — a scene that originally figured in the painted decoration Pius VI added to Clement's long gallery.[16]

By night, on the other hand, the *gabinetti* increased the suspense of those torchlit tours that confirm Winckelmann's aesthetic legacy. The theatrical potential of Simonetti's portico was fully realized in Heinrich Meyer's nocturnal visit to the courtyard in 1783. As Meyer's party advanced with their flickering brands, statues hidden in the portico's dark corners seemed to move and nod, as if awakened by the light. Finally, as the visitors approached the principal *gabinetto*, Apollo himself 'seemed to descend from his pedestal and advance towards us in the air, haughtily raising his head, where shines an eternal youth to dissipate the ancient night of chaos and to allow the day to triumph'.[17] Compared to the long gallery, an important shift occurred in the museum paradigm: instead of constituting the authority for whom the artefacts are disciplined and arranged, the viewer becomes an interloper in a divinely inhabited space. For Meyer, as later for Butler, a visit to the Vatican had become a theatrical but enlightening pilgrimage to the gods' private abode in the heart of the papal palace.

Without suggesting that such readings of the courtyard be attributed directly to its papal patrons, I do want to emphasize the coherence of visitors' reactions and the way in which their interpretations were sustained, even encouraged, by the new portico. Meyer's floating Apollo neatly prefigures Butler's levitating vision: both establish an opposition between chaos and organization, night and day, darkness and light, but blur the distinction between real and ideal, art and life, past and present, viewer and viewed. These same ambitions animated much of the papal museum, with its free adaptation of ancient plans, reuse of ancient materials, full integration of sculptural fragments and choreographed path through a potentially confusing jumble of pagan remains. At the same time, Meyer's light-giving sun god parallels the popes' expanding self-conception as Christian custodians of classical culture, guides who enlighten our journey

---

[16] This scene, painted by Christoph Unterberger (now covered over), was paired with another showing Pius's discovery and acquisition of the group consisting of Apollo and the Muses at Tivoli (see below), a further link between the octagonal court and the Sala delle Muse and an early example of Pius's attempt to associate himself with Julius II; see O. Michel, 'Peintres autrichiens à Rome dans la seconde moitié du XVIIIe siècle', *Römische Historische Mitteilungen* 13 (1971), 193–4.

[17] F.J.L. Meyer, *Darstellung aus Italien* (Hamburg, 1792), quoted by E. Chevallier, 'L'oeuvre d'art dans le temps. Comment on a vu le Laocoön e l'Apollon du Belvédère à la fin du XVIIIe siècle, d'apres la relation d'un voyagur allemand venu à Rome en 1783', in *Aiôn. Le temps chez les romains*. (Paris, 1976), 344 (my translation). Goethe refers to Meyer's description in his *Italian Journey*. Hester Piozzi remarked in 1789: 'It is the fashion for every body to go see Apollo by torch light' — *Observations and Reflections Made in the Course of a Journey through France, Italy and Germany* (London, 1789), I, 249.

through the glories of Western civilization. Pius VI, certainly, liked to see himself as a new Apollo, eternally young and the herald of a new dawn. Not surprisingly, the portico remained central to this vision even after the museum's expansion, and it is no accident that in two of the eight *gabinetti* the light-bearing oculi are replaced with painted medallions extolling the pope's distinctly Apollonian virtues. In one oval, Pius's fame (symbolized by his name on a golden orb) 'fill[s] the world'; in the other, his ray-like breath causes the defeated arts to be reborn.[18] The Vatican portico, then, clearly functioned as a locus for linking the popes to their classical heritage, while also suggesting overarching political messages. And it did so, I believe, by responding to contemporary tourists' aesthetic expectations as conditioned by writers like Winckelmann.

I have emphasized Clement XIV's portico in an essay dedicated to his successor partly to address a problem in some recent scholarship on the Pio-Clementino and partly to raise the question of Cardinal Braschi's early involvement in the museum. Although Gianpaolo Consoli's new study of the Pio-Clementino's architecture provides helpful data on its construction and style, his divorce of the museum's bricks and mortar from its contents obscures the project's larger meaning. Museums cannot be studied in this fragmentary way. As a result, Consoli underestimates both the novelty of Simonetti's portico and the way it prepares the ground for the neo-classical 'period' rooms Pius soon added to Clement's museum. Moreover, Consoli's concern to distinguish the Pio-Clementino's two phases makes him reject the traditional idea that Braschi helped instigate and shape the new museum while still Clement XIV's General Treasurer. For Consoli, Braschi's involvement began only after his election as pope, when he strove both to absorb and to cancel his precursor's museum while taking credit for decisions in which he had played no part.[19]

Although hard evidence is scarce, several factors suggest that while Braschi may have inflated his claims, his role cannot be dismissed lightly. It is true that his bolder assertions date from after 1780 and served a clear propaganda purpose. Moreover, the museum's true scholarly genius was neither Clement nor Pius but Winckelmann's successor as Papal Commissioner of Antiquities,

---

[18] These medallions signal Pius's continuing involvement in the court, which he completed after his predecessor's death. Unterberger's depiction of Boreas in the second medallion (an element of Braschi heraldry) exploits the similarity between gusts of wind and light rays, suggesting that Pius's presence revives the defeated arts just as new oculi illuminate the forgotten sculptures.

[19] See n. 15. As an architect, Consoli is interested primarily in the three central 'Roman' rooms of Pius's museum and gives short shrift to later spaces like the Atrio delle Quattro Cancelli, the Sala della Biga and the Galleria dei Candelabri. Although he considers the architecture in largely abstract terms (my major criticism of the book), his use of construction records in the Fondo Sacri Palazzi Apostolici at the Archivio Segreto Vaticano enriches Pietrangeli's work with the *Giustificazioni* in the Archivio di Stato. For Consoli's discussion of Pius's involvement see *Il Museo Pio-Clementino* (above, n. 15), 20–2.

Giambattista Visconti, who, together with his son, Ennio Quirino, oversaw the museum's every detail and probably suggested its plan.[20] Nevertheless, Visconti himself explicitly attributes the new portico to Braschi, writing in the museum's catalogue, 'Treasurer Braschi invented the fine idea of surrounding the court with a majestic portico, giving the beautiful statues filling its niches greater protection and decorum, and the Museum Clementinum more fullness and extension'.[21] This could be a lie, but construction records reveal that Simonetti showed his full-scale model for the portico both to Clement and to Braschi for approval, and we know that, as Treasurer, Braschi was required to endorse all expenses relating to the museum.[22] Moreover, Braschi's unusual initiative as Treasurer caught the attention of his contemporaries and seems to have permanently expanded the parameters of this post. But, most importantly, we have seen how the new portico departs from the conservative late Baroque mood of the long gallery and moves towards the Museo Pio's archaeological spirit. Unless Clement himself underwent a fundamental change of heart, it seems likely that a new vision intervened. Since Pius ordered the museum's expansion from the same architect within months of his accession, the extension may well reflect his prior ambitions. In sum, I believe Simonetti's portico already marks a new conception of the Vatican museum, and that, instead of attempting to reverse this new direction, Gianangelo Braschi was involved in (or at least approved of) the change.

THE SALA DELLE MUSE

If the octagonal court inaugurated Braschi's personal vision of the papal museum, the Sala delle Muse represents its culmination (Fig. 2). Here, too, I must refute Consoli, who reads the adjoining Sala Rotonda as the Pio-Clementino's heart. While its planimetric role is fundamental, nicely disguising the awkward intersection of two axes, the Sala Rotonda was not where Pius chose to be depicted in official propaganda.[23] Instead, he was universally

---

[20] For the role of the Visconti at the Vatican and in transforming archaeology see important ongoing work by D. Gallo, including 'Ennio Quirino Visconti e il restauro della scultura antica tra Settecento e Ottocento', in P. Krageiund and M. Nykjaer (eds), *Thorvaldsen. L'ambiente, l'influsso, il mito* (Rome, 1991), 101–22; and 'Originali greci e copie romane secondo Giovanni Battista ed Ennio Quirino Visconti', *Labyrinthos* 21 (14) (1992–3), 215–51. I would like to thank Dr Gallo for her generous assistance at all phases of my work on Pius VI.

[21] G. Visconti and E.Q. Visconti, *Il Museo Pio-Clementino*, 7 vols (Rome, 1782–1807), I, 4; I quote this passage from Visconti's draft manuscript in the Vatican Library, Vat. lat. 10307, ff. 57–8.

[22] For Simonetti's models for the portico (one in painted cardboard and another, full size, in wood) see Archivio Segreto Vaticano, Fondo Sacri Palazzi Apostolici, busta 345, n. 313, 'Conto e misura delli lavori di pittura ...', mentioning that the former was 'shown to Mons. Treasurer and to His Holiness' (quoted in Consoli, *Il Museo Pio-Clementino* (above, n. 15), 64, n. 76; see also 63, n. 70).

[23] Consoli, *Il Museo Pio-Clementino* (above, n. 15), 53: 'The Sala Rotonda is the visual, compositional, and iconographic centre of the museum's itinerary ...'; and 48: 'Pius VI ... would

represented in the Sala delle Muse, which I take to be the museum's true conceptual core.[24] This more complex space is composed of a domed central octagon and two lower rectangular vestibules, in a plan that may derive from Hadrian's small baths at Tivoli, a logical link since the room was designed around a sculptural group of Apollo and the Muses excavated near Tivoli in 1774.[25] Although its ten sides suggest that each wall was originally meant to receive one figure, in the end the statues were clustered more tightly, as if in a conversational grouping. Between the Muses and in the vestibules are herms of Greek authors, politicians and philosophers, with additional Hellenic-themed reliefs set into the walls. The room's sculptural programme is clear: while the adjoining Pantheon-rotunda, focused on the deified Emperor Nerva, evokes Roman civilization, the Sala delle Muse celebrates Greek intellectual culture as inherited by both ancient and modern Rome. As if to demonstrate that 'Greek' could be defined in the most catholic terms, four oil paintings set in the corner walls show the Italian poets Tasso and Ariosto alongside Homer and Virgil.[26]

---

move the porphyry cup ... from the Clementine centre to the centre of his museum, the Sala Rotonda'. Consoli mistakenly claims (73–4, 79–80) that Simonetti copied this room from the Pantheon, repeating Visconti's comment that 'in the new edifice the architecture of the Pantheon and of the baths of the ancient Caesars seems to live again' (Visconti, Pio-Clementino, I, 4). In fact Simonetti's model was not the Pantheon but the so-called Temple of Minerva Medica in the southeastern part of Rome, from which he copied the two-storey interior elevation, arched clerestory windows, the series of ten identical niches and distinctive exterior buttresses (the Pantheon, by contrast, has no clerestory windows or buttresses and contains only eight alternating square and round niches, each screened by columns and separated by aediculae not present at the Vatican). Although the Sala Rotonda's planimetric role depends on this decagonal model, the Pantheon's importance as a notional reference emerges both from Visconti's remarks and from the way Gagneraux (Fig. 1) suppressed the offending clerestory to increase the resemblance to this archetype.

[24] I know no contemporary depictions of Pius in the Sala Rotonda; by contrast, he is shown in the Sala delle Muse in Gagneraux's painting and in a tempera lunette by Stefano Piale, both shown in the exhibition Grand Tour; in a gilt-bronze relief by P.P. Spagna (probably on designs by Giuseppe Valadier) ornamenting one of two monumental tables Pius donated to the Vatican Library; in a marble relief by Giovanni Pierantoni ornamenting the base of a full-length statue in the library of the German-Hungarian Seminary; and in an anonymous print in G.B. Tavanti, Fasti di S. P. Pio VI con note critiche, documenti autentici, e rami allegorici (1804), showing him seated under Conca's fresco.

[25] In fact, only seven muses were found, so it was necessary to substitute another from a different source and to fabricate the ninth from an unrelated female torso. See C. Pietrangeli, 'La provenienza delle sculture dei Musei Vaticani [part I]', Bollettino dei Musei, Monumenti e Gallerie Pontificie 7 (1987), 115–49, esp. pp. 117–32.

[26] For Conca's fresco, so far largely ignored, see a detailed contemporary description in the Vatican Library, ms. Ferraioli 910ff. 13r–14r and a published account in Giornale delle Belle Arti for 7 January 1786, 1–2. See also a brief description in Pietrangeli, 'Provenienza' (above, n. 24), 120, and preparatory drawings reproduced in Crosscurrents: French and Italian Neoclassical Drawings and Prints from the Cooper Hewitt Museum (Washington D.C., 1978), nos. 34–6, and in A Scholar Collects (Philadelphia, 1980) no. 76 verso. The most recent discussion of the fresco (with some errors) and the first colour illustration appeared in C. Pietrangeli et al., I dipinti del Vaticano (Udine, 1996), 551–2 and fig. 537.

Other aspects of the Sala delle Muse reveal its iconographic centrality. Apart from the portico and the staircase, it is the only room to employ free-standing columns, sixteen monoliths from Carrara topped with largely ancient capitals supporting a continuous entablature. Sadly, the point of this gesture is now obscured by the paint covering up the illusionistic landscapes that originally dissolved the corner walls to create the illusion of a free-standing, garlanded pavilion.[27] The room's architectural concept, then, was not a Roman bath, as Consoli believes, but an open temple on Parnassus, the Greek mountain that Apollo and the Muses share with the immortal poets. In the Museo Pio's original itinerary (now unfortunately reversed) the viewer moved from west to east, with the Sala delle Muse thus effecting a gradual transition between the interior space of the Sala Rotonda and the open-air peristyle beyond.

This Parnassian reading is confirmed by Tommaso Conca's astonishingly Baroque ceiling fresco (Fig. 6), the only such vault in the entire museum and a testament to the room's special status. In a nine-part illusionistic scheme descended from Raphael's Loggia, Conca executed a detailed programme planned by Giambattista Visconti, in which Apollo and his Muses consort with Mercury and Minerva, Homer, Aeschylus, Pindar and the seven sages of Greece. Significantly, the figures occupy an open circular portico with domed, top-lit *gabinetti* remarkably like Simonetti's peristyle next door — a connection enhanced by the ceiling's distinctive octagonal plan. By emphasizing both historical and formal links to Bramante's hilltop courtyard, Conca's vivid fresco drives home the parallel between Mount Parnassus and the Vatican Mount — one the origin of artistic inspiration and the other the font of a new artistic renaissance under Pope Pius. Indeed, the Muses' permanent migration from Greece to the Vatican is the subject of Vincenzo Monti's pompous 'Prosopopea di Pericle', a poem illuminated and framed beside the bust of Pericles in the room below. Pericles admits that his own Athens was nothing to Pius's Rome, which exceeds even the glories of the High Renaissance.[28] The fresco (and the room in general) implicitly poses Pius as a new Julius II, who completes his noble predecessor's work. Just as Julius first brought Apollo to the Vatican, Pius now honours him with a portico and restores his attendant Muses. What better centrepiece to Pius's museum than a muse-eum, or permanent temple to the Muses? Given his ambitions as a patron, is it any surprise that this is where he chose to be represented?[29]

---

[27] Pietrangeli illustrates a photograph of the room from *c.* 1860, before the alterations, in *Musei Vaticani* (above, n. 2), 179. The garlands above the landscapes, also painted over, suggest a special festive decoration of a ceremonial structure.

[28] For a discussion of the Prosopopea in the context of the Pio-Clementino see C. Springer, *The Marble Wilderness: Ruins and Representation in Italian Romanticism, 1775–1850* (Cambridge, 1987), ch. 1.

[29] The Ferraioli manuscript (f. 13r) emphasizes that because Conca was required to 'form a unity out of so many varied and distinct items, the painter conceived a circular room supported by columns and pilasters, open at its top' — a clear parallel to the adjoining sculpture court in both form and programme.

FIG. 6. Tommaso Conca, ceiling fresco in the Sala delle Muse, 1782–7. Vatican Museums neg. no. xxiv.18.54. (*Reproduced courtesy of the Vatican Museums*)

The Julian ambitions of the Sala delle Muse emerge most clearly in its reference to Julius's Stanza della Segnatura at the other end of the Vatican Palace, a connection educated Grand Tourists could certainly be expected to make. Not only had Raphael placed his own Parnassus above the window facing the Vatican Mount (populating it, like Conca, with both Greeks and Italians), but Raphael's Segnatura ceiling is also the source of Conca's central scene of Apollo flaying the satyr Marsyas, whose pupil Olympus begs for mercy.[30] A gruesome subject for the centre of a museum, the choice demands some explanation. Although I know of no definitive period explanation, the fable appears to have lost Raphael's neo-platonic overtones (by which it would symbolize the soul's escape from the body towards God) and reverted to a simple warning not to challenge the gods' artistic supremacy — and certainly not in their abode. This threat seems to be the point of Conca's central panel, which presents Apollo as a symbol of papal authority and perhaps of Pius himself. The message is even clearer when we consider the viewer's experience. For the visitor entering from the Sala Rotonda, as intended, Conca's ceiling establishes a neatly descending vertical, from victorious Apollo in the centre of the dome, through Apollo in his fictive niche below, down past Pius's oversized sculptured *stemma* supported by (and supporting) the attributes of the arts, and out to the actual courtyard through the doorway, where the 'real' Apollo stands. While on the one hand this axis suggests an Apollonian continuity between all three (courtyard, Pius, Apollo), on the other it sets up two analogous pairings in which symbols of artistic authority surmount sculptural representation of Apollo. In the painted upper pair, the scene of Apollo flaying Marsyas appears above a distinctly statue-like image of the god in his painted *gabinetto*; in the sculpted lower pair, Pius's 'artistic' heraldry crowns our view of the octagonal court, and thus the Apollo Belvedere itself. This celebratory programme may explain why Apollo appears twice in Conca's ceiling, once discreetly clothed (above) and once as a heroic nude (below); if the latter evokes a historical statue, the former works better as the symbol of a living pope. In any case, Conca's ceiling clearly announces the Pio-Clementino and the Vatican as a new papal Parnassus, and woe to the tourist or rival who thinks otherwise. Marsyas is presented as a caution, and Olympus reminds us that intercession will not mitigate papal wrath.

If Pius's cultural and political ambitions structured the Sala delle Muse, they also informed its reception. Here I want to return to the image with which I began and to the role of the Grand Tour in the museum's conception (Fig. 1).[31] It

---

[30] The ceiling's Parnassus theme may also be indebted to Mengs's central ceiling at the Villa Albani, although the room itself does not take up this analogy, nor does the flaying of Marsyas appear. Raphael's positioning of Parnassus on the room's north wall specifically equates Parnassus with the Vatican Mount and the Villa Belvedere, the future site of the Pio-Clementino.

[31] On Gagneraux see the exhibition publications *Bénigne Gagneraux (1756–1795): un pittore francese nella Roma di Pio VI* (Rome, 1983), esp. pp. 98–9, with extensive bibliography; *Bénigne Gagneraux 1756–1795: un peintre bourgignon dans le Rome néo-classique (*Dijon, 1983); and,

is no accident that Bénigne Gagneraux portrayed one of the most illustrious Grand Tourists of all in Pius's Sala delle Muse; the room's novelty and sublimity make it the ideal venue for one enlightened sovereign (read culture, religion, nation) to show off his patrimony to another. At the same time, his picture documents the complex issues at stake in that intersection. Underlying the protagonists' appearance of easy fraternity is a meticulous choreography that shows how central both portraits and museums were to late eighteenth-century diplomacy. Gagneraux's painting (which exists in two versions, one for King Gustavus and one for the Pope) is clearly at pains to establish the two monarchs' 'separate but equal' status by highlighting each in different ways. Gustavus, for instance, steps slightly forward of the group and is more perfectly framed by the arch overhead. Pius, however, with his brighter costume and an attendant's raised cross pointing to him like an arrow, stands out more forcefully from the crowd and seems closer to the painting's visual centre. In fact the canvas's centre line passes directly between Pius and Gustavus, as if to demonstrate their perfect compositional and political equilibrium.

Nevertheless, there are subtle suggestions of seniority that befit Pius's presence on 'home turf' as well as his status as the senior monarch. Although the relative height of Pius and Gustavus varies according to whose copy one examines, in both versions Gustavus looks towards his older colleague, whose inviting gesture indicates that he is the museum's proprietor and the leader of the parade. This may be the gods' abode, but it is also Pius's headquarters. This hierarchical relationship is playfully repeated in the pair of hounds in the left foreground of both versions, where a smaller dog looks up expectantly at an indulgent larger friend. Gagneraux cements this distinction in the Pio-Clementino's own classicizing terms by introducing carefully chosen statues on the margins of the main group. On Gustavus's side of the canvas the painter places a statue of Ganymede, the youthful cup-bearer to the king of the gods, while on the left Pius is juxtaposed with a sculpted Amazon, fearless warriors renowned for their courage in battle. Neither work ever appeared in this room, but both serve to characterize and position the painting's principal human subjects. The same correlative technique explains the presence of two far more famous statues that Gagneraux has relocated from Bramante's courtyard into positions against the rear wall of the Sala delle Muse. The Swedish King's hand-

---

most recently, Wilton and Bignamini (eds), *Grand Tour* (above, n. 3), 80. For the circumstances of the event see also C. Pietrangeli, 'Gustavo III di Svezia a Roma', *Capitolium* 36 (10) (1961), 13–21 and n. 12. The picture was commissioned by Gustavus during a visit to the artist's studio in April 1784; in March of the following year the finished picture was sent to the Pope, who kept it for four days and was so pleased with the result he ordered a copy for himself (this copy was taken by the French in 1798 and is currently in Prague). Gagneraux complained of the commission's difficulty, writing 'c'est un tableau extrèmement compliqué' and 'je sacrifie tout pour me tâcher de m'attirer de plus en plus la bien-veillance de la Cour de Suède' (see *Un pittore francese* (above), 98).

FIG. 7. Giovanni Volpato, engraving after Raphael's *School of Athens*, Stanza dells Segnatura, c. 1780. (*Reproduced by kind permission of the Istituto nazionale per la grafica, Ministero per i beni culturali e ambientali, Rome*)

on-hip pose mimics that of the Belvedere Antinous behind him, while Pius's outstretched arm and *contrapposto* stance echo the Apollo Belvedere. Whereas Gustavus is figured as the youthful foreign companion of the great patron-emperor Hadrian (a figure Pius later claimed as a model in his Pinacoteca), the Pope is again conflated with the most famous and important deity from Julius II's sculpture garden. Pius again becomes Apollo, and it may be significant that the beam of light streaming from the Sala Rotonda's oculus traces a path immediately between the Apollo Belvedere and the Holy Father.

But Gagneraux's appreciation of the Pio-Clementino's layered messages does not end there. Besides altering the contents of the Sala delle Muse, he has also changed its architecture, opening up the arched passage to the Sala Rotonda and regularizing its strange decagonal shape (compare Figs 1 and 3). The painter was criticized for this in the Roman press, which felt he should either have invented an entirely fictional space or respected the museum's noble architecture.[32] Why did Gagneraux prefer this middle ground, and what does it express? Julian precedent is again the key. In a move that must have delighted the Pope, Gagneraux has silently blended Pius's Sala with Raphael's *School of Athens* from the Stanza della Segnatura. Not just the painting's regular architectural backdrop but its balanced, linear disposition of the figures are adapted from Raphael's canonical model, which Pius was busy diffusing through a suite of lavish engravings by Giovanni Volpato (Fig. 7).[33] Gagneraux's formal glance at Raphael has occasionally been noted, but its meaning has never been explored. Was it just an artistic crutch or did Gagneraux appreciate the inherent parallels between the subjects, using the quotation as a way to explain Pius's cultural ambitions? More specifically, is Gagneraux's casting of Pius VI as Plato the idealist and of Gustavus III as Aristotle the materialist an intentional comment on the relation between spiritual and worldly authority, a primary issue during the visit of a Protestant king and a focus of Pius's policy? Such a political reading would correspond well with the symbolic divisions made elsewhere in Gagneraux's painting.

What is clear is that the canvas's explicit reference to the Stanza della Segnatura recasts Pius's entire museum as the new 'School of Athens', appropriately centred on the most Greek space in the ensemble. As we have seen, it was here among all the museum's rooms that the themes of artistic inspiration, authority and transmission were treated most directly and most legibly for a tourist audience. The room's message depended on a transfiguring, experiential conception of the museum pioneered in Simonetti's octagonal portico, and on the creation of an itinerary structured to encourage historical and conceptual connections between the scattered spaces of the Vatican Palace. The gods' abode was the key to this larger matrix. Whatever his own sympathies, Gagneraux

---

[32] *Memorie per le belle arti* (March 1785), 35–8.
[33] For this series see G. Marini (ed.), *Giovanni Volpato 1735–1803* (Bassano del Grappa, 1988).

understood that the Sala delle Muse (and by extension the entire museum) aimed to summarize, absorb and perfect classical civilization with Christianity. Just as Raphael had made Bramante's Saint Peter's the setting for a similar cultural alchemy, Gagneraux transfigures the Pio-Clementino into the ideal classical 'muse-eum'.

CONCLUSION

Understanding the papal museum in relation to the Grand Tour, then, means studying more than its architecture or any one of its component parts. Instead the Pio-Clementino is a nexus of architecture, decoration, restoration, display and marketing, at the vanguard of Pius's ambitious artistic politics. While containing elements of a traditional princely collection, the papal museum's new outreach towards the viewer, its manipulation of the visitor's experience, its symbolic unification of the palace and its expression of public rather than private meaning all mark the birth of the modern Vatican Museum. We should return to the question of what constitutes a 'modern' museum. If Pius's construction of a custom-designed building around an art collection is fundamentally forward-looking, his invention of a Vatican museum none the less meant situating the papacy within the entire Western cultural tradition. Pius conceived his gods' abode as the new centre of art, learning and culture controlled by Rome — a goal I believe one sees expressed less in the soaring Sala Rotonda than in the octagonal courtyard and the Sala delle Muse.

What is a museum? As Fanny Butler points out, museums are places where a society reflects on itself, considers its past and plots its future. They are places where the dead meet the living and divinities meet mortals. The audience is essential for this encounter. I have suggested that Pius's museum responded actively to foreign tourists, not only in that their wealth catalysed its existence but also that their tastes conditioned its evolving character and reception. Inaugurated by Clement XIV as another Roman noble gallery, the project was transformed by his successor into an archaeological fantasy centred on a papal Parnassus. Bénigne Gagneraux read the ensemble as a modern 'School of Athens', while Butler experienced it as a liberating space of transfiguration. Although the museum was built by Italians, these models all depended in part on the Grand Tourists' vision of the papal city —romantic, associationist, prone to emotional rapture.

Yet the abode that Pius VI constructed for his gods was ultimately a fragile one. Just years after receiving his portico and his Muses, the Apollo Belvedere began his own 'Grand Tour' to the Louvre, while 'Citizen Pope' died in a French jail. Their destinies were again intertwined; but that is another story.[34]

[34] I would like to thank the American Academy in Rome, the National Endowment for the Humanities and the University of Washington for supporting my research on this subject.

'AFTER' THE 'GRAND TOUR'

10

Dickens And The Figures Of
Pictures From Italy

JOHN BOWEN

I

At four o'clock on 30 January 1845, Charles Dickens entered the Eternal City, not as a Grand Tourist but as one of their countless Victorian bourgeois successors. He entered as travellers from the North did, through the Porta del Popolo, into the piazza, and on to the Hotel Meloni, later the Hotel des Iles Britanniques, recommended by Coghlan's handbook as 'first-rate'.[1] It was, appropriately enough for the great comic, festive, popular novelist of the language and the century, the time of carnival. The weather was 'atrocious', a 'dark muddy day' with 'heavy rain'.[2] Entry into Rome for anyone hailing from its former colonies and provinces is a strange and often disturbing affair. Dorothea Brooke, from George Eliot's *Middlemarch*, fictionally visiting the city in 1830 on her disastrous honeymoon, found her provincial Protestant piety overwhelmed by 'the gigantic broken revelations', the 'stupendous fragmentariness' and 'dreamlike strangeness' of Rome.[3] Three-quarters of a century later, Sigmund Freud spent several journeys to Italy missing, evading, finding excuses, failing to go to Rome, overwhelmed not merely by the historical spectacle but by the richness of the psychic tropes and figures it released in his own deep unconscious identification with the Hannibal who also had halted short of Rome.[4] And many other visitors have testified to their trepid awe at the uncanny force of the sublime spectacle of imperial power in ruins. Charles Dickens, it seems, felt no such emotions, or if he did, did not record them. Rome

---

[1] K. Tillotson (ed.), *The Letters of Charles Dickens: Volume Four 1844–1846* (Oxford, 1977), 257.

[2] Charles Dickens, *American Notes and Pictures from Italy* (ed. F.S. Schwarzbach and L. Ormond) (London, 1997), 396. All references will be to this edition and placed in the text. See also Dickens's letter to John Forster, 31 January 1845, Tillotson, *Letters of Charles Dickens* (above, n. 1), 257.

[3] George Eliot, *Middlemarch* (ed. R. Ashton) (Harmondsworth, 1994), 192–3.

[4] S. Freud, *The Interpretation of Dreams* (ed. J. Strachey) (Harmondsworth, 1976), 282–7.

from a distance, he confessed, was 'like LONDON!!!' with 'no great ruins, no solemn tokens of antiquity to be seen ... no more *my* Rome: the Rome of anybody's fancy, man or boy, degraded and fallen and lying asleep in the sun among a heap of ruins than the Place de la Concorde in Paris is' (395–6).

1845 was a time of peculiar importance to Dickens. Two years before, he had suffered what he called 'the Chuzzlewit agonies'.[5] Until that time, he had had a unique set of artistic and popular successes from the age of 24: *Pickwick Papers*, *Oliver Twist*, *Nicholas Nickleby*, *The Old Curiosity Shop*, *Barnaby Rudge* — hit after hit. Translated into Russian, French, Polish and German, received with hysterical adulation in the United States, their young author had an unprecedented standing within the literature of his age. And then he wrote *Martin Chuzzlewit*, a novel of remarkable linguistic and metaphorical innovation, whose moral scepticism is unknown before Nietzsche and whose linguistic invention can only be compared with Shakespeare or Joyce. It was perhaps too strong a poison for the mid-Victorian mind and it did not sell well after the first few numbers. So, after an astonishing decade of literary production — not just six novels and two plays but also *Sketches by Boz*, *American Notes* and the editing of two journals —, Dickens decided to take a break for a full twelve months and come to Italy. And his entry into Rome on that wet day in January 1845 came at a particularly sensitive time in his life. He had felt, for perhaps the first time, the fear of the unbinding of that remarkable intimacy and rapport with his popular audience. It had been, it is true, restored in part by the appearance at Christmas 1843 of perhaps his greatest ever popular success, *A Christmas Carol*, the first of many Christmas books and stories; and, indeed, as he came to Rome he had just learned of the tremendous success of its sequel, that 'great blow for the poor', *The Chimes*; but later that year he could still fear 'failing health or fading popularity'.[6]

Dickens had lived in Italy, with his wife Kate and five children, for four months before he came to Rome, for the most part in a magnificent, shabby, flea-ridden villa outside Genoa, which he called 'the Pink Jail' (321), where he learnt enough Italian to 'talk to all the Italian boys who go about the streets with organs and white mice, and give them mints of money *per l'amore della bell'Italia*',[7] to relish the rich idioms of Genoese social life, and to record the complex cultural interchanges between his own cook and servant and the Genoese, which began with his servants speaking 'with great fluency in English (very loud: as if the others were only deaf; not Italian)'[8] and culminated in his cook accepting a

[5] J. Forster, *The Life of Charles Dickens* (London, n.d), bk 4, II, 219. Letter of 10 November 1843.

[6] Tillotson, *Letters of Charles Dickens* (above, n. 1), 200, 423.

[7] G. Storey and K. Tillotson (eds), *The Letters of Charles Dickens: Volume Five 1847–1849* (London, 1981), 154n. For an example of Dickens's 'fair command of the language' see Tillotson, *Letters of Charles Dickens* (above, n. 1), 308.

[8] Tillotson, *Letters of Charles Dickens* (above, n. 1), 157.

proposal of marriage from a Genoan and her staying behind in Italy to set up a restaurant with her new husband.[9] The encounters of the English and Italians were a matter of supreme delight to the novelist and were later to issue in the sublime comedy of John Baptist Cavalletto and Mrs Plornish in *Little Dorrit*, as when Cavalletto comes to live in Bleeding Heart Yard, and gradually (after a good deal of initial suspicion) he is accepted and the Bleeding Hearters start to speak to him:

> in very loud voices as if he were stone deaf. They constructed sentences, by way of teaching him the language in its purity, such as were addressed by the savages to Captain Cook, or by Friday to Robinson Crusoe. Mrs Plornish was particularly ingenious in this art; and attained so much celebrity for saying 'Me ope you leg well soon,' that it was considered in the Yard but a very short remove indeed from speaking Italian. Even Mrs Plornish herself began to think that she had a natural call towards that language.[10]

Gradually the other inhabitants of the yard try to develop Cavalletto's vocabulary so that

> whenever he appeared in the Yard ladies would fly out at their doors crying, 'Mr Baptist — teapot!' 'Mr Baptist — dust-pan!', 'Mr Baptist — flour dredger!' 'Mr Baptist — coffee — biggin!'. At the same time exhibiting those articles, and penetrating him with a sense of the appalling difficulties of the Anglo-Saxon tongue.[11]

After Genoa, Dickens and his entourage slowly wended their way through northern and central Italy — through Piacenza, Parma, Modena, Bologna, Ferrara, Verona, Mantua, Carrara, Pisa and Siena, with a side excursus for Dickens himself to Venice. Shortly after he returned to England in 1846, he edited a new national newspaper, *The Daily News*, from which he resigned after a few days, but continued with a set of 'Travelling Letters', detailed, first-hand accounts of his Italian journey, based in part on letters to friends written at the time. The travelling letters become the core of *Pictures from Italy* which, illustrated by Samuel Palmer, appeared later in 1846.

So there is a rich cache of material about Dickens and Italy, and Dickens and Rome — letters, journalism and finished book. Dickens was, of course, by no means the first English literary traveller in Italy. From Chaucer onwards, English poets and novelists have been paying their debts to the warmer South. But the 1840s saw some sort of peak of Italian literary adventuring, for in the same year as Dickens's book, there also appeared two works by Browning set in

---

[9] Tillotson, *Letters of Charles Dickens* (above, n. 1), 306. On Dickens's general relationship to Italy, see M. Hollington, 'Dickens and Italy', *Journal of Anglo-Italian Studies* 1 (1991), 126–36.

[10] Charles Dickens, *Little Dorrit* (ed. H.P. Sucksmith) (Oxford, 1982), 255.

[11] Dickens, *Little Dorrit* (above, n. 10), 255.

Italy, Hawthorne's *Rappaccini's Daughter*, Leigh Hunt's *Stories from the Italian Poets*, Edward Lear's *Illustrated Excursions in Italy*, Frances Trollope's *The Robertses on their Travels* and the second volume of Ruskin's *Modern Painters*; the decade saw (among many other Italian-inspired works) much more Browning, Macaulay's *Lays of Ancient Rome*, as well as travel journals by the veteran Romantics William Wordsworth and Mary Shelley.[12] Dickens, though, is markedly different from these other writers for, as Kenneth Churchill puts it in his wide-ranging study of *Italy and English Literature*, *Pictures from Italy* is 'quite unlike any other English book on Italy'.[13] This is partly because Dickens is drawn to the life of Italy's people and streets more than to its monuments and works of art, but also because of the very close affinity there is between the characteristic forms of his rhetoric and imagination and those of Italian popular life. It is not true, I think, to say, as G.K. Chesterton did, that Dickens 'never travelled out of England' because 'his travels are not travels in Italy but travels in Dickensland',[14] but there is nevertheless a striking similarity between the world of Dickens's imagination which we see in his novels — that characteristic mix of the sentimental, theatrical, hyperbolic, grotesque and absurdly funny — and the world he discovers or creates in Italy. Mario Praz has described *Pictures from Italy* as 'a funeral symphony ... culminating like the Symphonie Fantastique of Berlioz in a *"marche au supplice"*'.[15] But the darkness that is undoubtedly there in *Pictures from Italy* is matched by an equally powerful rhetorical and figurative exuberance.

Reading his account of the early months of residence in Genoa and travel in the north before coming to Rome, one is struck by Dickens's constant recourse to the hyperbolic. Nothing is ever simply large, beautiful or interesting: his first house in Genoa, despite the fleas, 'is in one of the most splendid situations imaginable' (321); the sky there is of 'the brightest and most intensely blue' (329); the houses of Genoa town are 'immensely high' (328); a yard is not merely 'deserted', but seems 'to have been unvisited by human foot, for a hundred years', and one hears only 'the dismallest and most lonesome echoes' (330) there. When he moves house to the Palazzo Peschiere, 'there is not in Italy a lovelier residence' (341) with 'one of the most fascinating and delightful prospects in the world' (342). Good and bad are pushed to equal extremes: although 'there never was anything so enchantingly graceful and full of beauty' (352) as the road from Piacenza to Parma, at Piacenza itself he finds only 'the sleepiest and shabbiest of soldiery ... the dirtiest of children and the gauntest of dogs' who 'trot in and out of the dullest of doorways' (351). Everything is in the superlative degree: from Pisa's leaning tower and Cathedral, 'perhaps the most remarkable and beautiful' group of buildings 'in the whole world' (389), to the

[12] K. Churchill, *Italy and English Literature 1764–1930* (London, 1980).
[13] Churchill, *Italy and English Literature* (above, n. 12), 137.
[14] G.K. Chesterton, *Charles Dickens* (London, 1906), 153.
[15] M. Praz, *The Hero in Eclipse in Victorian Fiction* (London, 1956), 449.

little fishing town of Camoglia, 'the saltiest, roughest, most piratical little place that ever was' (384).

This love of hyperbole draws Dickens to the search for the most treasured experience of nineteenth-century travellers, that of the sublime, to the tremendous, the awful, the incomprehensible, the terrifying, those experiences which take consciousness and language themselves to the edge of the impossible and inexpressible.[16] Just before crossing the papal frontier on the journey to Rome, after a night in a 'ghostly, goblin inn' (393), Dickens and his party encounter a 'dark, awful and solitary' storm, 'wrathful, rapid, violent, tumultuous' (394). Such moments reach a climax in his astonishing and near-fatal ascent of Vesuvius, in which, after 'looking down into the hell of boiling fire', Dickens and his companions descend 'rolling down; blackened, and singed, and scorched, and hot, and giddy: and each with his dress alight in half-a dozen places' (449). If it was natural for nineteenth-century travellers to go in search of the sublime, so too they usually looked for the picturesque, that quality of pleasing disorder or roughness in nature, that irregular or rugged beauty that was so highly praised in landscape and art.[17] Dickens at first seems quite conventional in his praises: the shore at Genoa is 'picturesque and beautiful' (323), as are the rocks (321) and the heights above (319). But Dickens shows his difference in often looking not for the picturesqueness of a landscape fit for artistic representation, but for the picturesqueness of popular life. His coach-driver, for example, from Nice to Genoa is 'a meteor of gallantry and cheerfulness' until there is some small difficulty, at which he stops the coach and falls into 'an ecstacy of despair ... as if there were no ray of hope to lighten his misery'. Once it is fixed, he proceeds, 'as if it were not in the power of misfortune to depress him' (347). The *cicerone* of Bologna, his face 'all shining teeth and eyes', shows Dickens the town graveyard and then suddenly reveals that his own five children are buried there, looks Dickens hard in the face, takes a pinch of snuff 'and made a little bow; partly in deprecation of his having alluded to such a subject, and partly in memory of the children and of his favourite saint. Immediately afterwards, he took his hat off altogether, and begged to introduce me to the next monument; and his eyes and teeth shone brighter than before' (356).

These are characteristic moments from the book, for they unite the picturesque with another leading figure of Dickens's rhetoric — his love of the

---

[16] There is an extensive literature on the literary sublime. See, for example, S.H. Monk, *The Sublime: a Study of Critical Theories in XVIII Century England* (Ann Arbor, 1935), and P. de Bolla, *The Discourse of the Sublime: Readings in History, Aesthetics and the Subject* (Oxford, 1989).

[17] J.H. Hagstrum, *The Sister Arts: the Tradition of Literary Pictorialism in English Poetry from Dryden to Gray* (Chicago, 1958), 157–8. Praz, *The Hero in Eclipse* (above, n. 15), 149, argues of Dickens that 'what, in him, may seem to be realism is merely delight in the picturesque'. See also M. Hollington, *Dickens and the Grotesque* (Beckenham, 1984), 138–52.

paradoxical and oxymoronic.[18] Genoa is full of the 'strangest contrasts, things that are picturesque, ugly, mean, magnificent, delightful and offensive, break upon the view at every turn' (327), and its palaces are 'so lively and yet so dead: so noisy and yet so quiet: so obtrusive, and yet so shy and lowering: so wide awake, and yet so fast asleep' (329). So, too, is Venice, whose buildings are 'high, and low, and black, and white, and straight, and crooked, mean, and grand; crazy and strong' (368): each epithet seems to call forth its opposite, to give birth to seemingly endless chains of contradictory particulars. And at times for Dickens it reaches beyond conscious experience itself to the logic of dreams. The sheer lack of resemblance to the familiar makes him fall into a 'dismal reverie' (320) at Genoa, for it is 'a bewildering phantasmagoria, with all the inconsistency of a dream, and all the pain and pleasure of an extravagant reality' (330). Like dreams, such experiences can be good or bad, painful and pleasurable without restraint. The prospect from the Palazzo Peschiere is 'like a vision ... a perfect dream of happiness' (342); just as all of Venice in one of the most beautiful chapters of the book is 'An Italian Dream', but visiting the prisons there a 'monstrous and unlikely' dream (367). The churches in Rome melt into one another like dreams, but the Mamertine prison remains 'a dream within a dream, a small wave by itself, that melts into no other wave, and does not flow on with the rest' (415). Dickens in Italy, as so often when he is moved, goes back to figures and scenes from his earliest and favourite reading — to fairy-stories and the *Arabian Nights* in particular.[19] The Peschiere Palace that he moves to is 'more like an enchanted palace in an Eastern Story than a grave and sober lodging' (342). Walking round a ruined palazzo, Dickens thinks of the cats and chickens in the outhouses as 'transformed retainers, wanting to be changed back again' (326). A palace in Piacenza would be 'a good home for the king with marble legs, who flourished in the time of the thousand and one Nights' (352) and the narrow valley of Carrara makes Dickens think of 'the deep glen ... where the Roc left Sinbad the Sailor' (386).

But these sublime, picturesque and fantastical moments are always liable to turn over rapidly, in a characteristically Dickensian way, into something much more absurd and comical. Visiting Verona, he is shown, like every good tourist, the balcony said to have been Juliet's. Dickens yields to no one in his love of Shakespeare, but at the Capulets' house it is the 'grim-visaged dog, viciously panting in a doorway' who draws his attention, a dog 'who would certainly have had Romeo by the leg, the moment he put it over the wall, if he had existed and

---

[18] On Dickens's rhetoric, see J.H. Miller, 'The genres of *A Christmas Carol*', *Dickensian* 89 (1993), 193–206.

[19] See H. Stone, *The Invisible World: Fairy-Tales, Fantasy and Novel-Making* (London, 1979), and M. Slater, 'Dickens in Wonderland', in P.L. Caracciolo (ed.), *The Arabian Nights in English Literature: Studies of the Reception of the Thousand and One Nights into British Culture* (London, 1988), 130–42.

been at large in those times' (370).[20] In another transformation of the serious and tragic, a Jesuit on a coach 'with a gash of pink leg between his black stocking and black knee-shorts' looks 'like Hamlet in Ophelia's closet' (349). It is this that goes some way to explaining Dickens's delight in the puppet theatre at Genoa, a spectacle simultaneously fantastical, sublime, picturesque and wholly absurd, something in popular life that takes one to superlative and inexpressible states. The puppets play 'St Helena or the Death of Napoleon' in an 'unspeakably ludicrous' way: 'Buonaparte's boots were so wonderfully beyond control ... doubling themselves up, and getting under tables, and dangling in the air, and sometimes skating away with him, out of all human knowledge, when he is in full speech' and the Doctor treating Napoleon 'in consequence of some derangement of his wires, hovered about his couch like a vulture, and gave medical opinions in the air' (341). It is, wrote Dickens, 'without any exception the drollest exhibition I ever beheld in my life' and the puppets 'absolutely insupportable ... prodigious ... tremendous ... the triumph of art' (339–41). Sublime and absurd, utterly false and a triumph of art: these paradoxical and picturesque puppets, this popular, pantomimic life and art, stand (and fail to stand) as representative figures of Dickens's time and writing in Italy.

II

What of the pictures of *Pictures from Italy*, that strange title for a book which has so few pictures, almost none at all? Dickens is the most copiously illustrated of all Victorian novelists, and he took a deep and persistent interest in the visual appearance of his books, commissioning artists and exercising a good deal of control over their work.[21] But *Pictures from Italy* is an exception; the much briefer text of the Christmas story of 1846, *The Cricket on the Hearth*, for example, had fourteen illustrations by five different artists (including John Leech and Edwin Landseer), as did its successor, *The Battle of Life*.[22] And yet in *Pictures from Italy*, a book whose title and genre both seem to demand a visual complement, we have only four small-scale woodcuts by Samuel Palmer, one at the beginning and at the end, and two more, of the Colosseum (Fig. 1) and 'Pompeii: The Street of the Tombs', poked rather furtively in the text. Even where the text seems to cry out for illustration and Dickens gives explicit visual cues — as in the opening 'The Reader's Passport' (Fig. 2) and the chapter called 'A Rapid Diorama' — there is no matching response from the artist and later

---

[20] On Dickens and Shakespeare, see V.L. Gager, *Shakespeare and Dickens: the Dynamics of Influence* (Cambridge, 1996).

[21] There is a considerable literature on Dickens and illustration. See, in particular, J. Cohen, *Dickens and his Original Illustrators* (Ohio, 1988), and M. Steig, *Dickens and Phiz* (Indiana, 1978). Also J.H. Miller, *Illustration* (London, 1992), 96–111. Praz, *The Hero in Eclipse* (above, n. 15) discusses Dickens's work in relation to genre painting and Biedermeier art.

[22] Charles Dickens, *The Christmas Books* (ed. M. Slater) (Harmondsworth, 1971).

FIG. 1. Samuel Palmer, *The Colosseum*, from *Pictures from Italy*, 1846. *(Reproduced by kind permission of The Dickens House)*

editors have sometimes felt it necessary to supplement the original woodcuts with other work by Palmer or by other artists.[23] In Dickens's own lifetime, the work was re-published with extra illustrations by Marcus Stone (Fig. 3), now best known as the illustrator of *Our Mutual Friend*. Yet Stone's rather grim work sits oddly both with Palmer's original work and the exuberance and pleasure in Italy of Dickens's writing.

     If there were no illustration at all to the book, we could point to the paradox of the title and compliment Dickens on his sophisticated highlighting of the difficulty of the passage from text to image, by creating a text called *Pictures* with no pictures in it. Dickens, though, is clearly not consciously or deliberately pointing the gap between the text and its pictures, or making an ironic point at the artist's (or Art's) expense. We know that he wanted the book to be illustrated, and that he imagined something akin to the illustrations to his old friend Samuel Rogers's *Italy* (a copy of which he lent to Samuel Palmer)[24] or

---

[23] Charles Dickens, *Pictures from Italy* (ed. D. Paroissen) (London, 1973) includes watercolours by James Holland, William Callow, J.D. Harding and David Roberts, as well as Palmer himself.
[24] Tillotson, *Letters of Charles Dickens* (above, n. 1), 546.

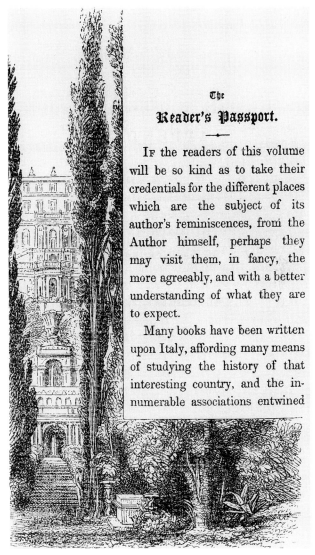

The

Reader's Passport.

IF the readers of this volume will be so kind as to take their credentials for the different places which are the subject of its author's reminiscences, from the Author himself, perhaps they may visit them, in fancy, the more agreeably, and with a better understanding of what they are to expect.

Many books have been written upon Italy, affording many means of studying the history of that interesting country, and the innumerable associations entwined

FIG. 2. Samuel Palmer, *The Villa D'Este at Tivoli from the Cypress Avenue*, from *Pictures from Italy*, 1846. *(Reproduced by kind permission of The Dickens House)*

indeed his own Christmas books (Fig. 4). Dickens's original intention was for his friend Clarkson Stanfield to illustrate *Pictures from Italy* with a dozen or so illustrations, but Stanfield found some of Dickens's remarks on the papacy offensive, and withdrew.[25] It was at this point, at short notice, that Palmer was approached. It was an interesting choice, for Palmer was of course the most important follower of William Blake, the great visionary radical of an earlier

---

[25] Tillotson, *Letters of Charles Dickens* (above, n. 1), 517n.

FIG. 3. Marcus Stone, *In the Catacombs*, from *Pictures from Italy*, Library Edition, 1862.
(Reproduced by kind permission of The Dickens House)

literary generation, and here, if ever, was an opportunity for literary greatness to touch hands through art across the generations.[26] But it was not to be, and Palmer's work with Dickens remains one of those great non-encounters of literary history, like Thomas Hardy's later encounter with Dickens in a coffee-

---

[26] See F.R. Leavis and Q.D. Leavis, *Dickens the Novelist* (Harmondsworth, 1972), 282–359.

house, when Hardy was too shy to speak and the elder novelist fussed over his change.[27]

FIG. 4. Clarkson Stanfield, *Peace*, from *The Battle of Life*, 1846. *(Reproduced by kind permission of The Dickens House)*

It is, of course, unfair to be too critical of Palmer. He was obliged to work at speed in a medium (wood-engraving) to which he was unaccustomed and which gave a result 'not of a kind to which the artist could look back with much

---

[27] P. Ackroyd, *Dickens* (London, 1990), 1,022–3.

satisfaction'.[28] But Palmer's comparative failure does give us a sense of the challenge that Dickens's work presents to any visual complement or translation. For it is hard to imagine any set of illustrations adequate to the demands of Dickens's extraordinarily mobile and evocative prose, which simultaneously seems to cry out for forms of visual response and illustration but at the same time to defy their possibility. Stephen Bann has recently argued that Dickens's work needs to be seen as part of 'a radical mutation in the act of seeing' in the nineteenth century, which he links to the development of optical devices, such as the Phenakistiscope and the Stereoscope, that anticipated and in many way pre-empted the invention of photography.[29] But it is to film, more than photography, that we should look for a good visual analogue to Dickens's work. Since Eisenstein's celebrated discussion in *Film Form*, which argues that Dickens's work anticipates cinema in important ways, the close relationship between Dickens's writing and film narrative has been clear.[30] His use of montage, cross-cutting, parallel plotting and the mixing of different genres, all have direct influence on early film-makers, most notably D.W. Griffiths and Eisenstein himself. *Pictures from Italy* contains many proto-filmic elements — there is the restless mobility of the camera eye, the metonymic selection of significant details, the rapid cutting and montage that characterize film grammar and narrative. Perhaps more than any other of Dickens's books, even more than *A Tale of Two Cities* or *Oliver Twist*, this is a cinematic text. And, in the important chapter 'A Rapid Diorama', it explicitly evokes one of cinema's most important precursors.[31]

And yet, unsurprisingly enough, *Pictures from Italy* is also one of the very few books by Dickens not to have been filmed. And to film it would be a quixotic affair, as it lacks even the elementary requirements of narrative, characterization and plot. So we have the paradoxical situation of a book which seems to demand a new relationship of word and image, and to prefigure later technical and conceptual developments in visual understanding, and yet lacks in the most radical way adequate contemporary or later visual reinterpretation by painters, illustrators or film-makers. In a way, of course, this does not matter: we are not short of pictures of Italy, in cinema or the visual arts. But its effect on

---

[28] R. Lister, *Samuel Palmer and his Etchings* (London, 1969), 122. See also D. Paroissen, '*Pictures from Italy* and its original illustrators', *Dickensian* 67 (1971), 87–90, and Tillotson, *Letters of Charles Dickens* (above, n. 1), 521.

[29] S. Bann, 'Visuality codes the text: Charles Dickens's *Pictures from Italy*', in J.B. Bullen (ed.), *Writing and Victorianism* (London, 1997), 204. See also J. Crary, *Techniques of the Observer: on Vision and Modernity in the Nineteenth Century* (London, 1990).

[30] S. Eisenstein, *Film Form: Essays in Film Theory* (ed. J. Leyda) (New York, 1949). See also G. Petrie, 'Dickens, Godard, and the film today', *Yale Review* 64 (1975), 185–201, and A.L. Zambrano, 'Charles Dickens and Sergei Eisenstein: the emergence of cinema', *Style* 9 (1975), 469–87. Both of these are reprinted in M. Hollington (ed.), *Charles Dickens, Critical Assessments* (Sussex, 1995), IV, 385–411.

[31] See R. Hyde, *Panoramania: the Art and Entertainment of the 'All-Embracing' View* (London, 1988).

this book is important; we can contrast, for example, the earlier *Sketches by Boz*, where Dickens's verbal sketches and clues are echoed and amplified by more than 40 engravings by Cruikshank, to create a much more ample dialogue of text and image. Hillis Miller has recently explored the complicated interactions of narrative and illustration in Dickens's fiction, which he argues lead to a strange uncanny doubling between the two, not a relation of mutual reinforcement, but 'an irreconcilable doubleness of text and picture'.[32] This doubleness, in which the illustrations intended to support a verbal text set up an alternative and competing order of representation, is also at work, in ghostly form, in *Pictures from Italy*. In the gap between the text and Palmer's illustrations, in the many differences between Palmer's and Stone's work, but above all in the pictures and films that do not exist but which are nevertheless constantly invoked by the text, we find an equally paradoxical situation, constituted by Dickens's most filmic and unfilmable text, his pictures without pictures.

Dickens's response to the great Renaissance and post-Renaissance art that he saw in Italy is equally double and complex. As one might expect, he is robust in his preferences and judgements. Although the Vatican, for example, has 'many most noble statues, and wonderful pictures ... there is a considerable amount of rubbish there too' (422). In Verona, there had been 'a gallery of pictures: so abominably bad, that it was quite delightful to see them mouldering away' (372). Dickens had little time for the pieties of guidebooks and connoisseurship: passing by 'a dismal sort of farmyard' on the way to the picture-gallery at Mantua, Dickens is waylaid by a flock of geese at which he remarks: 'I would take their opinion on a question of art, in preference to the discourses of Sir Joshua Reynolds' (375).[33] Elsewhere in Dickens's fiction, both classical civilization and connoisseurs of the fine arts do badly. In *Dombey and Son*, the first novel he wrote on his return to England, there is the dreadful Dr Blimber's academy: 'a great hothouse, in which there was a forcing apparatus incessantly at work ... mental green peas were produced at Christmas, and intellectual asparagus all the year round ... Every description of Greek and Latin vegetable was got off the driest of twigs, under the frostiest of circumstances'.[34] Blimber is aided in this by his daughter Cornelia, 'dry and sandy with working in the graves of dead languages. None of your live languages for Miss Blimber. They must be dead — stone dead — and then Miss Blimber dug them up, like a Ghoul', and by Mrs Blimber, who if she 'could have known Cicero, and been his friend and talked with him in his retirement at Tusculum (beau–ti–ful Tusculum) ... could have died contented'.[35] Meagles in *Little Dorrit* returns from his Italian tour with 'morsels of tessellated pavement from Herculaneum and Pompeii, like

[32] Miller, *Illustration* (above, n. 21), 96.
[33] For a more detailed discussion, see L. Ormond, 'Dickens and painting: the Old Masters', *Dickensian* 79 (1983), 131–51.
[34] Charles Dickens, *Dombey and Son* (Oxford, 1982), 119.
[35] Dickens, *Dombey and Son* (above, n. 34), 120, 124.

petrified minced veal' and has an entire picture-room 'devoted to a few of the regular sticky old Saints, with sinews like whipcord, hair like Neptune's, wrinkles like tattooing, and such coats of varnish that every holy personage served for a fly trap, and became what is now called in the vulgar tongue a Catch–em–alive O'.[36]

What is most striking about Dickens's writing on art in Italy itself is the contrast between his judgements on paintings and the way in which he himself writes. Describing the Correggio frescoes in the cathedral at Parma, he writes: 'Connoisseurs fall into raptures with them now; but such a labyrinth of arms and legs: such heaps of foreshortened limbs, entangled and involved and jumbled together: no operating surgeon, gone mad, could imagine in his wildest delirium' (353).[37] Michelangelo's *Last Judgement* in the Sistine Chapel lacks 'any general idea, or one pervading thought in harmony with the stupendous subject' (423). Giulio Romano's figures at Mantua are 'immensely large, and exaggerated to the utmost pitch of uncouthness; the colouring is harsh and disagreeable; and the whole effect more like (I should imagine) a violent rush of blood to the head of the spectator than any real picture set before him by the hand of an artist' (376). It is the 'exquisite grace and beauty' of Canova that Dickens admires, whereas Bernini and his followers create: 'the most detestable class of products in the wide world ... breezy maniacs; whose every fold of drapery is blown inside-out; whose smallest vein, or artery, is as big as an ordinary forefinger; whose hair is like a nest of lively snakes; and whose attitudes put all other extravagance to shame' (424). Dickens is here evoking not merely a more conservative aesthetic than that of his own novels, but one that seems overtly hostile to it. Dickens's writing is consistently interested in the grotesque,[38] and yet this is precisely what he rejects in painting; his plots at least until this point in his career have not been noted for their coherence, or his prose for a lack of exaggeration. Grotesqueness, lack of unity, incoherence, confusion, lack of correspondence to life, extravagance, fancifulness, exaggeration: these are the charges that Dickens made against Bernini and Correggio, and that his detractors have always made against him.

But it was, as always for Dickens, not art, but the life of the streets that interested him most, and he had timed his arrival just as street life was at its height, and the Rome carnival became his most central experience of the city. He had already encountered a rather sad carnival at Siena whose 'secret lay in a score or two of melancholy people walking up and down the principal street in common toy-shop masks, and being more melancholy, if possible, than the same sort of people in England' (391) and an even sadder one at Acquapendente 'consisting of one man dressed and masked as a woman, and one woman dressed

---

[36] Dickens, *Little Dorrit* (above, n. 10), 163.

[37] On this passage, see J. Schad, 'Dickens's cryptic church', in J. Schad (ed.), *Dickens Refigured* (Manchester, 1996), 5–21, and Bann, 'Visuality codes the text' (above, n. 29), 207.

[38] Hollington, *Dickens and the Grotesque* (above, n. 17).

and masked as a man, walking ankle deep, through the muddy streets, in a very melancholy manner' (394). The Roman carnival at first seemed likely to disappoint as well; he had glimpsed the end of the maskings from his hotel window on his arrival and it had seemed mere 'muddy foolings' to him, but the Monday dawned brighter and after a procession down the Corso, Dickens and family found themselves in the middle of a carnival battle royal:

> anything so gay, so bright, and lively as the whole scene there, it would be difficult to imagine ... The buildings seemed to have been literally turned inside out and to have all their gaiety towards the highway. Shop-fronts were taken down, and the windows filled with company, like boxes at a shining theatre; doors were carried off their hinges, and long tapestried groves, hung with garlands of flowers and evergreens, displayed within; ... and in every nook and corner, from the pavement to the chimney-tops, where women's eyes could glisten, there they danced, and laughed, and sparkled, like the light in water (403–4).

The coaches are driven by men 'with enormous double faces' or dressed as women. Women, too, break the rules of decorum and propriety 'at this time of general license', 'free, good-humoured, gallant figures' with 'laughing faces' (404). On foot there are:

> maskers ... in fantastic exaggerations of court-dresses ... and always transported with an ecstacy of love, on the discovery of any particularly old lady at a window; long strings of Polcinelli, laying about them with blown bladders at the ends of sticks; a waggon full of madmen, screaming and tearing to the life ... gipsy-women ... a man-monkey on a pole, surrounded by strange animals with pigs' faces, and lions' tails ... carriages on carriages, dresses on dresses, colours on colours, crowds upon crowds, without end ... an abandonment so perfect, so contagious, so irresistible, that the steadiest foreigner fights up to his middle in flowers and sugar-plums, like the wildest Roman of them all (405).

Dickens adored this carnival, and not I think by chance. In recent years, following the work of the great Russian critic, Mikhail Bakhtin, literary critics have discovered in carnivals a rich popular repertoire of symbolic action, transformations and pleasures which exist within the most wide array of societies and cultures, not just in carnival proper — as in Rome — but in many other forms of cultural practice including literature.[39]

How carnival works, as is clear in Dickens's account of the Rome carnival, is as a form of temporary licensed suspension and reversal of order, when the low is made high and the high low, a time when, albeit briefly, the world can be

---

[39] M. Bakhtin, *Rabelais and his World* (Indiana, 1984).

turned upside down. There are particular forms of carnival language and behaviour, including profanities, oaths and, above all, parodies of dignified and serious forms of speech and writing; there are also carnival rituals, games and performances; the body in particular is inverted, and the genitals and anus privileged over the dignified and polite upper body. Dress and behaviour are taken to extremes, to excessive, hyperbolic and transgressive states, with men dressed as women or as animals, as the very old or the very young.[40] The language of carnival is characterized by the bringing together of contradictory things in oxymoronic and parodic verbal play and absurdity. All of these things exploit the way in which symbolic ordering and hierarchies within human culture can be reversed, parodied and turned upside down. And of course what goes with this is an endless overflowing of libidinal energy — an abundance, fertility and excess of erotic play and feasting. Carnival creates a world, capable of uniting the most apparently contradictory things, spilling over boundaries and inverting hierarchies, grotesque, comical, absurd. We see all this in the streets of Rome in 1845. The carnival streets become theatres, the insides of houses are turned outwards; the dignities of court dress, grotesquely exaggerated, walk the streets in absurd form; passion is parodic, a matter of age not youth; the boundaries and distinctions of human and animal, rich and poor, high and low, youth and age, self and other, affection and aggression temporarily shudder and quake. Men are transformed into those most carnivalesque and strangely human of creatures, pigs and monkeys. Inside becomes outside; authentic behaviour becomes absurd theatricality. Bourgeois propriety and restraint yield to the contagious abandonment of carnival spirit.

It is striking how close the linguistic forms that we have already seen in Dickens's descriptions of Italy — the love of the hyperbolic, the grotesque, the pantomimic and paradoxical — are also the dominant symbolic forms of carnival. For in Dickens's writing, too, both fictional and non-fictional, we find the world, albeit temporarily, turned upside down, yielding to the transforming energies of symbolic inversion, becoming a world of grotesquerie and parody, of hyperbolic and absurd inventiveness, of the creation and discovery of contradictory and paradoxical things. Dickens perhaps of all English novelists is the one closest to carnival and carnival spirit in his writing and much of its ambiguous transformative energy finds a home in his pages. Although in England, in this very decade, Bartholomew Fair, which had provided a veritable thesaurus of carnival and carnivalesque themes and matter for Ben Jonson and later writers, was being actively suppressed, carnival is a robust thing.[41] Dickens was profoundly in love with popular festivity and celebration, with the circuses and theatres, where carnival fragments, tropes and figures lived on, exerting their

---

[40] P. Stallybrass and A. White, *The Politics and Poetics of Transgression* (London, 1986).

[41] On the suppression of Bartholomew Fair, see P. Schlicke, *Dickens and Popular Entertainment* (London, 1985); Stallybrass and White, *Politics and Poetics of Transgression* (above, n. 40).

powerful discomfiting sway over the orthodoxies and pieties of nineteenth-century industrial England. In Dickens's work, fragments of the carnival appear all over the place. Little Nell travels with a strolling Punch and Judy and meets dwarfs, giants and other travelling show people; Nicholas Nickleby journeys with the remarkably carnivalesque theatrical troupe of Vincent Crummles.[42] Against the constraints and misery of Mr Gradgrind's utilitarianism and Bounderby's factory discipline, Mr Sleary's circus in *Hard Times* is the sole domain of freedom, transgression, bodily expression and pleasure in Coketown.

Dickens had already reached for metaphors and analogies from carnival and its close companions, circus, pantomime and theatre, in his Italian travels: his postilion is like a figure from Astley's circus in 'ludicrously disproportionate' jackboots (303). At Modena, he witnesses the arrival of a circus: 'six or eight Roman chariots, each with a beautiful lady in extremely short petticoats, and unnaturally pink tights, erect within, shedding becoming looks upon the crowd ... which gave me quite a new idea of the Ancient Romans and Britons' (355). On the boat from Genoa to Nice he had struck up a friendship with 'one of the best friars in the world' who first fasts, then eats 'prodigiously, drinking deep of the wine, smoking cigars, taking snuff' but then, from 'laughing lustily from pure good humour', is transformed in a religious procession into a figure of 'imperturbable serenity ... without the smallest consideration of bread and meat, wine, snuff, or cigars' (345–7), a walking oxymoron, a figure off the pages of Rabelais who found his way straight into Dickens's heart.

The carnival is notoriously likely to spill over its boundaries, and although there were clear restraints upon it on the streets of Rome (the soldiers gallop alongside the carnival procession, and any carriage stepping out of line was escorted back to the beginning) in Dickens's writing, carnival knows no such restraint, constantly spilling over metaphorical borders it did not transgress in practice. *Pictures from Italy* is irresistibly drawn to seeing the theatrical and carnivalesque in places where they do not properly belong. Although 'nothing can exaggerate' the beauty of the Piazza in front of Saint Peter's or the interior's 'expansive majesty and glory', the decorations for a festival in the Church itself are 'like one of the opening scenes in a very lavish pantomime'. Behind the altar, a large space 'was filled up with boxes, shaped like those of the Italian opera in England, but ... much more gaily'; the pope in his chair in the middle of it is 'like a stupendous Bonbon'; the Swiss guard are 'like theatrical supernumeraries' from the low London theatres (396–400). Joseph and Mary in the Church of the Aracoeli take a similar tumble: they are 'two delectable figures ... such as you would see at any English fair' (411). The Easter Week ceremonies are like a 'droll and tawdry' Guy Fawkes Day (401) and watching the pope take part in them, two cardinals smile to each other 'as if the thing were a great farce'

---

[42] J. Bowen, 'Performing business, training ghosts: transcoding *Nickleby*', *ELH: English Literary History* 63 (1996), 153–75.

(432). The whole of Rome, from its highest and most dignified pontiff downwards, is subject to the liberating and absurd inversions of carnival ritual and carnivalesque writing.

III

This, then, is one story of *Pictures from Italy* and Dickens's residence in Rome — of Dickens the tourist, finding in the Roman carnival analogies for his own popular and celebratory art, and in the great art and high religious dignity another occasion for carnival laughter. But the letters that he wrote over this same period, some of which had to wait for well over a century before they were published, tell another, and quite different, story of his time in this city. Not of free, frank, public festivity, of happy licence and pleasure, but of strange nocturnal meetings, curious spasms, sexual jealousy and suffering, a story which is also a titanic struggle between good and evil, between the novelist and a 'Phantom'. This sounds rather a melodramatic way of putting it, but they are Dickens's terms. For the majority of Dickens's surviving letters from Rome are little about the city and much about Augusta de la Rue. Dickens had met the de la Rues, Emile and Augusta, a prosperous Swiss banker and his wife, early in his stay in Italy and they had rapidly become close friends. Augusta was troubled, however, by a nervous disorder characterized by convulsions, headaches, insomnia and a facial tic. Dickens had been acquainted with a number of celebrated mesmerists in London, including such serious practitioners as John Elliotson, a professor of medicine at London University, and so the untrained but charismatic novelist decided to treat Augusta de la Rue with the two leading mesmeric techniques — mesmeric sleep to settle the patient, and then mesmeric trance to explore fantasies, dreams and symptoms.[43] Dickens, whose later readings of his work transfixed huge audiences, was, unsurprisingly, an extremely successful hypnotist, and within a short space of time he and his patient were in a relationship of quite unprecedented intimacy and mutual dependency. We have one quite detailed account of a mesmeric session, which Dickens sent to Emile de la Rue. Dickens is speaking first:

> 'Well! where are you today? On the Hillside as usual?' — 'Yes' —
> 'Quite alone?' — 'No.' — 'Are there many people there?' — 'Yes.
> A good many.' — 'Men, or women?' — 'Both' ... Suddenly, she
> cried out, in great agitation. 'Here's my brother! Here's my
> brother!' — and she breathed very quickly, and her figure became
> stiff ... 'What Brother? The Brother I know?' 'No no. Not the

---

[43] The fullest discussion of this episode is in F. Kaplan, *Dickens and Mesmerism: the Hidden Springs of Fiction* (Princeton, 1975). There is an interesting fictional treatment of Dickens and mesmerism in P. Carey, *Jack Maggs* (London, 1997).

Brother you know. Another.' — 'What is his name?' — 'Charles. Oh how sad he is!'[44]

The parallels with Sigmund Freud's work of 50 years or so later are too close not to be drawn. Freud too, in his early cases, had used hypnotism to treat the intelligent and cosmopolitan women who people the *Studies on Hysteria*.[45] They too had nervous tics, bodily symptoms and inexplicable nervous disorders. Freud and his co-author Breuer also found themselves getting into sexual depths which they could not easily fathom. We cannot carry the parallels too far, as we lack detailed knowledge of what went on in those strange sessions in which Dickens magnetized Augusta de la Rue 'under olive trees, sometimes in vineyards, sometimes in the travelling carriage, sometimes at wayside taverns'.[46] We will never know what haunted her — the detailed case-notes her husband took are lost, as perhaps are other of Dickens's letters, which may have revealed more exactly what went on in those strange prefigurative exchanges, and how responsible or wild a mesmerist he was on his holiday from fiction.[47] Nor will we ever know how, if at all, Dickens linked the strange carnival maskings he lived with in those early days in Rome, and the daily epistolary reports on the hysterical terrified woman, stalked by an imaginary phantom, whom he was trying to help. But it is worth remembering how, as White has written in one of the most fascinating analyses of Freud's early cases, 'carnival debris spills out of the terrified Viennese women in Freud's *Studies in Hysteria*' and 'broken fragments of carnival glide through the discourse of the hysteric'.[48] On Dickens's first Tuesday in Rome, he awoke in the middle of the night, thinking of his patient, haunted by fears, feeling inexplicable anxiety, in 'a state of indescribable horror and emotion'.[49] It was the last day of carnival.

Rome itself, as well as Dickens's private life, also had another, disturbing and haunting, face. Dickens was concerned throughout his life with what we can call a discourse of spirit, fascinated by and drawn to metaphors and narratives to do with haunting, ghosts and spirits. They are there in the interpolated tales of *Pickwick Papers*, in the extraordinary haunting of Bill Sikes by the ghosts of Nancy's eyes in *Oliver Twist*, in the many uncanny repetitions of *Barnaby Rudge* and, perhaps most of all, in the obsessive concern with all those who tread the boundaries of life and death in *The Old Curiosity Shop*. Crossing the Campagna,

---

[44] Tillotson, *Letters of Charles Dickens* (above, n. 1), 247–9.

[45] S. Freud and J. Breuer, *Studies in Hysteria* (Harmondsworth, 1974).

[46] Charles Dickens, *Nonesuch Letters* (ed. W. Dexter) (London, 1938), III, 752.

[47] There is a strange, little-known, Dickens story of 1852, '*To be Read at Dusk*', written as an occasional piece for *The Keepsake* (edited by a certain Miss Power), which seems to use material from the mesmerism sessions. It is most easily found in the Oxford Illustrated Edition of *The Uncommercial Traveller and Reprinted Pieces* (London, 1958), 622–34. See M. Slater, *Dickens and Women* (London, 1983) 124–5.

[48] Stallybrass and White, *Politics and Poetics of Transgression* (above, n. 40).

[49] Tillotson, *Letters of Charles Dickens* (above, n. 1), 264.

then still malarial, it is for Dickens 'a world of terrible and gloom', 'the aptest and fittest burial ground for the Dead City' (395) — Rome. Rome itself is constantly compared to a world of ghosts and the living dead. It is conventional enough to call the Colosseum 'the ghost of old Rome' (397). But it is a much more profound metaphor for Dickens who so often thinks of human thought and imagination, even human life itself, as a ghostly business. Venice is 'a ghostly city' (363) inhabited by 'a host of spectres' (368). The Fort at Genoa is thought to be haunted, and Dickens writes 'my memory will haunt it, many nights, in time to come' (345). There is a theatre in the Farnese Palace at Parma where 'if ever Ghosts act plays, they act them on this ghostly stage' (354). Ferrara, where Dickens visits Ariosto's home and Tasso's prison, is at half an hour before sunrise 'as picturesque as it seemed unreal and spectral' (360), like a 'city of the dead without one solitary survivor' (360). Between Bologna and Ferrara, in a strange and uncanny threshold scene, Dickens is suddenly struck by 'the perfect familiarity' of a landscape he had never seen before: 'if I had been murdered there, in some former life, I could not have seemed to remember the place more thoroughly, or with a more emphatic chilling of the blood' (359). In that most uncanny of experiences, the unfamiliar seems suddenly and strangely familiar, and fatal.[50] Carnival, as we have seen, crosses and questions symbolic boundaries, but so too do ghosts, and ghosts too inhabit the carnival. Perhaps the most touching of all moments in Dickens's depiction of the carnival is the mock mourning for its end, in which all the participants light little candles and attempt to snuff out everyone else's:

> As the bright hangings and dresses are all fading into one dull, heavy, uniform colour in the decline of the day, lights begin flashing, here and there: in the windows, on the house-tops, in the balconies, in the carriages, in the hands of the foot-passengers: little by little: gradually, gradually: more and more: until the whole long street is one great glare and blaze of fire. Then, everybody present has but one engrossing object; that is, to extinguish other people's candles, and to keep his own alight; and everybody: man, woman, or child, gentleman or lady, prince or peasant, native or foreigner: yells and screams, and roars incessantly, as a taunt to the subdued, 'Senza Moccolo, Senza Moccolo!' (without a light! Without a light!) until nothing is heard but a gigantic chorus of those two words, mingled with peals of laughter ... The game of the Moccoletti ... is supposed by some to be a ceremony of burlesque mourning for the death of the Carnival (406–8).

---

[50] 'The "Uncanny"', in S. Freud, *Art and Literature. Jensen's Gradiva, Leonardo da Vinci and Other Works* (ed. A. Dickson) (Harmondsworth, 1985), 335–76. But ghosts and the uncanny, as always with Dickens, can also appear in more comic form, as in his description of the archetypal English tourist, Mr Davis, who appears 'slowly emerging out of some sepulchre or other, like a peaceful Ghoul, saying "Here I am!"', whereupon, 'Mrs Davies invariably replied, "You'll be buried alive in a foreign country, Davis. And it's no use trying to prevent you!"' (409).

Rome, then, is for Dickens a matter of carnival and ghosts, and they are not perhaps such different things. Dickens's favourite sight in Rome, its 'greatest sensation', was the Colosseum, 'the most impressive, the most stately, the most solemn, grand majestic, mournful sight, conceivable' such as 'no language can describe' (397). The final image of Rome, as Dickens departs for Naples and Pompeii, is of a last view of this great ruin, viewed as so often for nineteenth-century travellers, by moonlight. 'The ghostly pillars in the Forum; the Triumphal Arches of Old Emperors; ... even these were dimmed, in their transcendent melancholy, by the dark ghost of its bloody holidays, erect and grim; haunting the old scene' (437). And then in a final gesture of departure, Dickens places a stone by a wooden cross at the scene of a murder in the Campagna. A final act of mourning for a Rome of ghosts and holidays, festive celebrations and uncanny dreams, of sublime monuments and unearthly maskings: carnival and haunting; pictures from Italy; spirits of Rome.

11

The Impact Of The Archaeology Of Rome On British Architects And Their Work *c.* 1750–1840

FRANK SALMON

For Professor Robert MacLeod

The Grand Tour exhibition held in London and Rome in 1996–7 and the academic conferences which accompanied it provided opportunities for historians to reassess the nature of cultural relations between different European countries and in particular, of course, between Italy and Britain. One area of debate concerned the question of whether 'The Grand Tour' can be defined satisfactorily as an educational institution for male aristocrats approaching or early into their majority. Such a circumscription not only discounts wealthy mature men (such as the thrice-travelled Charles Townley or the expatriate diplomat Sir William Hamilton), men who were responsible for establishing some of the closest cultural connections between Italy and Britain, it also overlooks the significance of travellers from altogether different constituencies, such as women, middle-class professionals, writers and established or student artists. The differing circumstances and objectives of such travellers meant that they perforce had different experiences: in other words there were in reality many different 'grand tours'. The 1996–7 exhibition rightly aimed for a 'complete overview' of this complex subject area and a wide range of objects of outstanding quality was assembled.[1] But there was one important group of travellers which scarcely featured: the diverse activities of the 50 or so British architects who visited Italy in the eighteenth century were represented visually only by two topographical sketches by Robert Adam and a cartoon of an

---

[1] N. Serota, in A. Wilton and I. Bignamini (eds), *Grand Tour: the Lure of Italy in the Eighteenth Century* (exhibition catalogue, Tate Gallery, London, 1996), 7.

expedition to Tivoli by the younger George Dance.[2] Whilst it must be acknowledged that there are practical and perceptual difficulties involved in the display of architectural exhibits, it is none the less ironic that architecture should not be regarded as integral with the other cultural manifestations of Anglo-Italian travel, not least because buildings framed the display of paintings and statues with which many travellers returned and represented focal points in the Arcadian landscapes they sought to recreate at home.[3]

A second respect in which traditional assumptions about the Grand Tour have come under debate concerns its definition as a phenomenon particular to the eighteenth century. The parameters of the 1996–7 exhibition were set so as to include the seventeenth century as a sort of 'flash-back', and to take the Napoleonic invasion of the Italian peninsula in 1796 as a terminal date, thus aiming to create a 'self-contained topic which is susceptible of coherent exposition'.[4] The level of scholarly interest in pre-eighteenth-century Anglo-European relations may be gauged from the recent reissue of John Stoye's classic 1952 study of seventeenth-century travellers, as well as from ongoing research.[5] But it is the notion of 1796 as a significant terminal date which is of particular concern in the present paper.[6] For decades prior to its recent publication, Sir Brinsley Ford's remarkable archive of the British and Irish who visited Italy between 1701 and 1800 provided a tremendous resource for scholars seeking to establish such travel as a central element of eighteenth-century culture.[7] The absence of any parallel resource for the two or three decades after 1815, however, should not preclude consideration of the respects in which the British resumed eighteenth-century travel traditions after the Napoleonic era. It may be true that in the early nineteenth century a far larger number of middle-

---

[2] Wilton and Bignamini, *Grand Tour* (above, n. 1), 121, 222–3. Dance's measured drawings of the circular temple at Tivoli are in Sir John Soane's Museum, London, Dance Slider 3, Set 1, nos. 1–6. For Giovanni Stern's collaboration with Dance, Soane's copies of Dance's drawings and something of their importance in the history of English neo-classical architecture see P. du Prey, *John Soane: the Making of an Architect* (Chicago, 1982), 148–51.

[3] The description of how Lord Charlemont's Grand Tour resulted in the finest collection of paintings in Dublin, for example, might have been augmented by noting that it also led to the commission to William Chambers (whom Charlemont had surely met in Italy) to design the Casino at Marino, just outside Dublin, a key building in the history of European neo-classical taste (see Wilton and Bignamini, *Grand Tour* (above, n. 1), 61; J. Harris and M. Snodin (eds), *Sir William Chambers: Architect to George III* (New Haven and London, 1996), 35–9; and J. Ingamells, *A Dictionary of British and Irish Travellers in Italy 1701–1800* (New Haven and London, 1997), 198).

[4] Serota, in Wilton and Bignamini, *Grand Tour* (above, n. 1), 7.

[5] J. Stoye, *English Travellers Abroad 1604–1667: their Influence in English Society and Politics* (revised edition, New Haven and London, 1989). See also E. Chaney, *The Evolution of the Grand Tour: Anglo-Italian Cultural Relations since the Renaissance* (London, 1998).

[6] The use of the end of the eighteenth century as a terminal date for the Grand Tour was called into question by both John Brewer and Lawrence Klein during 'Going Places: Travel, Education and Identity in Eighteenth-Century Europe', the exhibition-related conference held at the Tate Gallery, London, on 6 December 1996, but discussion did not develop on that occasion.

[7] See now Ingamells, *Dictionary* (above, n. 3).

class men and women travelled to Italy, but a significant proportion of the travellers, perhaps the majority in fact, continued to be the young sons of the wealthy and aristocratic, completing their educations.[8] Just as in the second half of the eighteenth century, these young men included most of those who were to become leading statesmen including, as Trevelyan pointed out in 1919, the 'Italian Triumvirate' of Lord John Russell, Viscount Palmerston and William Ewart Gladstone.[9] We have perhaps lost sight of what was so obvious to an historian connected, as Trevelyan was, with the nineteenth century, namely that Italy continued to exert profound cultural influence over Britain until late in the Victorian age.[10] Moreover, until the advent of the railways in the 1840s, travel was still accomplished by private or public carriage in the manner of the previous century, or in the case of students often on foot.[11] For evidence of the re-establishment of eighteenth-century traditions we might also look to the travel literature produced as a direct result of experience in Italy. Upwards of 40 books of travel diaries, letters and guides dealing with Italy were published in English in the first decade after 1815.[12] The people who wrote these books were doing much the same things as their eighteenth-century counterparts: visiting the museums of antiquities and modern art, restored to their pre-Napoleonic state under the terms of the Congress of Vienna; acquiring art-works; studying foreign languages and manners; attending the salons and local festivals; behaving outlandishly; writing poems, and so forth. Their travel accounts provide evidence of continuities easily overlooked if we concentrate too exclusively on formal differences between the works of eighteenth- and nineteenth-century professional artists and writers, differences which in any case depend to an extent on an assumption of stylistic homogeneity in the eighteenth century.[13]

Whether or not one accepts the argument that the Grand Tour as a whole continued in the early nineteenth century, it can hardly be denied that, from the point of view of architectural students, the 1796 Napoleonic invasion of Italy merely indicates the beginning of a kind of double hiatus. Yes, there was a

---

[8] The only book-length study about the British in Italy in the early nineteenth century is C. Brand, *Italy and the English Romantics: the Italianate Fashion in Early Nineteenth-Century England* (Cambridge, 1957), in which see especially pp. ix, 9, 213–14.

[9] G.M. Trevelyan, 'Englishmen and Italians: some aspects of their relations past and present', *Proceedings of The British Academy* (1919–20), 104.

[10] See D. Cannadine, *G.M. Trevelyan: a Life in History* (London, 1993), 81.

[11] The architect George Ledwell Taylor first travelled to Italy in 1817–19, revisiting it in the 1850s and 1860s. In his autobiography he contrasted travel in post-Napoleonic Italy with the ease of travel after the introduction of railways, causing visitors to confine themselves to the cities and overlook the intermediate towns. In 1817–19 he calculated that he had covered 4,000 miles on foot, the same means by which James 'Athenian' Stuart, Robert Mylne and no doubt many more fine arts students had made much of their journeys in the eighteenth century (G.L. Taylor, *The Autobiography of an Octogenarian Architect*, 2 vols (London, 1870–2), I, iii, iv, and II, 267).

[12] See R. Pine-Coffin, *Bibliography of British and American Travel in Italy to 1860* (Florence, 1974).

[13] See C. de Seta, in Wilton and Bignamini, *Grand Tour* (above, n. 1), 18.

period of five years between 1797 and the Treaty of Amiens in 1802 when no British architects made the journey to Italy: but five of them were back between 1802 and the Battle of Trafalgar in 1805, doing much the same things as before. And yes, there was a period between Trafalgar and Waterloo when hardly any British architects travelled in the Mediterranean. But after 1815 they returned in great numbers. In fact, more British architects went to Rome in the two decades from 1815 to 1835 than in the entire eighteenth century, and in 1819 there were no fewer than twenty present in that one year.[14] This paper will outline the involvement of British architects in the archaeological research on ancient Roman buildings in the later eighteenth and early nineteenth centuries, the period when travel to Italy was virtually imperative for any ambitious British architectural student. It will then consider how their experience of the Roman monuments affected architectural design in Britain in the same years and suggest some contexts for the developments that occurred. It should be recalled, however, that archaeology only represented one aspect of what interested architectural students in Italy, and there is no room here for discussion of their involvements with the various Italian academies, their studies of modern Italian architecture and building technology, or their attempts to impress the potential patrons to whom the Grand Tour gave them a social access they would not have enjoyed in England. But architects' relations with the antique were, of course, a central factor both in their activities as students in Rome and in their design work as professionals once they returned to Britain. What I hope to show is that if we take the year 1796 as the endpoint of the Grand Tour we miss one of the most interesting episodes in the cultural linkage between Britain and the ancient Roman world. The early nineteenth-century British interest in the ancient *Greek* world is a well-known topos for historians: there have been at least eight substantial books on the subject since 1980.[15] There has been far less study of the way that the Romans were regarded in nineteenth-century Britain, although the exhibition 'Imagining Rome', held at Bristol City Art Gallery in 1996, represented a welcome reappraisal of the influence of Rome on Victorian painters.[16]

---

[14] See F. Salmon, 'Storming the Campo Vaccino: British architects and the antique buildings of Rome after Waterloo', *Architectural History* 38 (1995), 147.

[15] See R. Jenkyns, *The Victorians and Ancient Greece* (Oxford, 1980); F. Turner, *The Greek Heritage in Victorian Britain* (New Haven and London, 1981); F.-M. Tsigakou, *The Rediscovery of Greece* (London, 1981); T. Webb (ed.), *English Romantic Hellenism, 1700–1824* (Manchester, 1982); D. Constantine, *Early Greek Travellers and the Hellenic Ideal* (Cambridge, 1984); G. Clarke (ed.), *Rediscovering Hellenism: the Hellenic Inheritance and the English Imagination* (Cambridge, 1989); H. Angloumatis-Tsougarakis, *The Eve of the Greek Revival: British Travellers' Perception of Early Nineteenth-Century Greece* (London, 1990); I. Jenkins, *Archaeologists and Aesthetes in the Sculpture Galleries of the British Museum 1800–1939* (London, 1992). In addition, J. Mordaunt Crook's *The Greek Revival: Neo-Classical Attitudes in British Architecture 1760–1870* (London, 1972) was republished in 1995.

[16] M. Liversidge and C. Edwards (eds), *Imagining Rome — British Artists and Rome in the Nineteenth Century* (exhibition catalogue, Bristol City Museum and Art Gallery, 1996). See also

It has become a truism of English architectural historiography to say that archaeology represents one of the defining characteristics of the whole neo-classical idiom. What historians have meant by this is that the spirit of enquiry and personal verification so typical of Enlightenment thought led eighteenth-century students of ancient architecture to question the canonical authority of Renaissance architects, such as Palladio and Vignola, on matters of rule and proportion. The process is generally agreed to have commenced with Antoine Desgodetz, sent to Rome by Jean-Baptiste Colbert and the French Académie Royale d'Architecture to measure the surviving ancient buildings. He did this with considerable success, even making a few excavations, and publishing the results in *Les édifices antiques de Rome* in 1682. It might be expected that British architects would have continued in this vein in the eighteenth century, and to a certain extent they did. Between the summer of 1755 and September 1756, for example, Robert Adam set his team of assistants the task of measuring all the same buildings Desgodetz had measured. He proposed to publish a corrected version using red lines to show where Desgodetz had made an error — the hint of francophobia here perhaps reminding us that Adam was in Italy on the eve of the Seven Years War.[17] Nor was it was just the British who were eager to question the accuracy of Desgodetz's surveys. In 1760 Giambattista Piranesi wrote to his Scottish acquaintance, the architect Robert Mylne, by then settled in London, to say that he had taken to the Temple of Castor and Pollux 'diversi di questi Sig. Inglesi, e quivi col Desgodet alla mano ho mostrato Loro, che questo autore ha diversificato tutti gli ornamenti, e in consequenza ne ha altevate per lo più Le misure'.[18] Piranesi's study of the remains of this famous temple was made alongside that of the British architectural student George Dance the Younger, both men benefiting from the advantage of the scaffolding which had been erected around the columns by the Roman *Conservatori* who feared that collapse was imminent. The exceptional nature of this opportunity can be judged from Piranesi's comment to Mylne that it was 'una delle più rare occasioni'. Most architects, Italian and British alike it seems, had to conduct their surveys by leaning a ladder against a monument, mounting with a yard ruler in one hand (no doubt with considerable trepidation) and calling down the measurements to an assistant. This was precisely the method deployed by John Soane and Thomas Hardwick in the later 1770s and which Soane exhibited in graphic form to the students who attended his second lecture on architecture at the Royal Academy in 1819.[19]

The remeasuring of extant ancient buildings seems almost to have been an obsession for a number of later eighteenth-century British architects. But at the

---

R. Jenkyns, *Dignity and Decadence: Victorian Art and the Classical Inheritance* (London, 1991), and N. Vance, *The Victorians and Ancient Rome* (Oxford, 1997).

[17] J. Fleming, *Robert Adam and his Circle in Edinburgh and Rome* (London, 1962), 170.

[18] British Architectural Library (Royal Institute of British Architects), London, MyFam/4/55.

[19] See Salmon, 'Storming' (above, n. 14), fig. 2, 151 and n. 24, 170.

FIG. 1. Robert Adam or Charles-Louis Clérisseau, *View of the Temple of Venus and Rome and the Basilica of Maxentius from the Colosseum*, 1755–8. *(Courtesy of Sir John Clerk of Penicuik)*

same time, Britons such as Gavin Hamilton, Thomas Jenkins and Robert Fagan were busy obtaining licences from the Reverenda Camera Apostolica to excavate promising sites in search of Roman statuary. Their activities make a stark contrast with those of the 40 or so British architects who resided in Rome between 1750 and 1797. In my searches at the Archivio di Stato I have found only one application for a licence to make excavations from these men, an application made by Charles Cameron in 1768.[20] Cameron wanted permission to investigate the bath complex below the church of Santa Cecilia in Trastevere, as part of his project to revise *Fabbriche antiche,* Lord Burlington's mid-1730s publication of Palladio's drawings of the Roman baths. But although Cameron had the support of Jenkins, who endorsed the request, it was refused. At the so-called 'Baths of Titus', however, Cameron was able to fulfil some of his excavational ambitions: by passing through one of the vaulted substructures below the Baths of Trajan he was able to enter the room of Nero's Domus Aurea now famous for its central vault image of 'Achilles at Skyros', but unknown to Renaissance explorers and not properly represented in plan until Giuseppe Lugli published *The Classical Monuments of Rome and its Vicinity* in 1929. The room was full of earth, almost to the vault, so it was the fluted niche with its 'trophies of Musick' that the architect saw. In Cameron's own words, 'it was with great difficulty that I got into this room. I was obliged to cut a hole through the wall ... and to let myself down by a rope, and afterwards to creep through a hole in the

---

[20] Archivio di Stato, Roma, Camerale II, Antichità e Belle Arti, Busta 3, Fasc. 133 (Scavi: Roma 1756–68), transcribed and fully discussed in F. Salmon, 'Charles Cameron and Nero's Domus Aurea: una piccola esplorazione', *Architectural History* 36 (1993), 69–93.

FIG. 2. Willey Reveley, *View of the Temple of Venus and Rome and the Basilica of Maxentius from the Colosseum*, 1784–8. *(Courtesy of the Yale Center for British Art, Paul Mellon Collection)*

wall ... upon my hands and knees. It was nearly full of earth to the ceiling'.[21] Now that was real archaeology! But it was the exception rather than the rule among eighteenth-century British architects. The only other late eighteenth-century British architectural excavation known to me was a minor one made at the base of the Colosseum by Hardwick in 1777, the same year that he made drawings of the painted room discovered below ground at the Villa Negroni.[22] The high labour costs of mounting an excavation other than in the search for statues, for which some financial return might be expected, no doubt placed this method of studying antique Roman buildings beyond the often extremely limited means of most British architectural students.

The newly-discovered Roman cities of Herculaneum and Pompeii were a different matter again for the British. There are very few plans, perspectives or decorative details of these sites surviving from the hands of British eighteenth-century architects, largely because the Bourbon authorities in Naples denied them even supervised access to all but the most familiar parts. In the early nineteenth century Soane told the students of the Royal Academy that his own sketches of the Temple of Isis at Pompeii had had to be made in 1779 'by stealth by moonlight'.[23] For details on the design and colour of Roman ceiling and wall paintings it was far simpler to turn to a number of well-known published sources, such as Nicolas Ponce's *Description des bains de Titus* of 1786, immediately adopted by Joseph Bonomi as the source for his gallery at Packington Hall in Warwickshire.[24] Moreover, for grotesques, *rinceaux* and the other devices of neo-classical interior décor one could also turn to easily accessible Renaissance exemplars, such as the loggias of the Vatican or of the Villa Madama.

Now, if archaeology is to have any intrinsic purpose, I take it that it must aim to be scientific in its methodology and honest in the presentation of data. In the 1750s 'truth' was a clearly stated aim of the antiquarian Robert Wood in his investigations of the eastern Mediterranean Roman cities of Palmyra and Balbec, and of the architect James Stuart at Athens (although doubts have now been cast on their claims to accuracy of hundredths of an inch with 2,000-year-old

---

[21] C. Cameron, *The Baths of the Romans Explained and Illustrated with the Restorations of Palladio Corrected and Improved* (London, 1772), 54 n.

[22] Hardwick's drawings of his Colosseum excavation and of the Villa Negroni paintings are in the Royal Institute of British Architects Drawings Collection, London [hereafter RIBA DC] E3/40 and E3/27–28 respectively. See also T. Hardwick, 'Observations on the remains of the Amphitheatre of Flavius Vespasian at Rome, as it was in the year 1777', *Archaeologia* 7 (1785), 369–73, and H. Joyce, 'The ancient frescoes from the Villa Negroni and their influence in the eighteenth and nineteenth centuries', *The Art Bulletin* 65 (1983), 423–40.

[23] D. Watkin, *Sir John Soane: Enlightenment Thought and the Royal Academy Lectures* (Cambridge, 1996), 525.

[24] See J. Wilton-Ely, 'Pompeian and Etruscan tastes in the neo-classical country-house interior', in G. Jackson-Stops *et al.* (eds), *The Fashioning and Functioning of the British Country House* (Washington, 1989), 66–9. For a recent general study of antique sources for neo-classical interior décor see I. Bristow, *Architectural Colour in British Interiors 1615–1840* (New Haven and London, 1996), 78–91 and ch. 6.

masonry).[25] But Robert Adam's ostensibly similar publication of the *Ruins of the Palace of the Emperor Diocletian at Spalatro* in fact represents an altogether different approach, as the capricious frontispiece (with at least one element introduced to Split in Dalmatia from the site of Pola in Istria) immediately shows.[26] Some small excavations were made by Adam's party at Split, but only to assist in a conjectural restoration of the palace. Whilst happy to accept a reputation as a scrupulous archaeologist, Adam was really after novelties, such as the so-called 'Diocletian Capital' which he found at Split and used as a sort of trademark in some of his subsequent buildings, in the entrance hall at Osterley in 1767, for example. For him, Roman antiquity represented a source which he could mine at will. The way he came to look at the ancient ruins under the tutelage of Charles-Louis Clérisseau was picturesque, in the sense that he perceived them as he wished them to be, rather than as they actually were. This can be seen if we compare a view of the Temple of Venus and Rome and the Basilica of Maxentius drawn by Adam or Clérisseau (Fig. 1) with one by their near-contemporary, Willey Reveley (Fig. 2). Reveley, later to take on the scholarly editorship of the third volume of Stuart's and Revett's *Antiquities of Athens,* produced a straightforwardly topographical view, framed by the lower arcade of the Colosseum; the Adam/Clérisseau view simply ignored the inconvenient medieval intrusion of the *campanile* of Santa Francesca Romana, even though the higher vantage point on the west side of the amphitheatre ought to have made more of the tower visible.[27] This selective approach to sources underpinned Adam's subsequent design method and, because of its great commercial success, much other later eighteenth-century architectural and interior design. When Roman buildings were used as precedents in that period, as with the Arch of Constantine surmounted by a Pantheon dome in the south front of Adam's Kedleston, they were generally used eclectically and transformed well beyond their original context. The saloon behind the Kedleston south front, the plan form of which relates to Diocletian's Palace at Split as well as to the Pantheon, takes its recesses from the apse of the Temple of Venus and Rome and the coffers of its cupola from the adjacent Basilica of Maxentius (Fig. 3).[28] These rearranged fragments allude to antiquity in the same way as the

---

[25] E. Kaufman, 'Architecture and travel in the age of British eclecticism', in E. Blau and E. Kaufman (eds), *Architecture and its Image* (Montreal, 1989), 74.

[26] See I. Gordon Brown, *Monumental Reputation: Robert Adam and the Emperor's Palace* (Edinburgh, 1992).

[27] Fig. 1 is from an album in the collection of Sir John Clerk of Penicuik entitled 'Views of antiquity in and about Rome and other parts of Italy', no. 72, and was reproduced as an Adam drawing of 1756 by Fleming in *Adam* (above, n. 17), pl. 50. More recently it has been attributed to Clérisseau by his biographer, Thomas McCormick. The Reveley drawing is in the Yale Center for British Art, B1977.14.19455.

[28] The lozenge-shaped coffers of the Temple of Venus and Rome do not feature in Adam's 1760 initial scheme for the recesses of the saloon and were probably added at the time of the room's eventual completion in 1787–9 (see L. Harris, *Robert Adam and Kedleston* (The National Trust, 1987), 58–9).

selection of statues in the background of a Batoni portrait do, or in the same way that Members of Parliament in the eighteenth century liked to stud their speeches with quotations from Latin authors. British eighteenth-century patrons wanted an architecture which offered the veneer of ancient culture but also something new, or modern, and distinctively British. Of course there were buildings which made very literal rather than eclectic use of Roman buildings in the eighteenth century, such as William Chambers's Temple of the Sun at Kew (1761) and Henry Flitcroft's Temple of Apollo at Stourhead (1765), both closely based on the Temple of Venus at Balbec as published by Wood in 1757. But such literalism tended to be frowned upon in architectural discourse. The Royal Academy's first Professor of Architecture, Thomas Sandby, for example, said of Kedleston's domical sky-lighting that it had 'a noble effect but such rooms have too much the appearance of Roman temples about them'.[29]

We should bear Sandby's dislike of buildings that too closely resembled Roman temples in mind as we turn now to consider the British architects who visited Rome after 1815. They found it, of course, a much altered city. In just five years, from 1809 to 1814, the government of the occupying French had put into practice a dramatic programme of excavations and restorations, especially in the Forum area, where the Temples of Saturn and Vespasian had been cleared to their bases. Moreover, Giuseppe Valadier, the *Architetto Direttore* of the French Commissions, was busy publishing minutely detailed and measured engravings of the newly exposed parts in his periodic *Raccolta delle più insigni fabbriche di Roma antica*.[30] The British were eager to participate in these ongoing activities. In the Archivio di Stato I found sets of documents in which six British architects made eleven separate requests to erect scaffolding on six different monuments within just nine months in 1821–2.[31] All of these licences were granted, largely thanks to the support of Valadier, by then one of the government *Consiglieri* along with the *Commissario delle Antichità* Carlo Fea. A sketch of 1816 by John Goldicutt shows how such scaffolding functioned: a painter's cradle cantilevered from the cornice of a temple enabled the student to study the entire upper parts of the monument at eye-level, a great improvement on the nature of access possible in the eighteenth century.[32] One result of this was that architects became closely aware of the great sculptural richness of Roman architectural carving. Another was that, if they were so inclined, they could resume the eighteenth-century tradition of measuring the buildings. The most comprehensive response to this new situation came from George Ledwell Taylor and Edward Cresy, who

---

[29] See Watkin, *Soane* (above, n. 23), 49.

[30] See R. Ridley, *The Eagle and the Spade: Archaeology in Rome During the Napoleonic Era* (Cambridge, 1992).

[31] Archivio di Stato, Roma, Camerlengato I (1816–24), Antichità e Belle Arti, Busta 42, Fasc. 231, items 1 and 4; Busta 43, Fasc. 260, item 4, transcribed and fully discussed in Salmon, 'Storming' (above, n. 14), 146–75.

[32] RIBA DC, J6/230, reproduced in Salmon, 'Storming' (above, n. 14), fig. 5.

FIG. 3. Robert Adam, *The Saloon at Kedleston Hall*, 1760–89. *(Courtesy of The National Trust)*

in 1818 and 1819 proceeded to make detailed surveys of fifteen buildings in Rome (as well as the Temple of 'Vesta' at Tivoli and the Arch of Trajan at Ancona). In 1821–2 Taylor and Cresy published their great two-folio work *The Architectural Antiquities of Rome,* presenting actual state perspective views of the monuments and their newly-excavated parts, minute surveys in English feet and inches together with huge lithographic images showing their sculptural enrichment, and restorations based on all the available evidence. This work perhaps represents the single most comprehensive new archaeological survey of the major Roman monuments to have been published in any language since that of Desgodetz in 1682. The English architects were also particularly interested in the excavations of podia. This is significant, as it marks a realization that Roman temples in their original form could not have been perceived as columns protruding from the ground but must have been seen as magnificently elevated structures enjoying superb urban locations. Public buildings in general could now be conceptualized, as James Cockburn put it in 1827, 'not in a detached and isolated state, but as they form an essential part of a populous city'.[33] It should come as no surprise, therefore, to find that the imaginative restorations of the entire forum complex made by British architects, such as Charles Robert Cockerell and James Pennethorne, date from this period rather than from the later eighteenth century (Fig. 4).[34]

The idea of imaginative reconstructions of antique buildings or complexes based on detailed archaeological study was, of course, close to the spirit of the *envois* which the early nineteenth-century *pensionnaires* of the Académie de France à Rome were required to send back to Paris. One of the most celebrated of such *envois* was the 1825 restoration of the Baths of Caracalla by Guillaume-Abel Blouet.[35] Blouet was one of four or five intimate French friends in Rome of the English architectural student Thomas Leverton Donaldson, who later recorded how influential their approach to antiquity had been on him when producing the design for a 'Temple à la Victoire', for which he gained honorary election to the Accademia di San Luca in Rome in 1822. Donaldson in fact made explicit use in this design of an equally famous French project, Jean-Nicolas Huyot's 1811 restoration of the Temple of Fortune at Palestrina.[36] British architects were fulsome in their praise for what the French had achieved in the

---

[33] In T.L. Donaldson, *Pompeii, Illustrated with Picturesque Views,* 2 vols (London, 1827), I, 2.

[34] For one of Cockerell's Forum sketch restorations see Salmon, 'Storming' (above, n. 14), fig. 13; the final version seems to have been the one sold at Sotheby's on 30 April 1987, lot 561. For Pennethorne see G. Tyack, *Sir James Pennethorne and the Making of Victorian London* (Cambridge, 1992), fig. 7 (Fig. 4 here) and colour plate 1.

[35] Discussed and illustrated in P. Rossetto *et al., Roma antiqua — 'Envois' degli architetti francesi (1786–1901): grande edifici pubblici* (Rome, 1992), 234–49.

[36] RIBA DC W15/23 and OS 5/5/1–4. Engraved versions of some of these drawings were later published by Donaldson, together with an account in French of their genesis, as *Temple à la Victoire* (Paris, 1876). Two of the engraved plates are reproduced in F. Salmon, 'British architects, Italian fine arts academies and the foundation of the RIBA, 1816–43', *Architectural History* 39 (1996), figs 4 and 7. I also reproduce Donaldson's later copy of Huyot's Palestrina plan (fig. 6).

FIG. 4. James Pennethorne, *Drawn Restoration of the Forum Romanum*, 1825. Private collection.

field of Roman archaeology, George Basevi actually going as far in 1816 as to regret the cessation of French rule: 'What a deal of good the French did in that respect. Had they but held Italy for two or three years more the antiquarians would have no need to dispute on any of the remains here'.[37] The British also shared the French interest in the debate about the role of polychromatic colouring in ancient architecture. The interest in colour extended to the ancient treatment of interiors, and here the British were no doubt partly inspired by the great clearances undertaken at Pompeii during the Napoleonic period and the improved degree of access they received to the site during the decade following 1815. There are several hundred drawings of Pompeii surviving from the early nineteenth-century travels of Goldicutt, Joseph Woods, Richard Sharp, Donaldson, Henry Parke and Ambrose Poynter.[38] British studies there bore fruit with Sir William Gell's and John Peter Gandy's topographical *Pompeiana,* published 1817–19, and Donaldson's *Pompeii* (1827), recognized as an important work of archaeological scholarship by Franz Christian Gau when producing the third and fourth volumes of François Mazois's *Les ruines de Pompéi,* the standard early nineteenth-century work on the ancient city.[39] Moreover, in 1825 Goldicutt published some of his drawings as *Specimens of Ancient Decorations from Pompeii,* in which he commented that the Romans' 'arrangements of colour appear to have been as happy as their combination of forms, and may, I think, be as useful to the Artist or Amateur who may study them'.[40]

Having given some consideration to the activities of British architectural students in Rome after 1815 and into the 1820s, what remains to be asked is whether or not their studies had any subsequent effect on the character of British architecture itself. I think that they certainly did, and in a way hitherto little recognized, perhaps because it undermines the sequential model many historians have adopted for explaining the major ideological developments in early nineteenth-century British architecture. According to the traditional view, the ending of Italian cultural hegemony by French military action at the end of the eighteenth century opened the way in Britain for the powerful development of the Greek Revival and, coevally, for the acceleration of the Gothic Revival as a form of Nationalist opposition to France. Then, in 1836, came what was perhaps the single most important architectural commission of nineteenth-century

---

[37] Soane's Museum, 'George Basevi 1794–1845 ... Home Letters from Italy and Greece' (typed transcript ed. A.T. Bolton), 57.

[38] RIBA DC J6/1–61 (Goldicutt); RIBA DC Y3/63 (154 drawings by Woods, Sharp and Donaldson); RIBA DC Poynter Sketchbook and Portfolio (see J. Lever, *Catalogue of the Drawings Collection of the Royal Institute of British Architects, O–R* (Farnborough, 1976), 97, [12]7; RIBA DC W5/43/1–37 (Parke).

[39] See, for example, F. Mazois, *Les ruines de Pompéi,* 4 vols (1824–38), III, 37, n. 1, where Gau discusses Donaldson's plan of Pompeii and calls him 'savant architecte anglais et auteur de plusieurs ouvrages estimés'.

[40] J. Goldicutt, *Specimens of Ancient Decorations from Pompeii* (London, 1825), 1.

England for the new Palace of Westminster. The undoubted splendour of this great Gothic Revival building generally has been seen, hardly surprisingly, as marking a turning point in British public architecture, establishing the dominance of revived indigenous medieval forms and the marginalization of the classical tradition. Vigorous reinforcement of this view of history comes when we read the work of one of the most successful polemicists of the period, A.W.N. Pugin. Pugin's book, *Contrasts*, also of 1836, places classical and Gothic forms in such opposition to one another, so much to the detriment of the former, that it seems impossible to countenance any legitimate continuing use of the classical idiom for great public buildings. But one has to ask whether the undoubted significance of the Palace of Westminster competition and the forceful rhetoric of Pugin in fact might have misled us a little.[41] Of the other major architectural competitions held during the 1830s how many resulted in the choice of medievalizing designs? Perhaps even more significantly, how many led to buildings as explicitly Greek as those of the 1820s, pre-eminently Robert Smirke's British Museum and General Post Office? In fact, the Greek Revival was dying out in London at the end of the 1820s (although not, perhaps, in the provinces and certainly not in Scotland). The Fishmongers' Hall at London Bridge, begun by Smirke's pupil Henry Roberts in 1832, and William Wilkins' widely criticized National Gallery, begun in 1834, perhaps mark its last throes in the capital.

Although the British interest in Greek archaeology was to continue throughout the nineteenth century, there was something of a caesura between the appearance of the revised fourth volume of *The Antiquities of Athens* in 1830 and that of the third volume of *Ionian Antiquities* in 1840.[42] During that decade, however, the renewed interest in Roman topography was sustained. In 1831 Richard Burgess, the Anglican minister at Rome, published *The Topography and Antiquities of Rome, Including the Recent Discoveries Made about the Forum and the Via Sacra*. This was followed in 1832 by two new volumes of *Pompeiana* by Gell, who then in 1834 published *The Topography of Rome and its Vicinity*. Alongside this series of books came, in 1834, a key event with the foundation of the Institute of British Architects. Many of the young professionals involved in the foundation of the Institute were those who had travelled to the Mediterranean as students in the years after 1815, with Donaldson as the most active figure. As secretary of the new Institute, Donaldson opened active

---

[41] For a recent reappraisal of the symbolism of the Palace of Westminster see R. Quinault, 'Westminster and the Victorian constitution', *Transactions of the Royal Historical Society*, 6th series, 2 (1992), 79–104.

[42] Also in 1830 came W. Kinnard, *Antiquities at Athens and Delos*, a work supplementary to *The Antiquities of Athens*. William Leake's two extensive works of Greek topography, *Travels in the Morea*, 3 vols (1830) and *Travels in Northern Greece*, 4 vols (1835) were accounts of journeys made between 1799 and 1815. Christopher Wordsworth's *Athens and Attica: Journal of a Residence There* (London, 1836), however, was a contemporary descriptive account which included three views by Cockerell.

correspondence with foreign architects and archaeologists. A number were elected honorary members, including Gau, Huyot, Blouet, Valadier and Luigi Canina, by the time of his election in 1838 the leading Roman architect in the archaeological study and publication of antique buildings.[43] A year later we find Canina writing to the Institute of British Architects describing recent discoveries made near the Porta Maggiore, a paper which Donaldson read out at a general meeting. There is no doubt that the advance of classical archaeology was one matter about which the new Institute intended to extract as much information as it could from the distance of London. It also provides a context for the succession of quite explicit Roman public buildings which appeared in England during the 1830s, some based on prototypes made visible by the progress of archaeology since the Napoleonic interlude.

The sequence starts with George IV's triumphal arches: the Marble Arch, built by Nash in 1825–30; and the Arch at Constitution Hill, erected by Decimus Burton from 1827 but never receiving the full sculptural programme intended for it. Triumphal arches had not, I think, been erected in London before as part of royal processional routes.[44] The Marble Arch stood at the entry to the forecourt of the King's new Buckingham Palace, and the Constitution Hill Arch in its original location stood between Hyde Park and the gardens of Buckingham Palace.[45] At the same moment, Soane published his vision of a series of arches as part of an elaborate processional route leading the King from Windsor to a new royal palace at Hyde Park Corner and from thence to the Palace of Westminster for the State Opening of Parliament.[46] In all this there was, of course, a close correspondence with the work George IV's rival, Napoleon, had carried out in First Empire Paris: the Arc du Carrousel had been constructed in 1805 between the palaces of the Louvre and Tuileries, and the Arc de Triomphe was begun at the same time at the west end of the Champs Elysées. It was through the Arc de Triomphe that Napoleon and Marie-Louise had processed on the day of their dynastic marriage. The rather obvious imperial symbolism of the triumphal

---

[43] See Salmon, 'British Architects' (above, n. 36), appendix C, pp. 100–1. Under the date 21 May 1838 it should read that Giuseppe rather than Luigi Valadier was elected.

[44] Between 1636 and 1638, however, Inigo Jones had proposed an explicitly Roman arch to serve at Temple Bar, the point at which Charles I would enter the City of London from Westminster (see J. Harris and G. Higgott, *Inigo Jones: Complete Architectural Drawings* (New York, 1989), 251–3). I am grateful to Professors Edward Chaney and Michael McCarthy for bringing this example to my attention. There were also eighteenth-century precedents for George IV's arches in John Gwynn's proposals in *London and Westminster Improved* (London, 1766) and in plans of George III (see D. Arnold, 'George IV and the metropolitan improvements: the creation of a royal image', in D. Arnold (ed.), *Squanderous and Lavish Profusion: George IV, His Image and Patronage of the Arts* (London, 1995), 53–6), and an engraving of a 'Triumphal Arch. Proposed to be erected at Hyde Park Corner, commemorative of the victories achieved by the British arms during the reign of King George the Third', published in 1813 by William Kinnard.

[45] A. Saint, 'The Marble Arch', *The Georgian Group Journal* 7 (1997), 75–93; D. Arnold, 'The arch at Constitution Hill: a new axis for London', *Apollo* 138 (September, 1993), 129–33.

[46] S. Sawyer, 'Sir John Soane's symbolic Westminster: the apotheosis of George IV', *Architectural History* 39 (1996), 54–76.

arches utilized by both Napoleon and George IV was echoed by the 1839 selection of William Railton's column to commemorate Nelson in Trafalgar Square, although there is a closer similarity between Napoleon's Colonne Vendôme of 1806–10 and the precedent honorific column for a soldier-emperor, that of Trajan in Rome.[47] The clearances of the Forum of Trajan and of the Arches of Septimius Severus and Titus in the first quarter of the nineteenth century lay behind the renewed interest shown in these Roman building types by both the French and the British. But perhaps the single greatest commission of Napoleon's reign was the church of the Madeleine, occupying a prime urban space at the north end of the Rue Royale. The Emperor personally chose Pierre Vignon's design, inspired by the Maison Carrée at Nîmes, because he wanted it to appear more like a 'Temple de la Gloire' than a Christian church, and the interior design of 1828 by Jean-Jacques-Marie Huvé is thought to have been inspired by Blouet's restoration of the Baths of Caracalla which reached published form that year.[48]

As with the London triumphal arches, the Madeleine also has an English counterpart: the Town Hall in Birmingham, built from 1832 and modelled, by the architect Joseph Hanson's own account, on the Temple of Castor and Pollux in Rome. The capitals are closely derived from those of the Roman prototype, as are the mouldings of the entablature, although the cost of emulating the richly carved decoration of the Roman original proved prohibitive. Hansom had never visited Rome and must, I think, have got the detailed information he required on the temple from Taylor's and Cresy's *Architectural Antiquities*. The podia of the two buildings are almost exactly the same height. It is even conceivable that the arched openings in the rough Anglesea 'marble' basement of Birmingham Town Hall were derived from the way Taylor and Cresy depicted the arches linking the travertine podium piers of the Roman prototype. Being left blank, these better suggested windows than Valadier's representation of the same excavation in his *Raccolta delle più insigne fabbriche*.[49] The building of Birmingham Town Hall came about as the result of a competition. Other entries proposed buildings in a range of different styles of architecture, as one would expect in a period with as many formal possibilities as the 1830s. But it was the most archaeological Roman building which was chosen by the town's Commissioners for Street Improvements. Three further major public buildings of the 1830s, similarly erected after competitions, exemplify the triumph of an essentially literal Roman

---

[47] For a general study of such monuments in this period see A. Yarrington, *The Commemoration of the Hero 1800–1864* (London, 1988). In 1821 William Burn had designed the Melville Monument, a version of Trajan's Column in St Andrew's Square, Edinburgh, commemorating the Lord Advocate Henry Dundas, Viscount Melville.

[48] L. Hautecoeur, *Histoire de l'architecture classique en France,* 7 vols (Paris, 1943–57), V, 206–7.

[49] See Salmon, 'Storming' (above, n. 14), 163–5 and figs 6, 8, 17.

style over all others proposed: the Fitzwilliam Museum in Cambridge, Saint George's Hall in Liverpool and the Royal Exchange in London.

FIG. 5. Harvey Lonsdale Elmes and Charles Robert Cockerell, *St George's Hall, Liverpool*, 1840–54.

The competition for the Fitzwilliam Museum was held in 1835 and resulted in the commission being awarded to Basevi, one of the architects who had studied in Rome immediately after the Napoleonic Wars. With its laterally-extended portico, Basevi's design related generically to Smirke's Greek Revival British Museum, but it has a more specific source in the Vespasianic Capitolium at Brescia, which had been excavated from 1822. Basevi himself had left Italy well before that date, but he could have known of the excavation from a number of sources: the part plan published in Giovanni Labus's *Antichi monumenti scoperti in Brescia* of 1823, for example, or the perspective view in Paolo Brognoli's *Nuovo guida di Brescia,* published in 1826.[50] Basevi's design was chosen in an election in which initially 140 of the Senate members present voted for Basevi and 105 for Ambrose Poynter, another architect with first-hand experience of post-Napoleonic Rome. The style of Poynter's design is unfortunately unknown. Certainly he would have had the knowledge to produce a sophisticated classical scheme, although by the 1830s he was already working predominantly in the idiom of the Gothic Revival. In any event, the preference for classical

---

[50] It was Robert Willis, a member of the University Syndicate appointed in 1835 to oversee the building of the Museum, who reported on hearsay that Basevi had based his portico on that at Brescia, although the published source referred to by Willis actually post-dates the design of the Fitzwilliam Museum (R. Willis and J. Willis Clark, *The Architectural History of the University of Cambridge,* 3 vols (Cambridge, 1886), III, 206).

architecture shown by the academics in selecting Basevi's design is consistent with other Cambridge buildings of the period, and it is worth noting that the study of classics at Cambridge was under intense review during the same period, having been introduced as a semi-independent tripos in 1824.[51]

In 1839–40 two competitions were held in Liverpool to produce designs for a public assembly hall and a set of Assize Courts, each brief specifying that the architectural style had to be Greek or Roman. The victor in both was Harvey Lonsdale Elmes, who subsequently combined the two buildings into the outstanding Saint George's Hall (Fig. 5). It has often been asserted that Elmes drew inspiration for his design from the work of Karl Friedrich Schinkel, specifically from the Prussian architect's Altes Museum in Berlin. If this was so, however, the influence must have come from the plates of the building published in the 1825 fascicle of Schinkel's *Sammlung Architektonischer Entwürff,* since Elmes's visit to Belgium, Germany and Austria (which in any case took place in 1842 when Saint George's Hall was already under construction) did not extend to Berlin. More recently scholarship has focused instead on the British sources available to Elmes at the end of the 1830s: it seems clear that his competition design for the assembly hall was a paraphrase of a Greek Revival design for Cambridge University Library by C.R. Cockerell; it has been suggested that his competition design for the Assize Courts was a Greek Doric version of Basevi's Fitzwilliam Museum; and it has been suggested that the distinctive arrangement of the final building, with its temple portico to the south and square piers along part of the east longitudinal axis, was derived generically from William Wilkins' Grange Park in Hampshire.[52] Such attempts to identify the sources, however, run the danger of suggesting that Saint George's Hall can be understood as little more than an exercise on the young Elmes's part in synthesizing the work of architects a generation older. But surely what we see in Liverpool is a powerful representation of a new architectural mode. Elmes never had the opportunity of visiting Rome himself, although it was his dearest wish to see 'the innumerable wonders of the Eternal City'.[53] None the less, he was so steeped in the archaeological publications and imagery that flowed from the Napoleonic excavations there that he could produce a building in an English context which bears a striking resemblance to Pennethorne's 'restoration' of the Temple of Castor and Pollux in his Roman Forum vision of 1825 (Fig. 4, left).

---

[51] See D. Watkin, *The Triumph of the Classical: Cambridge Architecture 1804–1834* (Cambridge, 1977); E. Leedham-Green, *A Concise History of the University of Cambridge* (Cambridge, 1996), 126–7.

[52] See J. Olley, 'St George's Hall, Liverpool, Part I', *The Architects' Journal* 183 (26) (18 June 1986), figs 3 and 32 for Saint George's Hall and Cockerell's Cambridge Library, and figs 4 and 33 for the Assize Courts and the Fitzwilliam Museum. See S. Bayley, 'A British Schinkel', *Architectural Association Quarterly* 7 (2) (April–June 1975), 32, for Saint George's Hall and Grange Park. Bayley's comparison depends partly on the use of piers in the side elevations of the two buildings, but Wilkins had used antae (in direct emulation of his archaeological source, the Choragic Monument of Thrasyllus in Athens), whereas Elmes's piers have full capitals.

[53] See R. Rawlinson, *Correspondence Relative to St George's Hall Liverpool* (London, 1871), 46.

Pennethorne had identified this building as the Graecostasis, linking the multi-stepped octastyle portico of the temple to a great hall centrally set on the longitudinal axis and surmounted by a high attic, the very features which characterize Saint George's Hall.[54]

Although Pennethorne had not displayed this work at the Royal Academy and it is not known to have been engraved, there is no reason why it should not have been known in London when Elmes was a student in the early 1830s or subsequently. The possibility that Pennethorne's scheme represented Elmes's inspiration is strengthened by the fact that, after settling on the form of Saint George's Hall, Elmes developed several schemes for using the building as the western boundary of a Liverpool 'forum'. His perspectives show the site from the south to the north, so that Saint George's Hall is placed on the left of the urban space in identical fashion to the building in Pennethorne's Roman Forum.[55] In execution, Saint George's Hall contains a number of Grecian features, although the Corinthian order itself is from a late Roman Republican or early Imperial exemplar. Moreover, it is widely accepted that in planning the great hall and its interior treatment Elmes (and, after his early death, Cockerell) made use of Blouet's restoration drawings of the Baths of Caracalla as published in 1828.[56] The sense that Saint George's Hall might represent the central building of a 'forum' for the merchant princes of Liverpool was reinforced by the fact that the corporation and subsequent architects respected the Roman and Renaissance traditions when designing the four public buildings which face it to the north, even in the 1870s when the Gothic Revival was at its height in England.[57]

When the Royal Exchange in London was destroyed by fire in 1838 a competition to design a replacement was organized by the City of London Common Council and the Mercers' Company. The brief specified that the style of the new Exchange should be 'Grecian, Roman, or Italian' and the building eventually erected by William Tite, an architect not known to have visited Rome, depended to a considerable extent on the competition entry of Donaldson, one of the most avid British students of ancient Rome in the Napoleonic period whose design had been placed first by the three architect-referees 'for magnificence and

---

[54] Pennethorne was misled into thinking that the remains of the Temple of Castor and Pollux were part of the Graecostasis (the place where foreign ambassadors waited to address the Roman senate) by his prior erroneous assumption about the site of the Curia (British Architectural Library, Royal Institute of British Architects, London, PeJ/1/3).

[55] Illustrated by Olley, 'St George's Hall' (above, n. 52), 42 and fig. 18.

[56] See, for example, R. Middleton and D. Watkin, *Neoclassical and Nineteenth Century Architecture,* 2 vols (London, 1987), II, 259. Cockerell's decoration of the great hall includes lictor's rods in the plasterwork of the vault and the initials 'S.P.Q.L.' in the bronzework of the doors.

[57] The four buildings are the William Brown Library and Museum (by T. Allom and J. Weightman, 1857–60); the Walker Art Gallery (C. Sherlock and H. Vale, 1874–7); the Picton Reading Room (C. Sherlock, 1875–9); and the Sessions House (F. and G. Holme, 1882–4).

beauty'.[58] The great portico, the widest in London, is based on that of the Pantheon, complete with deep arched central recess and frieze inscription referring to the building's predecessor, Sir Thomas Gresham's Exchange, as Hadrian's Pantheon does to Agrippa's. But Tite removed Donaldson's rather Greek stylobate, replacing it with a Roman frontal arrangement of steps between projecting podia, and raising the columns on pedestals to increase the more elevated Roman effect of the whole.[59] The reorientation of the Exchange, so that the principal façade lay to the west rather than the south, coupled to the coeval clearance of the space in front of the new building, meant that it effectively bounded the east side of what Cockerell is said to have called the 'Forum Londinium', onto which the Mansion House and the Bank of England already faced.[60] That the commercial heart of the city might be conceived as its major public space seems to have been an idea deliberately engendered by the government as early as 1809. In that year the area in front of the Mansion House had been chosen as the site for the national celebrations of the jubilee 50th year of George III's reign.[61]

Now, the Royal Exchange and Birmingham Town Hall seem to have been disliked by almost every historian who has written on nineteenth-century architecture in Britain, no doubt because they have been thought to represent what I recently heard described by one as 'the dog-ends of neo-classicism': they are judged to be the products of second-rate architects who responded to the stylistic dilemma of the mid-nineteenth century by having no more imagination than to restate outmoded ancient Roman prototypes. Despite his admiration for the 'exciting architecture' and sculptural character of the Fitzwilliam Museum, Henry-Russell Hitchcock, in his standard history of architecture in this period, sided with Pugin by describing the building's façade as 'the most complete sham possible'.[62] Even a building of such self-evident quality as Saint George's Hall still tends to be perceived and assessed in terms of the Prussian classicism of Schinkel. I hope I have shown, however, that these buildings do have a real vitality, a vitality deriving from the archaeological revelation of Rome which followed the Napoleonic excavations and the subsequent fresh studies and publications of ancient Roman buildings by the tens of British students who flooded back to the Eternal City after 1815. But is that all they are — inspired

---

[58] M. Port, 'Destruction, competition and rebuilding: The Royal Exchange 1838–1884', in A. Saunders (ed.), *The Royal Exchange* (London Topographical Society, 1997), 285 and 290.

[59] See Salmon, 'Storming' (above, n. 14), figs 14 and 15.

[60] Quoted in Port, 'Destruction' (above, n. 58), 297. For Cockerell's 1858 association of this area with the Roman history of London see D. Abramson, 'C.R. Cockerell's architectural progress of the Bank of England', *Architectural History* 37 (1994), 113, 120–1.

[61] See the engraving reproduced in L. Colley, *Britons: Forging the Nation 1707–1837* (New Haven and London, 1992), fig. 48, p. 219, also in S. Jeffery, *The Mansion House* (Chichester, 1993), fig. 208.

[62] H.-R. Hitchcock, *Early Victorian Architecture in Britain,* 2 vols (New Haven, 1954), I, 302–3.

academic efforts? Or do they belong to a broader symbolic and cultural context within the society which opted for their design and paid for their construction?

We need to recall that the 1830s was one of the most turbulent, but also invigorating, periods in British history. The decade began with the accession of William IV, who reigned for only seven years before being succeeded by the young Queen Victoria in 1837. This was not a period when British domestic or foreign policy was driven by a domineering or demanding monarch. Indeed, on the contrary, the Whig party under Earl Grey took the opportunity to head off constitutional unrest by introducing the Great Reform Bill in 1832, thereby moderately extending the franchise. On the other hand, Britain had been victorious over France in 1815, and moved to consolidate its position of imperial power. Ancient Rome, with its part Republican and part Imperial history, could be seen as a model for those of radically different political persuasions. The Tory *Quarterly Review*, for example, for which the Reform Bill was tantamount to a revolution, consoled itself by the thought that 'the Romans after a great calamity did not waste their energies in complaints nor bury them in gloomy torpor; and ... that heroic spirit saved the state in many emergencies'.[63] This editorial line was translated into repeated arguments against Greek and Gothic and in favour of a Romano-Renaissance architectural revival:

> In proportion as pseudo-Greek is in the ascendant, so is Roman art slighted, and falling into disrepute; but it is well to remember this truth, that we, who approximate nearer the wealth of old Rome than any other modern nation, not only do not rival her greatness and taste in our edifices, but are actually falling behind other states, whose resources are as limited as ours are boundless.[64]

For Liberals and Radicals, however, the extended nature and degree of representation of the citizenry in Parliament was a democratic triumph rather than a disaster. This was especially so in Birmingham, where, in 1830, Thomas Attwood had founded the Political Union to campaign for parliamentary reform. The laying of the foundation stone of the new Town Hall fell within a month of the passage of the Reform Bill and the virtual apotheosis of Attwood, who was addressing rallies of tens of thousands on Newhall Hill and leading processions

---

[63] 'Stages of the Revolution', *The Quarterly Review* 47 (94) (July 1832), 588.

[64] Review of Thomas Hope's *History of Architecture* in *The Quarterly Review* 53 (106) (April 1835), 370. See also an article on the competition for the new Palace of Westminster in *The Quarterly Review* 58 (115) (February 1837), 77, in which the Romano-Renaissance style is said to deserve 'to be well examined before we discard it, either for the fantastic incongruities of the Tudor, or the superior purity of a Grecian style which prevailed when arches and domes were not invented ... No style has been so completely adapted to the abodes of modern opulence and luxury, — none invented in which the effect of richness and graceful grandeur can be better displayed in a large or public building, and elegance and propriety in a small one. Devised for habitation, there is no difficulty in its application, or appearance of imposture in its design. Its houses look like dwellings, its halls are civic, and its palaces are royal'.

of supporters waving not just Union banners but also fasces. Benjamin Haydon, who painted one of the Newhall Hill meetings, perceived that the people of Birmingham were 'high in feeling — <u>Roman</u> quite — and will be immortal in their great struggle'.[65]

In the field of intellectual and political history one of the key figures of the 1830s was the Headmaster of Rugby School and Regius Professor of Modern History at Oxford University, Thomas Arnold, whose *History of Rome* was published in three volumes from 1838 to 1843. This work was partly based on Barthold Niebuhr's monumental *Römische Geschichte* of 1827–32, the translation into English of which had begun immediately.[66] Arnold, who became a member of the *Instituto di Corrispondenza Archeologica* founded at Rome in 1828–9 by his friend the Prussian minister Karl Bunsen (to whom his own *History of Rome* was dedicated), drew a quite explicit connection between ancient Rome and modern Britain. In the preface to the first volume, dated 1838, he offered no apology for presenting a subject some might have felt to be exhausted, pointing out:

> We have lived in a period rich in historical lessons beyond all former example; we have witnessed one of the great seasons of movement in the life of mankind, in which the arts of peace and war, political parties and principles, philosophy and religion, in all their manifold forms and influences, have been developed with extraordinary force and freedom. Our own experience has thus thrown a brighter light upon the remoter past ... it is not claiming too much to say, that the growth of the Roman Commonwealth, the true character of its parties, the causes and tendencies of its revolutions, and the spirit of its peoples and its laws, ought to be understood by none as well as by those who have grown up under the laws, who have been engaged in the parties, who are themselves citizens of our kingly commonwealth of England.[67]

Arnold's text found a public already widely familiar with the drawing of allusions between the archaeological remains of Roman antiquity and contemporary political debate through its reading of Canto 4 of Byron's *Childe Harold's Pilgrimage* of 1818 and Shelley's *Ode to Naples* of 1820. In 1834 this linkage was reinforced by the newly-elected, reforming, Liberal Member of Parliament Edward Bulwer-Lytton in *The Last Days of Pompeii,* apparently the most popular historical novel since *Waverley.* Although the moral supremacy in the novel lies throughout with a small band of first-century Christians, the

---

[65] Cited in C. Flick, *The Birmingham Political Union and the Movements for Reform in Britain 1830–1839* (Hamden Connecticut, 1978), 93.

[66] See F. Walter, *The Roman History ... Translated from the German* (London, 1827); J. Hare and C. Thirlwall, *The History of Rome ... Translated*, 2 vols (Cambridge, 1828); T. Twiss, *An Epitome of Niebuhr's History of Rome* (Oxford, 1836).

[67] T. Arnold, *History of Rome* (fifth edition), 3 vols (London, 1848), I, vi–vii.

Roman characters look back from their vantage point of AD 79 to the 'good old days' of the Republic and, in a conspicuous authorial interjection, Lytton makes an impassioned objection to Italian unification: 'Italy, Italy ... listen not to the blind policy which would unite all your crested cities, mourning for their republics, into one empire'.[68] The political significance of the novel was sufficiently apparent at the time of its publication for Lady Blessington to tell Lytton gleefully that she had persuaded 'an ultra Tory' to read it,[69] but in truth the book's tremendous popularity was due more to its ability to bring the ancient Romans, as Lytton imagined them, powerfully to life for a British readership ranging from the most scholarly to the most frivolous. On the basis of its Greek protagonists and philhellenic ideas, some historians have interpreted the novel as the literary equivalent of the Greek Revival in architecture.[70] But Lytton was no admirer of that genre of architecture, which he attacked in his great social and cultural survey *England and the English* in 1833.[71] Lytton's *Last Days of Pompeii,* like Thomas Babington Macaulay's equally successful *Lays of Ancient Rome* (1842), appealed to a reading public of which many individuals had acquired an interest in Roman topography and architecture when visiting Italy during that great period of travel for the British which followed on from 1815.

This paper has endeavoured to show that the years from 1815 to 1840 should be considered to be at least as interesting as the better-known eighteenth century from the point of view of the relationship between the architecture of ancient Rome and that of modern Britain, if not more so. The great archaeological advances made in Rome during the Napoleonic era, coupled to the cooperative and international character of research they engendered, fired the imaginations of British architectural students who visited the city after 1815, and their publications in turn fired the imaginations of and provided design information for those architects who had not travelled. If we look beyond the very conspicuous decision to build the new Palace of Westminster in a Gothic style in the 1830s and the rhetoric surrounding that decision, we find that a series of the major public buildings erected from the late 1820s to the early 1840s were in fact explicitly Roman in their forms. But the character of architecture at any given time and place does not, of course, depend solely on the impulses of architects. Despite the complexities and contradictions of architectural debate during the 1830s, these buildings point to the emergence of a kind of consensus among clients as diverse as Cambridge University academics, City of London bureaucrats and the citizenry of burgeoning industrial towns such as Birmingham

---

[68] E. Bulwer-Lytton, *The Last Days of Pompeii,* 3 vols (London, 1834), I, 46, 220.

[69] Earl Lytton, *The Life of Edward Bulwer Lytton, First Lord Lytton,* 2 vols (London, 1913), I, 447.

[70] See, for example, Jenkyns, *Victorians and Ancient Greece* (above, n. 15), 84–5.

[71] E. Bulwer-Lytton, *England and the English,* 2 vols (London, 1833), II, 226–9. Lytton's preference was in fact for a revival of British architecture from the Saxon to the Elizabethan periods.

and Liverpool, a consensus that public buildings and urban spaces reflecting a vision of ancient Rome might best serve their practical and symbolic purposes. Ancient Rome could be perceived as a sort of parallel state to modern Britain, in a way which offered no threat, and the symbolism of Roman buildings could become as much a part of a specifically British national identity as the supposedly indigenous Gothic.[72] Indeed, these buildings can be seen as the physical embodiment of the interest in ancient Rome that touched every area of intellectual and cultural life during the 1830s. It was an interest surely supported by the first-hand experiences of the many thousands of Britons, from young aristocrats to middle-class professionals, who had travelled in Italy since 1815, travellers who give us good cause for considering whether a definition of the Grand Tour as an exclusively eighteenth-century phenomenon might not be a little too narrow. It has been argued that the 1763 Treaty of Paris, which concluded the Seven Years War, led to a period of peace fully exploited by the British during 'the Golden Age' of the Grand Tour.[73] Perhaps the Congress of Vienna, which concluded the Napoleonic Wars, should be perceived as ushering in a second golden age for the British traveller to Italy, even if we do not actually call it the Grand Tour.[74]

---

[72] It might be added that the death of Henry Stuart in 1807 and Catholic Emancipation in 1829 finally must have severed the Jacobite associations which had made Rome symbolically an unsuitable source of influence for some eighteenth-century Grand Tourists and patrons of architecture.

[73] Wilton and Bignamini, *Grand Tour* (above, n. 1), 33.

[74] Preparation of this paper was aided by members of staff at the British School at Rome, especially Clare Hornsby, Valerie Scott and Tommaso Astolfi. I would like to acknowledge a research grant from my former colleagues in the Manchester School of Architecture. For their kind assistance in gathering the illustrations I wish to thank Honor Clerk, Julia Marciari-Alexander and Tim Knox.

BIOGRAPHICAL NOTES ON CONTRIBUTORS

ILARIA BIGNAMINI was born in Milan and received her Ph.D. from the Courtauld Institute in 1988. She is a historian of art and classical archaeology. She was Visiting Curator at the Tate Gallery, London, from 1994 to 1996 and Leverhulme Trust Research Fellow at the Department of History of Art, University of Oxford, in 1996–9. Her publications include the catalogue *Grand Tour: the Lure of Italy in the Eighteenth Century* (Tate Gallery Publishing, London, 1996) and she has edited and contributed to *Archives and Excavations I. Essays on the History of Archaeological Excavations in Rome and Southern Italy from the Renaissance to the Nineteenth Century*, to be published by the British School at Rome in 2001. She is currently a Research Associate at the University of Oxford, and is preparing a monograph entitled *Digging and Dealing in the Eighteenth Century. The British Conquest of the Marbles of Ancient Rome*.

JOHN BOWEN is Senior Lecturer in English at Keele University, and is the author of *Other Dickens: Pickwick to Chuzzlewit* (Oxford University Press, 1999) and a number of articles on nineteenth- and twentieth-century literature and literary theory. A member of the editorial board of the *Journal of Victorian Culture*, he is currently editing *Barnaby Rudge* for Penguin.

CHLOE CHARD is a literary historian who works on travel writing and imaginative geography. Her recent publications include a book, *Pleasure and Guilt on the Grand Tour* (Manchester University Press, 1999), and a collection of essays, *Transports: Travel, Pleasure and Imaginative Geography, 1600–1830*, co-edited with Helen Langdon (Yale University Press, 1996). She has recently been a Visiting Fellow at the Centre for Cross-Cultural Research, Australian National University, Canberra, and a Visiting Scholar at the University of Tasmania, Hobart.

JEFFREY COLLINS studied at Yale and Clare College, Cambridge, as an undergraduate, and completed his Ph.D. at Yale in 1994. He is the author of *Arsenals of Art: Eighteenth-Century Rome and the Cultural Politics of Pope Pius VI*, forthcoming from Cambridge University Press. He is a Fellow of the American Academy in Rome and is Assistant Professor of Baroque Art at the University of Washington in Seattle.

CLARE HORNSBY studied history of art as an undergraduate and postgraduate at the University of Bristol. Her Ph.D. was on the life and work of Giovanni Servandoni (1695–1766) and she has published several articles based on this research. She was formerly Assistant Director for History of Art at the British

School at Rome where she is now a Research Fellow, working on a sketchbook of landscape drawings by Nicolas-Didier Boguet.

MICHAEL LIVERSIDGE is Dean of Arts and Senior Lecturer in History of Art at the University of Bristol. He specializes in British art of the eighteenth and nineteenth centuries. His publications include *Canaletto and England* (with Jane Farrington, 1993) and *Imagining Rome: British Artists and Rome in the Nineteenth Century* (edited with Catharine Edwards, 1996). He is a Fellow of the Society of Antiquaries.

MICHAEL MCCARTHY is Professor of the History of Art at University College, Dublin and the author of *The Origins of the Gothic Revival* (Yale University Press, 1987). He has published several articles on Piranesi and his relations with Grand Tourists in *The Burlington Magazine*, *Apollo* and other journals, and has been a principal contributor to J. Ingamells (ed.), *A Dictionary of British and Irish Travellers in Italy 1701–1800* (New Haven and London, 1997).

FRANK SALMON has been a lecturer in the School of Art History and Archaeology at the University of Manchester since 1997, prior to which he lectured in the University's School of Architecture for eight years. He has published many articles about architectural relations between Britain and Italy in the eighteenth and nineteenth centuries, and his book, *Building on Ruins: The Rediscovery of Rome in English Architecture*, was published by Ashgate in 2000.

LORI-ANN TOUCHETTE was Cary Fellow at the British School at Rome in 1997–8. Her D. Phil. from Oxford was in Classical Archaeology, on the topic of Roman copies of Greek relief sculpture. She has taught Greek and Roman art and archaeology in the USA and at University College, Dublin. In 1995 she published *The Dancing Meanad Reliefs: Continuity and Change in Roman Copies*. Forthcoming with Oxford University Press is *Sculpting the Difference: Roman Reception of Greek Classical Sculpture*.

DAVID WATKIN is Reader in the History of Architecture at the University of Cambridge and a Fellow of Peterhouse. His numerous publications include monographs on Thomas Hope, James 'Athenian' Stuart, and C.R. Cockerell. His most recent book, *Sir John Soane: Enlightenment Thought and the Royal Academy Lectures* (1996), received the Sir Banister Fletcher Award from the RIBA and the Society of Authors.

INDEX
of
People, Places and Works